THE ADULT ONLY JOKE BOOK

HB
HINKLER
BOOKS

Adult Only Joke Book
First published in 2002 by Hinkler Books Pty Ltd
45-55 Fairchild Street
Heatherton VIC 3202 Australia
www.hinklerbooks.com

32 31 30 29 28 27 26 25
14 13 12 11 10

ISBN 978 1 8651 5479 4

Cover designer: Sam Grimmer
Text by: Scribblers & Writers Pty Ltd
Typesetting: Midland Typesetters

Printed and bound in China

CONTENTS

INTRODUCTION

Consider one of the great ironies of life. These days, people regularly get on radio and television, and talk about their first sexual experience. Gurus write therapeutic columns giving advice to the impotent. Multi-degreed boffins travel the world, hectoring people about such things as "transmission of bodily fluids". They freely use phrases and terms that a generation ago, nobody would dream of mentioning in public.

Ah, but tell a joke about a bloke and a blonde having a shag at the drive-in, and bang! The Comedy Control Cops are down on you like a tonne of bricks. Before you know it, you are sitting in a cell deep in the bowels of the Chamber of Political Correction. There they force feed you the Cold Gruel of Seriousness, make you study the Gormless Book of Rigidity and let you out only for a daily one-hour session at the Ruthless Gymnasium of Self Righteousness.

Where's the justice in all this? On the one hand, they are allowed to say what they like about human relationships and bore everybody witless in that flat monotone that is favoured by the gloriously pompous. But if you or I put the same thing in a funny context, we end up in the Sin Bin. Well, we are not going to take it any more. If they can talk about sex, so can we! And Irishmen. And blondes. And politicians. And farting. And the differences between us. And the funny, peculiar attitudes we all have.

Anything we want. And in the way that we want. The joke way, the fun way, the way that brightens up our lives. Not necessarily in a crude or dirty way, but in a way that gets the party going and makes people realize that we all need a good laugh.

So be brave, be rebellious, read this book and storm the Bastille of Blandness. Let the Adult Joke throw off the shackles of the Comedy Control Cops and run free!

TELLING A JOKE

"So, said the archbishop, now maybe we can all get some sleep ..."

Hopefully, when you've rolled out the punch line of a joke, people will be rolling on the floor! Or at least, showing some form of appreciation for the fact that you've put your heart and soul on the line. Because that is what telling a joke is – it's putting your credibility as a story-teller to the test.

Telling a joke might sound easy and some people certainly make it look that way. But it is fraught with danger, as anyone who has been greeted with an icy, silent stare after he has delivered his number one, sure-fire rib-tickler knows. They did not get the joke – or worse still, the bastards got it but didn't find it funny ...

Telling a joke successfully is a combination of four major factors – the material, the audience you are telling it to, the moment you choose to tell it and the presentation. For starters, there is no end of material for you to work with! Jokes hinge on irony, incongruity, cultural differences and social attitudes. This takes you into the world of sex, religion, social customs, alcohol, driving, men, women, sport, habits (both behavioural and nuns' ...) and any number of other areas dealing with human peculiarities.

There's a whole heap of stuff out there, just waiting to be told.

There are always new jokes going around, as well as old jokes that never die and recycled versions of old gags that have been done up to suit the times. Gags are constantly being updated, starting from the time Adam said to Eve, "Stand back, I don't know how big this thing is gonna get!" As well as books like this, there are magazines with big joke sections, and the Internet is also becoming a prime source for material.

How do you know what is a good joke? Simply, if it makes you laugh. If it makes you laugh, then you can be pretty sure it will make a lot of other people laugh too. Or at least groan in an ironic sort of way. If a joke doesn't make you laugh, forget it.

Once you've come across a few gags you like, the next step is deciding who you are going to tell them to. Friends are a great start. If they are good friends and it is a good joke, they will laugh. If it is a bad joke they will tell you, saving you from further humiliation and embarrassment. Family? Hmmm, family is tricky. Uncle Bert, who wears a naked lady print on his tie and calls his penis The Great One, might laugh uproariously at a gag about Monica, Bill and that dress. Whereas Aunty Ethel, who actually invites Mormons inside for tea, might be outraged. And the rich old bag who lives in the big house on the hill and gets around in a chauffer-driven 1928 Rolls Royce Silver Shadow, might write you out of her friggin' will!

A further test is an assembled group of people who you are not too familiar with, and you are unaware of all their backgrounds. Many a would-be party comic has been found in the kitchen, banging his head against the pantry door, lamenting, "How was I supposed to know that the little fat guy in the dark suit is the local Godfather? That's the last Mafia gag I'm telling ..."

The greatest test of your skills is the moment you suddenly find yourself at the rostrum with a microphone. Sprouting, "Hey, just think – if Mama Cass had not eaten that ham sandwich and Karen Carpenter had instead, they'd both be alive today," might not be a wise opening line at the annual general meeting of the Anorexia and Bulimia Survivors Association!

So, you've got your gag and you've picked your audience. What about the chosen time to present it? This is a crucial decision and could have a life-altering effect on you. A beautifully told joke at a poignant moment can do wonders. It can break up an awkward situation – especially when friends and family are gathered over an emotive issue – and get everybody back on track. It's a great feeling when somebody says to you later, "Thanks for jumping in at that point; everyone was so morbid and it just needed something to spark them up." However, you do this at your own peril. Pick the wrong type of gag and you'll be dismissed as a tasteless moron for the rest of your life.

In general conversation, especially when things start to lag amongst a group who has just met, a good joke can revive everyone's enthusiasm, particularly if it is intelligent and witty. Again, selection of the style and content is crucial. Notice how for some people, usually self-made blokes, telling a gag within the first few moments of a meeting (whether they know you well or have never met you before in their life) is their only form of communication. Often these types don't know or care about the risk they are taking if they tell the wrong joke. They always seem to blunder on with some really tasteless gag that many women in the group find offensive and not funny.

Good joke tellers are people who have a wide range of material at their disposal, are good at selecting what type of gag will suit the audience, and a combination of an innate sixth sense and experience to know when the time is right to fire one off.

Now it's all up to the presentation.

First up, it is not a good idea to tell a gag when everyone else is sober and you are totally, gloriously and outrageously pissed. No matter how much you giggle before, during and after the execution of the gag, they will not find it funny. They will, in fact, find it very annoying. Especially if you get to the punch-line and black out! Sometimes the reverse role is similarly dangerous. Here you are, sober as a judge, trying to get a gag out, and this bunch of sozzled saps is falling about giggling at a every syllable and falling about in each other's arms. They're pointing at you and shrieking things like, "But he's so serious about it!" You can guarantee that right at the punch-line, they will go totally silent, one will blurt, "I don't get it," and they will all burst into hysterical laughter again.

Go for a level playing field. If you are sober and they are sober, all well and good. If you have been ingesting vast quantities of alcohol and so has your audience, you are in with a big chance. Besides, it won't matter much – you will all have forgotten everything in the morning.

The basis of jokes is language – and the intelligent appreciation of it. If you've got a smart gag full of irony and a pretty clever, educated audience, then you are home and hosed. Good jokes have levels and layers of information presented in an enjoyable, accessible sequence, leading to a surprise finish.

It's interesting to watch how little kids respond to jokes. They struggle when they are tiny and often say, "But I don't get it," because the gag will involve situations they are not familiar with, characters they do not know, or true and/or ironic meanings and interpretations of words and phrases that they do not yet understand. Over the years, as they begin to grasp these notions and differences, their approach to humor becomes more sophisticated. Or morbid, or sex-oriented, or off-the-wall, or whatever, depending on their upbringing!

A key to a successful gag is how you introduce it. The instant you say, "Did you hear the one about …?" you have put yourself on the line. People are expecting something good and you have to deliver. They do not know whether it is a new gag, an old gag, whether it's clean, or pure smut. For you, there is no turning back.

A way of easing the pressure on yourself is to go straight into the opening line. "This bloke goes to the doctor, and …" No-one has time to say, "Oh, he's going to tell me a joke." You are already into it and the scene has been set.

A softer intro is to categorize the first gag, saying something like, "Did you hear the latest Clinton joke?" Then people have already got an idea of where you are going. They have heard many jokes from this category before, they may or may not like it and anyway, the joke might lead to other, more profound discussion.

A tricky one is to ask the direct question: "What's the

difference between ...?" the testing aspect of this is the response you get. Generally it's a mumbled "I dunno" and you have to really deliver the goods to get a positive response.

A clever way to introduce your joke is to shape the story so that it sounds, at the start, as though you are telling a real-life scenario. "I met this bloke the other day and ..." Only near the end, as the picture you are painting starts to get ludicrous, do people catch on that you are, in fact, spinning them a yarn.

Whichever way you go, the art is to be able to take control of your audience, whether it is one person or one thousand. You want to make them feel that you are delivering this to them personally and it is something that, once they have heard it, their lives will somehow be better for it. You need to have authority in your voice, and not a whimpering little simper. You need to know your material. Sometimes it's a good idea to practice by yourself in the bathroom. There is nothing worse than a joke-teller who fluffs lines, gets sentences out of order, or who delivers the punch with all the impact of sock full of custard.

Above all, as the best comics will tell you – it's all in the timing. You have to pace a gag, use softness and loudness to emphasise the right shading of the words, and employ that stand-out skill of all the brilliant speakers. The pause.

The pause is a vital weapon in your armory. It breaks up the gag, it gives people time to take the information in, and above all, it cranks up the expectation levels to fever pitch. A beautifully timed, hanging pause is worth a thousand badly-chosen words. You know you have got them when, during the pause, you see the sparkling glint of anticipation in their eye.

So, take this book, find some gags you like, practice them up a bit and go for it. And as the archbishop said to the actress, now maybe we can all get some sleep ...

GRAEME JOHNSTONE

JUST FOR FUN

Have you ever wondered the reason as to why we have an angel on the top of the Christmas tree? On one particular Christmas Santa was rushed and harried trying to get ready for his annual trip to deliver gifts to the world's children.

He asked Mrs. Claus to wake him at five a.m. and to have his breakfast ready with a lunch to take along on the journey.

He then went to his workshop and told the elves to have all the presents packed in the sleigh and the reindeer harnessed at 5:30 a.m.

At 5:30 the following morning he awoke. He jumped out of bed furious with Mrs. Claus for not awakening him on time. His mood worsened when he realized she had fixed neither his breakfast nor his afternoon meal.

He ran out to his sleigh only to find that the elves, drunk from partying all night, had no presents packed, and the reindeer were running loose in the pasture. About this time a little angel walked by dragging a large Christmas tree. Santa tried to ignore her since his mood was so foul, but the angel spoke up and said, "Santa what should I do with this Christmas tree?" And that, my children, is why there is an angel on the top of the Christmas tree …

A man who was installing carpet decides to take a cigarette break after completing the installation in the first of several rooms he has to do. Finding his ciggies missing from his pocket he begins searching, only to notice a small lump in his recently completed carpet-installation.

Not wanting to rip up all that work for a lousy pack of cigarettes he simply walks over and pounds the lump flat. He decides to forgo the break continues on to the other rooms to be carpeted.

At the end of the day he's completed his work and he is out in the drive-way loading his tools into his truck when the lady of the house returns home and admires her new carpet and thanks him for a job well done. He spies his pack of cigarettes on the dashboard of the truck when the lady of the house calls out, "Have you seen my parakeet, he's not in his cage?"

T wo goats are out behind a movie studio eating old movie film. One goat says to the other, "Pretty good, huh?"

The second goat says, "Yeah, but it's not as good as the book."

I t's a sunny morning in the Big Forest and the Bear family is just waking up. Baby Bear goes downstairs and sits in his small chair at the table. He looks into his small bowl. It is empty! "Who's been eating my porridge?" he squeaks.

Daddy Bear arrives at the table and sits in his big chair.

He looks into his big bowl. It is also empty! "Who's been eating my porridge?" he roars.

Mummy Bear puts her head through the serving hatch from the kitchen and yells, "For Pete's sake, how many times do we have to go through this? It was Mummy Bear who got up first. It was Mummy Bear who woke everybody else in the house up. It was Mummy Bear who unloaded the dishwasher from last night and put everything away. It was Mummy Bear who went out into the cold early morning air to fetch the newspaper. It was Mummy Bear who set the table. It was Mummy Bear who put the cat out, cleaned the litter box and filled the cat's water & food dish. And now that you've decided to come down stairs and grace me with your presence … listen good because I'm only going to say this one more time. I haven't made the bloody porridge yet!"

Did you hear about the two television aerials who got married? The wedding was rubbish but the reception was brilliant!

A teacher noticed that a little boy at the back of the class was squirming around, scratching his crotch and not paying attention. She went to find out what was going on.

He was quite embarrassed and whispered that he had just recently been circumcised and he was quite itchy.

The teacher told him go down to the principal's office

and to phone his mother, and ask her what he should do about it. He did that and he returned to the classroom, where he sat down in his seat. Suddenly, there was a commotion at the back of the room.

The teacher went back to investigate, only to find the lad sitting at his desk with his penis hanging out.

"I thought I told you to call your mum," she admonished

"I did," he said, "And she told me that if I could stick it out till noon, she'd come and pick me up from school."

"**H**e is so romantic. Every time he speaks to me he starts by saying 'Fair Lady'."

"Romantic my foot! He used to be a bus driver ..."

An insurance agent who was talking to a prospective client at her home pointed to an exquisite vase on the sideboard and asked, "Do you keep anything in it?"

"Yes, my husband's ashes," came the reply.

"I am sorry," apologized the agent, "I did not know he was deceased."

"He isn't – he is just too lazy to hunt for an ashtray."

A couple of fellers who were out of work were strolling past a shoe shop when they spotted a pair of crocodile-skin shoes in the window.

"Strewth!" one of the blokes exclaimed. "Will you look at the price of them! I tell you what, mate, there's money to be made in that business, no mistake."

So they decided to go up north and shoot a few crocs for a living.

They had it really rough for a whole week, wading through the mangrove swamps, and being eaten alive by mossies and leeches. But they bagged quite a few crocs.

By the week's end they had run out of ammo, but they kept at it, taking on the crocs by hand.

Come Saturday morning, they were both in a terrible state.

After one particularly vicious battle with a big old croc, one of the blokes had just about had enough.

"This is no good," he told his mate. "If the next one's not wearing shoes, I'm going home!"

Just wondering, what does it say under 'hair colour' on the driver's licence of a bald man?

The phone was ringing. I picked it up and said, "Who's speaking please?" And a voice said, "You are."

A man is walking down the street when he is approached by a prostitute.

"For $200, I'll perform any act for you," she tells him,

"provided that you can describe the act in three words."

The man thinks about the offer for less than a moment and gives the woman $200.

"OK, tell me what you want me to do, but remember, only in three words," she tells him.

The man, who has been quiet throughout the exchange says, "Paint my house."

A young polar bear came into his den and asked his mother, "Mum, am I a real polar bear?"

"Of course you are," his mother replied.

The young polar bear asked his father, "Dad, am I a real polar bear?"

"Yes, you are a real polar bear."

A week passed and the young polar bear asked his parents, "Are grandma and grandpa real polar bears?"

"Yes," said his parents.

Another week passed and the young polar bear asked his parents, "Are all my relatives real polar bears?"

"Yes, they are all real polar bears," said his parents.

Finally it came too much for the parents, "Why do you ask?" queried his mother.

"Because," said the young polar bear, "I'm bloody well freezing!"

A bloke rings triple zero and says, "Quick, quick, send an ambulance. My wife's having a baby! For God's sake, hurry!"

"Just calm down a moment," says the operator. "Is this her first baby?"

"No, you dill," says the bloke, "this is her husband, Frank."

Young Johnny was sitting on a park bench eating chocolate bars. A man sitting opposite watched him finish six of them off.

The man said, "Eating that many chocolate bars is bad for you."

Johnny replied, "My Grandad lived to be one hundred and five."

"Did he eat lots of chocolate bars at once?" asked the man.

"No," said Johnny "he minded his own bloody business."

I went into my bank the other day and asked the cashier to check my balance. She pushed me over!

So I was getting into my car, and this bloke says to me, "Can you give me a lift?"

I said, "Sure, you look great, the world's your oyster, go for it."

A man who lived in a block of apartments thought it was raining and put his head out the window to check. As he did so a glass eye fell into his hand. He looked up to see where it came from, just in time to see a young woman looking down.

"Is this yours?" he asked.

She said, "Yes, could you bring it up?" and the man agreed. On arrival she was profuse in her thanks and offered the man a drink.

As she was very attractive, he agreed. Shortly afterwards she said, "I'm about to have dinner. There's plenty. Would you like to join me?" He readily accepted her offer and both enjoyed a lovely meal.

As the evening was drawing to a close the lady said, "I've had a marvelous evening. Would you like to stay the night?"

The man hesitated then said, "Do you act like this with every man you meet?"

"No," she replied, "Only those who catch my eye."

Woman in crowd at a political rally where Sir Winston Churchill is speaking: "You mongrel Churchill, if you were my husband I'd put rat poison in your tea."

Churchill: "And if you were my wife, Ma'm, I'd drink it!"

One day a woman and her baby got onto a bus. As the woman paid the bus driver, he said to her, "That is one ugly baby!" The woman was furious and stomped to her seat.

"What's the matter?" asked another passenger.

"The bus driver just insulted me!"

"Well go up there and tell him off while I hold your monkey."

A man goes into the hairdressers.
He has only three hairs on his head.
The hairdresser says, "What would you like done?"
The man replies, "I'll have a side parting please."
The hairdresser tries that, but a hair falls out.
"Just make it a middle parting," says the man.
The hairdresser tries that, too, and another hair falls out.
The hairdresser apologizes.
"It's okay," says the man, "just leave it a mess!"

"Can I have a coffee without cream please?"
"We don't have cream, only milk."
"OK, I'll have it without milk then."

"I used to feel like a man trapped in a woman's body, but then I was born …"

A distinguished-looking man entered a Geneva bank and inquired about taking out a loan for 1000 Swiss francs.
"What security can you offer?" the banker asked.

"My Rolls-Royce is parked out front," he said. "I will be away for a few weeks. Here are the keys."

A month later, the man returned to the bank and paid off the loan, 1017 francs with interest.

"Pardon me for asking," the banker said, "but why a one-thousand franc loan for a man of your obvious means?"

"Very simple," he replied. "Where else can you store a Rolls for a month for seventeen francs?"

A duke is hunting in a forest with his men-at-arms and servants when he comes upon a tree. Archery targets are painted all over it, and smack in the middle of each is an arrow.

"Who is this incredibly fine archer?" cries the duke. "I must find him."

After continuing through the forest for a few miles, he comes across a small boy carrying a bow and arrow. Eventually the boy admits that it was he who shot the arrows plumb in the centre of all the targets.

"You didn't just walk up to the targets and hammer the arrows into the middle, did you?" asks the duke worriedly.

"No my lord. I shot them from 100 paces. I swear it by all that I hold holy."

"That is truly astonishing," says the duke. "I hereby admit you into my service. But I must ask one favour in return. You must tell me how you came to be such an outstanding shot."

"Well," said the boy, "first I fire the arrow at the tree, and then I paint the target around it."

A scientist was successful in cloning himself. He was asked to speak at a national convention of cloning scientists.

The meeting room was located on the 45th floor of a skyscraper.

The scientist arrived with his clone and proceeded to the podium.

The clone sat at the end of the head table. The scientist began the speech intending a tribute to the advances in the field of modern biology.

"My fellow scientists," he began. But before he could utter another word, the clone sprang to his feet and shouted out, "He's an asshole!".

The crowd began to murmur as the scientist commanded the clone, "Sit down and shut-up!" Apologizing for the interruption, the scientist began again, "My fellow scientists ..."

Again the clone sprang to his feet and yelled, "This dumb ass couldn't produce a copy on a Xerox. He's a fraudulent son-of-a-bitch!"

Incensed, the scientist rushed to the clone, grabbed him, and threw him out of the window.

A short while later the police arrived and were told of the events that had transpired.

The police chief thought about it for a while, and finally said to the scientist, "We are going to have to arrest you."

The shocked scientist replied, "For what? I have committed no crime. What fell from the window was a clone, not a person." The attending scientists nodded in agreement

"Well," retorted the police chief, "we cannot let this heinous act go unchallenged. We are holding you for making an obscene clone fall ..."

Inflation: When the buck does not stop anywhere.

Wally goes into an electrical store. "Do you have color TVs?"

"Yes."

"All right. I'll take a green one."

"**H**oney, there are some people at the door asking for donations to build a new swimming pool."

"Give them three ... no, two buckets of water."

A saw mill advertises for a timber worker. A skinny little bloke shows up at the camp the next day carrying an axe.

The head timber worker takes one look at the puny bloke and tells him to get lost.

"Give me a chance to show you what I can do," says the skinny feller.

"Okay, see that giant redwood over there?" says the foreman. "Take your axe and cut it down."

The guy heads for the tree, and in five minutes he's knocking on the foreman's door.

"I cut the tree down," says the bloke.

The foreman can't believe his eyes, and says, "Where did you learn to chop down trees like that?"

"In the Great Australian Forest," says the little man.

"You mean the Great Australian Desert," says the foreman, correcting him.

"Sure! That's what they call it now!"

Mrs. Perkins was talking to her hair stylist. "It's silly," she said, "but my daughter has some sort of crazy idea about losing her hair."

"What do you mean?" the beautician asked.

"Well, I overheard her on the phone the other day telling her best friend that she hoped she'd be 'balled' soon."

A few months ago, there was an opening with the CIA for an assassin. These highly classified positions are hard to fill, and there are many tests and background checks involved before you can even be considered for the position. After sending some applicants through the background checks, training and testing, they narrowed the possible choices down to two men and a woman, but only one position was available.

The day came for the final test to see which person would get the extremely secretive job. The CIA men administering the test took one of the men to a large metal door and handed him a gun.

"We must know that you will follow your instructions no matter what the circumstances," they explained. "Inside this room, you will find your wife sitting in a chair. Take this gun and kill her."

The man got a shocked look on his face and said, "You can't be serious! I could never shoot my own wife!"

"Well," says the CIA man, "you're definitely not the right man for this job then."

So they brought the second man to the same door and handed him a gun.

"We must know that you will follow instructions no matter what the circumstances," they explained to the second man. "Inside you will find your wife sitting in a chair. Take this gun and kill her."

The second man looked a bit shocked, but nevertheless took the gun and went in the room. All was quiet for about five minutes, then the door opened. The man came out of the room with tears in his eyes. "I tried to shoot her, I just couldn't pull the trigger and shoot my wife. I guess I'm not the right man for the job."

"No," the CIA man replied, "you don't have what it takes. Take your wife and go home."

Now they're down to the woman left to test.

They led her to the same door to the same room and handed her the same gun.

"We must be sure that you will follow instructions no matter what the circumstances, this is your final test," the CIA man said. "Inside you will find your husband sitting in a chair. Take this gun and kill him."

The woman took the gun and opened the door.

Before the door even closed all the way, the CIA men heard the gun start firing. One shot after another, for six shots. They heard screaming, crashing, banging on the walls. This went on for several minutes, then, all went quiet.

The door opened slowly, and there stood the woman. She wiped the sweat from her brow and said, "You guys didn't tell me the gun was loaded with blanks! I had to beat him to death with the chair!"

Education: A process in which knowledge passes from lecture notes of the professor to the exam paper of the student without passing through the heads of either.

The Cohens were shown into the dentist's office, where Mr. Cohen made it clear he was in a big hurry.

"No fancy stuff, Doctor," he ordered. "No gas or needles or any of that stuff. Just pull the tooth and get it over with."

"I wish more of my patients were as stoic as you," said the dentist admiringly. "Now, which tooth is it?"

Mr. Cohen turned to his wife, Jenny. "Show him your tooth, Honey."

The college professor had just finished explaining an important research project to his class. He emphasized that this paper was an absolute requirement for passing his class, and that there would be only two acceptable excuses for being late. Those were a medically certifiable illness or a death in the student's immediate family.

A prankster student in the back of the classroom waved

his hand and spoke up, "But what about extreme sexual exhaustion, professor?"

As you would expect, the class exploded in laughter.

When the students had finally settled down, the professor froze the young man with a glaring look.

"Well," he responded, "I guess you'll just have to learn to write with your other hand ..."

TOP 20 BOOKS WHICH HAVE NO CONTENT

ADULT ONLY

1. The Royal Family's Guide to Good Marriages.

2. Safe Places to Travel in the USA.

3. The Code of Ethics for Lawyers.

4. The Australian Book of Foreplay.

5. Contraception by Pope John Paul II.

6. The Book of Motivated Postal Workers.

7. Americans' Guide to Etiquette.

8. Bill Clinton: A Portrait of Integrity.

9. The Wit and Wisdom of George W. Bush.

10. Cooking Enjoyable Dishes with Tofu.

11. The Complete Guide to Catholic Sex.

12. Consumer Marketing Ethics.

13.   Popular Lawyers.

14.   John Howard: The Bourbon Years.

15.   Career Opportunities for History Majors.

16.   Everything Men Know about Women.

17.   Home Built Airplanes by John Denver.

18.   My Life's Memories by Ronald Reagan.

19.   Things I Love About Bill by Hillary Clinton.

20.   Things I Can't Afford by Bill Gates.

ABOUT A CERTAIN PRESIDENT . . .

Bill is out on his morning jog when he sees a hooker. As he passes her he says, "Twenty bucks?"

"No way," she answers.

The following morning Bill is jogging with Hillary.

They pass the same hooker on the street who says, "See what you get for twenty bucks?"

It has been reported that Monica Lewinsky had been in an accident with her Sports Utility Vehicle. These are our concerns:

1.   She must have blown a rod.
2.   Obviously, her driving sucks too.
3.   It's not the first time she flipped over something with a spare tyre.
4.   How badly did THIS accident stain her dress?

TOP TEN CLINTON MOVIE TITLES

1.   Free Willy.
2.   The Big Lewinsky.
3.   Neither an Officer nor a Gentleman.

4. Willy's Wonka and the Cigar Factory.
5. Citizen Stain.
6. Prince of Ties.
7. Saving Private Lyin'.
8. The Lying King.
9. Terms of Impeachment.
10. Waiting to Inhale.

Two of Bill's sperm were racing toward the cervix and the first one said, "How far do you think it is to the fallopian tubes?"

The other one said, "It can't be too far. I think we just passed the tonsils."

Bill & Hillary invited Al & Tipper Gore over for dinner at the White House. In the middle of dinner, Al excused himself to use the bathroom. After a couple of minutes, he came back. They finished dinner and left.

On the way home, Al turned to Tipper and said, "Did you know Bill has a solid-gold urinal in his bathroom? How can we tell the American people that we are serious about cutting the budget when the President has a solid-gold urinal?"

Tipper said, "There must be some mistake, I'll call Hillary when we get home and find out."

They get home and she calls Hillary and says, "Is it true that Bill has a solid-gold urinal in his bathroom?"

Hillary puts her hand over the receiver and says, "Bill!!! I found out who peed in your saxophone!"

During a recent staff meeting in Heaven, God, Moses and Saint Peter concluded that the behaviour of Ex-President Clinton has brought about the need for an Eleventh Commandment.

They worked long and hard in a brain-storming session to try to settle on the wording of the new commandment, because they realized that it should have the same style, majesty and dignity as the original ten. Finally, they came up with the 11th:

"Thou shalt not comfort thy rod with thy staff."

Hillary went in for her yearly check-up. When she was finished, she asked her gynaecologist how things looked.

He said he was pleased and that she is in great shape, and congratulated her on her pregnancy. She argued that she couldn't possibly be pregnant, but the doctor gave her a due date eight months in the future.

She stormed out of the office, went to the receptionist's desk, grabbed the phone and called the White House. When she finally got through the red tape and had Bill on the phone, she shouted, "You dirty bastard, you got me pregnant."

There was dead silence on the other end of the line. After a few seconds, she yelled even louder, "You dirty bastard, you got me pregnant!"

Finally Bill answered, "Who is this?"

President Clinton was being entertained by an African leader.

They'd spent the day discussing what the country had received from the Russians before the new government kicked them out.

Said the African leader, "The Russians, they built us a power plant, a highway, and an airport. Plus we learned to drink vodka and play Russian roulette."

President Clinton frowned, "Russian roulette's not a nice game."

The African leader smiled, "That's why we developed African roulette. If you want to have good relations with our country, you'll have to play. I'll show you how."

He pushed a buzzer, and a moment later six magnificently built, nude women were ushered in. "You can choose any one of those women to give you oral sex," he told Clinton.

"Unreal," Clinton said. "But it doesn't seem much like Russian roulette."

"Trust me, it is. One of them is a cannibal ..."

Bill Clinton and Chelsea are walking along a beach in California.

Summoning up all the courage a father can, he asks, "Chelsea, how is college going socially? Do you have any boyfriends, and are you being, um, nice?"

Chelsea thinks for a second, then replies, "Well Dad, if you're asking me, 'Am I having sex,' well, the answer is no, not as YOU define it ..."

Have you heard about the Monica Virus? It attacks laptops.

Bill Clinton and his driver were cruising along a country road one night when all of a sudden they hit a pig, killing it instantly. Bill told his driver to go up to the farm house and explain to the owners what had happened.

About an hour later Bill sees his driver staggering back to the car with a bottle of wine in one hand, a cigar in the other and his clothes all ripped and torn.

"What happened to you?" asked Bill.

"Well, the Farmer gave me the wine, his wife gave me the cigar and his 19-year-old daughter made mad passionate love to me," said the driver.

"My God, what did you tell them?" asks Clinton.

The driver replies, "I'm Bill Clinton's driver, and I just killed the pig."

This is the FBI summary of a conversation that took place between President Clinton and Megan, a brand new intern in the White House.

Megan walked into the White House for her first day of her internship and was greeted by the President. After a short tour of the White House the President asked, "Would you like to see the Presidential clock?"

Megan looked troubled and said, "I don't know Mr. President. I have heard some pretty bad things about you.

I don't think that would be a good idea."

"Nonsense," said the President. "It's just a clock."

Megan agreed and the President led her into the Oval Office where they were alone. He closed the door, dropped his pants, and pulled it out.

Megan gasped. "Oh that's not the Presidential clock," she said, "that's the Presidential cock!"

To which the President responded, "Megan honey, once you put a face and two hands on it, it's a clock!"

Clinton and the Pope die on the same day and, due to some administrative foul up, Clinton gets sent to heaven and the Pope gets sent to hell.

The Pope explains the situation to Hell Administration; they check their paperwork, and the error is acknowledged. They explain, however, that it will take 24 hours to make the switch.

The next day, the Pope is called in and the Hell Administration staff bid him farewell and he heads for heaven.

On the way up, he meets Clinton, on the way down, and they stop to chat.

Pope: "Sorry about the mix-up."

Clinton: "No problem."

Pope: "Well, I'm really excited about going to heaven!"

Clinton: "Why's that?"

Pope: "All my life I've wanted to meet the Virgin Mary."

Clinton: "You're a day late ..."

First Lady Hillary Clinton and an Australian cabinet Minister, who shall remain nameless, but let's call her Bronwyn, are having a girl-to-girl talk.

Hillary says to Bronwyn, "You're lucky that you don't have to put up with men having sex with you. I have to put up with Bill, and there is no telling where he last had his pecker."

Bronwyn responds, "Just because I am aesthetically challenged it doesn't mean I don't have to fight off unwelcome sexual advances."

Hillary asks, "Well, how do you deal with the problem?"

Bronwyn replies, "Whenever I feel that a guy is getting ready to make a pass at me, I muster all my might and squeeze out the loudest, nastiest fart that I can."

That night, Bill was already in bed with the lights out when Hillary slips into bed. She could hear him start to stir, and knew that he would be wanting some action. She had been saving her farts all day and was ready for him.

She tenses up her butt cheeks and forces out the most disgusting sounding fart you could imagine.

Bill rolls over and says, "Bronwyn, is that you?"

Bill Clinton and Al Gore went into a local diner for lunch. As they read the menu, the waitress came over and asked Clinton, "Are you ready to order, sir?"

Clinton replies, "Yes, I'd like a quickie."

"A quickie?!" the waitress replies with disgust. "Sir, given the current situation of your personal life, I don't believe that's a good idea. I'll come back later when you are ready to make an order from the menu."

Al Gore leans over to Clinton and says, "Sir, it's pronounced 'Quiche'…"

Once Bill Clinton visited an elementary school to talk to a group of third-graders. He said to them, "Today we are going to discuss the difference between a tragedy, a great loss and an accident".

Then he said, "Can anyone give me an example of a tragedy?"

A little boy raises his hand and says, "If a kid runs out in the street after a ball and gets hit by a car?"

Clinton says, "No, that would be an accident. Can anyone else try?"

A little girl raises her hand and says, "If a busload of kids drove off a cliff?"

Clinton says, "No, that would be a great loss. Come on, anyone else?"

A boy raises his hand and says and says, "If you and Mrs. Clinton were on a plane and it blew up."

Then Clinton says, "Well, yes, but can you tell me why it would be considered a tragedy?"

And the little boy says, "Well, it wouldn't have been an accident, and it sure as heck wouldn't have been a great loss."

Did you know that Bill Clinton is considering changing the Democratic seal from a donkey to a condom? It represents inflation, halts production, and gives you a false sense of security while you are being screwed.

Bill Clinton steps off Air Force One carrying a small dog. One of his Secret Service men says, "Nice dog, Sir."

Bill says, "Thanks. I got it for Hillary." The Secret Service man says, "Nice trade, Sir!"

Bill Clinton steps out onto the White House lawn in the dead of winter. Right in front of him, on the White House lawn, he sees "The President Must Die" written in urine across the snow.

Well, old Bill is pretty pissed off. He storms into his security staff's HQ, and yells, "Somebody wrote a death threat in the snow on the front damn lawn! And they wrote it in urine! Son-of-a-bitch had to be standing right on the porch when he did it! Where were you guys?!"

The security guys stay silent and stare ashamedly at the floor. Bill hollers, "Well, dammit, don't just sit there! Get out and find out who did it! I want an answer, and I want it tonight!"

The entire staff immediately jump up and race for the exits. Later that evening, his chief security officer approaches him and says, "Well Mr. President, we have some bad news and we have some really bad news. Which do you want first?"

Clinton says, "Oh Hell, give me the bad news first."

The officer says, "Well, we took a sample of the urine and tested it. The results just came back, and it was Al Gore's urine."

Clinton says, "Oh my God, I feel so... so... betrayed! My own vice president! Damn. ...Well, what's the really bad news?"

The officer replies, "It's Hillary's handwriting ..."

Bill and Hillary Clinton are at a baseball game. As the game is getting ready to start, Bill stands up, picks up Hillary, and throws her out onto the field.

When he sits down, his chief advisor leans over and says, "You know, Bill, you may have misunderstood me. I said you have to throw out the first pitch."

Clinton and Gore are sitting around in the Oval Office, having a chat.

After a while, as expected, the Lewinsky situation came up. Gore says, "You know Bill, I just think we have different mindsets about things. For example, I don't believe in premarital sex. I never slept with Tipper before we got married. How about you?"

Clinton paused and thought, then said, "I don't know Al, what was her maiden name again?"

Last summer, the President and Mrs. Clinton were vacationing in their home state of Arkansas.

One day, they stopped at a service station to fill up their car with gas. It seemed that the owner of the station was once Hillary's high school love.

They exchanged hellos and then the White House couple went on their way.

As they were driving on to their final destination, Bill put his arm around Hillary and said, "Well, honey, if you had stayed with him, you would now be the wife of a service station owner."

She smirked and replied, "No! If I had stayed with him, he would be the President of the United States …!"

TOP 10 TITLES FOR MONICA LEWINSKY'S NEW BOOK...

1. Me and My Big Mouth.
2. I Suck at My Job.
3. What Really Goes Down in the White House.
4. How I Blew It in Washington.
5. Going Down and Moving Up.
6. Testing the Limits of the Gag Rule.
7. Going Back for Gore.
8. Secret Services to the President.
9. Deep Inside the Oval Office.
10. Al Gore Is in Command, For The Next 30 Minutes …

RIDDLES

Q.   What do you call a man with no arms and no legs
who can play the drums?

A.   Clever Dick.

Q.   Why did the golfer have two pairs of pants?

A.   In case he got a hole-in-one.

Q.   What is the German word for constipation?

A.   Farfrompoopin.

Q.   What does a maths graduate say to a sociology
graduate?

A.   I'll have the burger and fries, please.

Q.   When is it much better to be a woman than a man?

A.   When you are in the lavatory and the plane hits
turbulence.

Q.   What's the difference between Jewish women and
Catholic women?

A.   Catholic women have fake jewellery and real
orgasms.

Q.   Why did Arnold Schwarzenegger and Maria Shriver get married?
A.   They're trying to breed a bullet-proof Kennedy.

Q.   Why don't Baptists make love standing up?
A.   Because it might lead to dancing.

Q.   What's grey, has four legs and a trunk?
A.   A mouse on vacation.

Q.   How are sex and air a lot alike?
A.   Neither one's a big deal unless you're not getting any.

Q.   How do you make an elephant fly?
A.   Start with a 3-foot zipper ...

Q.   How do you know when you pass an elephant?
A.   You can't get the toilet seat down.

Q.   What's the red stuff between elephant's toes?
A.   Slow pygmies.

Q.   What is more difficult than getting an elephant into the back seat of your car?
A.   Getting a pregnant elephant in the back seat of your car.

Q.   What is more difficult than getting a pregnant elephant in the back of your car?
A.   Getting an elephant pregnant in the back seat of your car.

Q.   Dad, what's a transvestite?

A.   I don't know, but ask your Mother, he'll know!

Q.   What happens if you play a country & western song backwards?

A.   The singer gets his wife, house, and his job back!

Q.   If a bra is an upper topper flopper stopper, and a jock strap is a lower decker pecker checker, and golden toilet paper is a super duper pooper scooper. then what is a Japanese boxer's father who has diarrhoea??

A.   A slap happy Jappy with a crap happy pappy.

Q.   When does a woman enjoy a man's company?

A.   When she owns it.

Q.   What did the leper say to the prostitute?

A.   You can keep the tip.

Q.   Why did the leper fail her driving test?

A.   She left her foot on the clutch.

Q.   Did you hear about the short-sighted circumciser?

A.   He got the sac.

Q.   What are a woman's four favorite animals?

A.   A mink in the closet, a Jaguar in the garage, a tiger in the bedroom, and a jackass who'll pay for it all.

Q. How did Pinocchio find out he was made of wood?

A. His hand caught fire.

Q. What did God say after creating Man?

A. I must be able to do better than that.

Q. What did God say after creating Eve?

A. Practice makes perfect.

Q. How are men and parking spots alike?

A. All the good ones are always taken. Free ones are mostly handicapped or extremely small.

Q. What is the one thing that all men at singles bars have in common?

A. They're married.

Q. Did you hear about the cannibal who had chronic indigestion?

A. He ate someone who disagreed with him.

Q. What do you get if you cross a dog with a Concorde?

A. A jet setter.

Q. Why are bull sperm and politicians the same?

A. In each case, only one in a thousand works!

Q. What do a Christmas tree and a Catholic priest have in common?

A. Their balls are just for decoration.

Q.   What does D.N.A. stand for?

A.   National Dyslexics Association.

Q.   Did you hear the one about the dyslexic pimp?

A.   He bought a warehouse!

Q.   Did you hear about the dyslexic Devil worshipper?

A.   He sold his soul to Santa!

Q.   What is a definition of a pessimist?

A.   Someone who takes a daily dish of prunes with his All-Bran.

Q.   Why was the washing machine laughing?

A.   Because it was taking the piss out of the knickers.

Q.   Why do nursing homes give Viagra to old men?

A.   To stop them rolling off the bed.

20 THINGS I WISH I'D SAID

1.   Depression is merely anger without enthusiasm.

2.   Black holes are where God is divided by zero.

3.   The only substitute for good manners is fast reflexes.

4.   I almost had a psychic girlfriend, but she left me before we met.

5.   I drive way too fast to worry about cholesterol.

6.   Shin: a device for finding furniture in the dark.

7.   Why do psychics have to ask you for your name?

8.   Support bacteria – they're the only culture some people have.

9.   When everything's coming your way, you're in the wrong lane.

10. Ambition is a poor excuse for not having enough sense to be lazy.

11. If everything seems to be going well, you have obviously overlooked something.

12. I couldn't repair your brakes, so I made your horn louder.

13. How do you tell when you run out of invisible ink?

14. Beauty is in the eye of the beer holder.

15. Everyone has a photographic memory. Some don't have the film.

16. Join the Army, meet interesting people, and kill them.

17. Laughing stock: cattle with a sense of humor.

18. Wear short sleeves! Support your right to bare arms.

19. Corduroy pillows: They're making headlines!

20. I tried sniffing Coke once, but the ice cubes got stuck in my nose.

THEN THERE WAS THE BLONDE THAT . . .

A blonde goes into the drug store to buy some condoms because her friend told her that she should learn about practicing safe sex.

She walks up to the pharmacist and asks, "How much for a box of rubbers?"

"They're six dollars for a box of three," he replies, "Plus sixty cents for the tax."

"Oh," replies the blonde, "I always wondered how they kept them on ...!"

A blonde and a redhead are watching the nine o'clock news, and come across an item about a man threatening to commit suicide by jumping from a bridge.

The blonde offers the redhead a bet that the man won't actually jump.

The redhead agrees to wager $50 on the outcome and then the announcer cuts to a commercial break.

When the news resumes, more footage is shown and the man actually jumps to his death. The redhead feels dreadful that she was so flippant as to bet on the outcome of such a gruesome incident and says that she feels bad about taking the money. She would feel better if the bet was called off.

"No, a bet is a bet," insists the blonde. "Besides, I saw the whole thing on the six o'clock news."

"What? Well, why did you offer me the bet then, if you knew the outcome?" asks the redhead.

"I honestly didn't think that he would do it the second time …"

Back in the Wild West, there are two blond cowboys, Frank and Jim. One day, the two are enjoying a drink in the local saloon, when a man walks into the bar with an Indian's head under his arm.

The barman shakes his hand and says, "I hate Indians; last week the bastards burnt my barn to the ground, assaulted my wife, and killed my children." He then adds, "If any man brings me the head of an Indian, I'll give him one thousand dollars."

The two blonds looked at each other and walk out of the bar and go hunting for an Indian.

They find one and Frank throws a rock which hits the Indian right on the head.

The Indian falls off his horse, but lands way down a ravine. The two blonds make their way down the ravine where Frank pulls out a knife ready to claim their trophy.

Jim calls urgently, "Frank, take a look at this."

Frank replies, "Not now, I'm busy."

Jim tries again with more panic in his voice and says, "I really think you should look at this."

Frank says, "Look, you can see I'm busy? I have a thousand dollars in my hand!"

But Jim is adamant, "Please, please, Frank, take a look at this."

Frank looks up and sees that standing at the top of the ravine are ten thousand red Indians in full battle gear, their bows and arrows aimed at them.

Frank just shakes his head and says, "Oh… my… God… we're going to be millionaires!"

A woman hired a contractor to repaint the interior of her house. The woman walked the man through the second floor of her home and told him what colors she wanted for each room. As they walked through the first room, the woman said, "I think I would like this room in a cream color."

The contractor wrote on his clipboard, walked to the window, opened it and yelled out, "Green side up!" He then closed the window and continued following the woman to the next room.

The woman looked confused, but proceeded with her tour, "In this room, I was thinking of an off blue."

Again, the contractor wrote this down, went to the window, opened it and yelled out, "Green side up!" This baffled the woman, but she was hesitant to say anything.

In the next room, the woman said she would like it painted in a light rose color. And once more, the contractor opened the window and yelled, "Green side up!"

Struck with curiosity, the woman mustered up the nerve to ask, "Why do you keep yelling 'Green side up' out my window every time I tell you the color I would like the room?"

The contractor replied, "Because, across the street, I have a crew of blonds laying instant lawn ..."

It was a really, really hot day and this blonde decided she would go buy a drink. She went to the vending machine and when she put her money in, a can of drink came out – so she kept putting money in.

It was such a hot day, a line beginning forming behind her. Finally, a guy on line said, "Will you hurry up? We're all hot and thirsty!"

And the blonde said, "No way. I'm still winning!"

How many blondes does it take to milk a cow? Eleven. One to hold the udders, and ten to lift the cow up and down.

A bloke walks into a pub with a crocodile on a leash and puts it up on the bar.

He turns to the amazed drinkers, "Here's the deal. I'll open this crocodile's mouth and place my genitals inside. Then the croc will close his mouth for one minute. He'll then open his mouth and I'll remove my wedding tackle unscathed. In return for witnessing this spectacle, each of you will buy me a drink."

After a few moments' silence the crowd murmurs approval.

The man stands up on the bar, drops his trousers, and places his privates in the crocodile's mouth.

The croc closes his mouth as the crowd gasps. After a minute, the man grabs a beer bottle and raps the crocodile hard on the top of its head.

The croc opens his mouth and the man removes his genitals – unscathed as promised.

The crowd cheers and the first of his free drinks is delivered.

The man calls for silence and makes another offer. "I'll pay anyone $1000 who's willing to give it a try". A hush falls over the crowd. After a while, a hand goes up at the back. It's a blonde. "I'll try," she says. "But only if you promise not to hit me on the head with the beer bottle …"

THE TOP 10 INVENTIONS BY THE WORLD'S MOST INTELLIGENT BLONDES

1.   The Pedal-Powered Wheel Chair.
2.   The Inflatable Dart Board.
3.   The Submarine Screen Door.
4.   The Waterproof Towel.
5.   The Solar Powered Torch.
6.   The Dictionary Index.
7.   The Helicopter Ejector Seat
8.   Powdered Water.

9.   The Waterproof Tea Bag.

10.   A Book on How To Read.

While out one morning in the park, a jogger found a brand new tennis ball, and, seeing no-one around that it might belong to, he slipped it into the pocket of his shorts.

Later, on his way home, he stopped at the pedestrian crossing, waiting for the lights to change. A blonde girl standing next to him eyed the large bulge in his shorts. "What's that?" she asked, her eyes gleaming with lust.

"Tennis ball," came the breathless reply.

"Oh," said the blonde girl sympathetically, "that must be painful. I had tennis elbow once."

A depressed blonde decided to commit suicide by hanging herself from a tree in the park. A few days later, a man was walking his dog and spotted her hanging from the tree. He asks the blonde what she is doing and she replies, "I'm hanging myself."

"You're supposed to put the noose around your neck, not your waist," said the onlooker

"I tried that," replied the blonde, "but I couldn't breathe …"

Three women are about to be executed – a redhead, a brunette, and a blonde.

The guard brings the redhead forward and the executioner asks if she has any last requests. She says no, and the executioner shouts, "Ready! Aim …"

Suddenly the redhead yells, "Earthquake!!!"

Everyone is startled and they all throw themselves on the ground for safety. When they look up the redhead has escaped.

The guard brings the brunette forward and the executioner asks if she has any last requests. She says no, and the executioner shouts, "Ready! Aim …"

Suddenly the brunette yells, "Tornado!!!"

Again, everyone is startled and dives for cover. When they look up, the brunette has escaped.

By now the blonde has it all figured out. The guard brings her forward and the executioner asks if she has any last requests. She says no, and the executioner shouts, "Ready! Aim …"

And the blonde yells, "FIRE!!"

A blonde with two very red ears went to her doctor. The doctor asked her what had happened.

"I was ironing a shirt and the phone rang," she said. "But instead of picking up the phone, I accidentally picked up the iron and stuck it to my ear."

"Jeezus!" the doctor exclaimed in disbelief. "So, what happened to your other ear?"

"The person rang back …"

A blonde was shopping at the supermarket. As she placed her groceries on the checkout stand, the assistant asked her, "Paper or plastic?"

"It doesn't matter" she replied, "I'm bisacksual."

B oyfriend: "Why do you never scream my name when you have an orgasm?"

Blonde: "Because you are never there."

T wo blond carpenters were working on a house. The one who was nailing down siding would reach into his nail pouch, pull out a nail and either toss it over his shoulder or nail it in. The other, figuring this was worth looking into, asked, "Why are you throwing those nails away?"

The first explained, "If I pull a nail out of my pouch and it's pointed toward me, I throw it away 'cause it's defective. If it's pointed toward the house, then I nail it in!"

The second blond got completely upset and yelled, "You moron! The nails pointed toward you aren't defective! They're for the other side of the house!"

T here is a spooky mirror in a women's restroom in a restaurant in downtown New York.

If you say something truthful while looking into the mirror, you receive one wish.

If you say some that's not truthful, the mirror will magically drag you in, and you disappear forever.

First, a beautiful brunette strolls in. She takes a look at herself in the mirror and says, "I think I'm the prettiest woman in the world." And, bang, she's sucked in.

Next, a very attractive redhead woman comes in, looks in the mirror, and says, "I think I'm the prettiest woman in the world." The mirror sucks her in.

Then a cute little blonde comes in, looks at herself in the mirror, and says, "I think ..."

And she's sucked in straight away.

What nursery rhyme do blondes know meticulously off by heart?

"Hump-me, dump-me ..."

A blonde goes into an electronics store, and asks one of the staff how much a TV is. The salesman says straight away, "Sorry we don't sell to blondes." She storms home, goes to the bathroom, pulls out some hair-color, and the next day comes back as a brunette.

She asks another salesman, "How much is that TV?"

He also says, "Sorry we don't sell to blondes."

She goes home and the next day comes back as a red-head, and asks yet another salesman, "How much is this TV?"

He says, "Sorry we don't sell to blondes."

She says, "How can this be? I have come back here as a

brunette and a red-head. How did you know I was a blonde?"

And he says, "Because that is not a TV, that is a microwave!"

Then there was a blonde who desperately needed some money, so she decided to kidnap a child and demand a ransom. At her local park, she grabbed a little boy and wrote a note: "I have kidnapped your son. Leave $100,000 in unmarked bills in a plain brown envelope at the foot of the cherry tree tomorrow at 6 am. Signed, The Blonde. " She pinned the note inside the boy's shirt, and told him to go straight home. The next morning, she returned to the park to find the $100,000 in a brown envelope, at the foot of the cherry tree, just as she had instructed. Inside the bag was another note: "Here is your money. I cannot believe that one blonde would do this to another!"

"I can't find the cause of your illness," said the doctor, "But, I think it may be due to drinking."

"In that case," replied the blonde, "I shall come back when you are sober."

A blonde is pulled over for speeding.
Cop: "Can I see your driver's license, please?"
Blonde: "What's that?"

Cop:"It's that card with your picture on it."

Blonde:"Oh! Here it is," said the blonde after searching in her purse.

Cop:"And can I have your registration?"

Blonde:"What's that?"

Cop:"It's those papers saying that this is your car."

Blonde:"Oh!" searching frantically again, "Here you go."

Then the cop unzips his fly and takes his penis out of his pants.

Blonde:"Oh-no! Not another breathalyser test!"

Why did the blonde have lipstick on her steering wheel? She was trying to blow the horn.

A blonde went outside to check her mailbox, and her neighbor kept an eye on her. She had no mail, so she went back inside her house.

Two minutes later, the same blonde went outside for the second time to check her mailbox, and still, she had no mail. The neighbor was confused. One minute later, again the woman comes outside to check her mailbox for the third time, and again, she had no mail.

This time, her neighbor went up to her and said, "The mailman won't be here for another three hours, why do you keep on checking your mail?"

The blonde said, "Oh, because my computer keeps on saying, 'You've got mail'."

There once was a blonde who had two horses. She couldn't tell her two horses apart so she decided to ask her neighbor to help her out.

She said to her neighbor, "I have two horses that I can't tell apart, can you help me?"

"Sure," said her neighbor, "maybe you should nick the ears of one, and then you could tell them apart."

So the blonde went home and did that. The next day the blonde went to check up on her horses. However she still could not tell them apart, because the other horse also had a nicked ear. She went back over to her neighbor.

"My other horse has a nicked ear, too." she said, "Do you have any other ideas as to how to tell them apart? They are both girls."

"Hmmmm," said her neighbor, "cut one's tail shorter than the other!"

So the blonde went home and did that. The next day, though, when she looked at them, both horses had the same length of tail!

As a last resort the neighbor suggested that she should consider measuring the horses. Maybe one stands taller than the other one.

The blonde did this and excitedly rushed home and phoned her neighbor. "You were right!" She said. "The black horse is bigger than the white one!"

Derek drove his brand new Mercedes to his favorite bar, and put it in the car park at the back. He went in inside, where the bar was being looked after by Beverley, the regular waitress.

Beverley was a pretty blonde, and as Derek walked into the bar, she happily greeted him. He bought a drink, and went and sat at a table.

A few minutes later, Beverley came running up to him yelling, "Derek! Derek! I was putting the trash out the back and saw someone driving off with your new Mercedes!"

"Dear God! Did you try to stop him?"

"No," she said, "I did better than that! I got the license plate number!"

Three blondes are stuck on a deserted island, when one of them finds a lamp on the beach. She picks it up and gives it a little rub and a genie pops out.

The genie looks at the three blondes and says, "I normally give three wishes, but since there are three of you, I will grant each of you one wish."

Well, the first one is tired of being on the island, so she wishes to go back home. POOF!! She disappears.

The second one said she, too, is tired of the island, and wishes to go home. POOF!! She also disappears.

The genie then turns to the last blonde and asks her what her wish is. "Gee," she says, "I'm awfully lonely here by myself. I wish my friends were still here."

Then there was the blonde who was complaining to her friend about constantly being called a dumb blonde. Her friend tells her, "Go do something to prove them wrong! Why don't you learn all the world capitals or something?"

The blonde thinks this is a great idea, and locks herself up for two weeks studying. The next party she goes to, some guy is making dumb blonde comments to her.

She gets all indignant and claims, "I'm NOT a dumb blonde. In fact, I can name ALL the world capitals!"

The guy doesn't believe her, so she dares him to test her.

He says, "Okay, what's the Capital of Monaco?"

The blonde tosses her hair in triumph and says, "That's easy! It's M!"

A young blonde woman is distraught because she fears her husband is having an affair, so she goes to a gun shop and buys a handgun.

The next day she comes home to find her husband in bed with a beautiful redhead

She grabs the gun and holds it to her own head.

The husband jumps out of bed, begging and pleading with her not to shoot herself. Hysterically the blonde responds to the husband, "Shut up ... you're next!"

On a plane bound for New York, the flight attendant approached a blonde sitting in the first class section and requested that she move to economy since she did not have a first class ticket. The blonde replied, "I'm blonde, I'm beautiful, I'm going to New York and I'm not moving."

Not wanting to argue with a customer, the flight attendant asked the co-pilot to speak with her.

He went to talk with the woman asking her to please move out of the first class section. Again, the blonde replied, "I'm blonde, I'm beautiful, I'm going to New York and I'm not moving."

The co-pilot returned to the cockpit and asked the captain what should he do. The captain said, "I'm married to a blonde. I know how to handle this."

He went to the first class section and whispered in the blonde's ear. She immediately jumped up and ran to the economy section mumbling to herself, "Why didn't anyone just say so?"

Surprised, the flight attendant and the co-pilot asked what he said to her that finally convinced her to move from her seat.

He said, "I told her the first class section wasn't going to New York …"

A blonde walks into a hairdresser's, wearing headphones. She says to the hairdresser, "Please cut my hair, but, whatever you do, don't knock the headphones off!"

Alas, during the cutting, the hairdresser slips, and the headphones accidentally fall off.

The blonde falls over dead.

The shocked hairdresser picks up the headphones and listens.

The taped voice is saying, "Breath in, breath out, breath in, breath out …"

Eleven blondes and one brunette are hanging on a rope If one of them does not let go of the rope, it will break and they will all die.

The brunette says she will sacrifice herself and let go because the blondes are such good friends that they would all grieve too much if one of them was to die and wreck their lives.

She finishes her speech and the blondes are so touched by her generosity that all they begin to clap.

Two blondes are walking down the street when they find a makeup compact.

The first blonde opens it and looks in the mirror.

She says, "That face is familiar. But I can't put a name to it."

The second blonde grabs the mirror, looks into it, then looks at her friend and says, "Duh, silly, it's ME"!

SHE WAS SO BLONDE THAT:

- She sent me a fax with a stamp on it.
- She tried to put M&M's in alphabetical order.
- She thought a quarterback was a refund.
- If you gave her a penny for her thought, you'd get change back.
- She tripped over a cordless phone.
- She took a ruler to bed to see how long she slept.
- At the bottom of the application where it says, "sign here" she put, "Sagittarius."

- If she spoke her mind, she'd probably be speechless.
- She studied for a blood test – and failed.
- It takes her two hours to watch 60 Minutes.
- She sold the car for petrol money.
- When she took you to the airport and saw the sign that said, "Airport Left" she turned around and went home.

How do you brainwash a blonde? Give her a douche and shake her upside down.

This blonde decides to try horseback riding, for the first time.

She mounts the horse unassisted, and it springs into motion. It gallops along at a steady pace, but the blonde begins to slip from the saddle. In terror, she grabs for the horse's mane, but cannot get a firm grip.

She throws her arms around the horse's neck, but slides down the side, while it gallops on.

The blonde tries to leap from the horse to safety. But her foot becomes entangled in the stirrup, and she is now in all sorts of trouble, with her head repeatedly banging against the ground as the horse continues its gallop.

The blonde starts to lose consciousness.

But luckily, one of the checkout girls sees her predicament, rushes over, and unplugs the horse …

This blonde walks into a telephone office and tells the man behind the counter that there has been a family emergency, and she has to immediately call her mother, who is holidaying in a remote part of Africa.

After looking up the charge list, the man says that such a call to such a remote place is not easy to set up, and just three minutes on the phone would cost her 120 dollars.

The blonde is shocked, saying she just couldn't afford that much.

The man looks at her very kindly, and says gently: "Maybe we can work something out between us. Let's go to the back room."

They go out the back, where the man tells her to get on her knees in front of him, which she does.

He says, "Unzip my pants".

She unzips his pants.

He says, "Take it out."

She takes it out.

He says, "Put it to your lips".

She puts it to her lips.

After waiting for a bit, with nothing happening, the man looks down and says, "Well, go ahead!"

The blonde looks up at him puzzled, and then finally, slowly, holds it again to her mouth.

And says, "Hello? Mum?"

Did you hear about the figure-conscious blonde who had square boobs?
She forgot to take the tissues out of the box.

Then there was the blonde working at Reception. A fellow worker came up and said, "Would you like to buy a raffle ticket? Janice in Production died suddenly last week. It's for her husband and four children."

"No thanks," the blonde says. "I've already got a husband and two kids of my own."

20 GREAT PHILOSOPHICAL STATEMENTS

1. A miss is as good as a Mr.
2. Better to be safe than punch a 5th grader.
3. When the blind lead the blind ... get out of the way.
4. Laugh and the whole world laughs with you. Cry and you have to blow your nose.
5. Strike while the bug is close.
6. It's always darkest before daylight savings time.
7. Never underestimate the power of termites.
8. Don't bite the hand that ... looks dirty.
9. No news is impossible.
10. None are so blind as Helen Keller.
11. You can't teach an old dog.
12. Love all, trust ... me.
13. An idle mind is the best way to relax.
14. Where there is smoke, there's ... pollution.
15. Happy is the bride who gets all the presents.
16. If you lie down with dogs, you will stink in the morning.
17. A penny saved is not much.
18. Two is company, three's The Musketeers.
19. Children should be seen and not spanked or grounded.
20. If at first you don't succeed get new batteries.

MILITARY

A young officer was posted to a British army detachment in the desert.

On his tour of the facility with the master sergeant, he noticed a group of camels.

"What are those for?" he asked.

"The men use them when they want to have sex."

"Don't say another word, sergeant. That is the most disgusting thing I have ever heard. Get rid of those camels immediately!"

"Yes, sir."

A few weeks went by and the young officer began to get rather horny.

He called the sergeant over and asked, "Where are the camels we used to have?"

The sergeant replied that he had sold them to a Bedouin that camped nearby.

"Take me to them, please."

The officer and the sergeant went over to the Bedouin camp and found the camels.

The officer told the sergeant to leave him alone with the camels, then picked out the most attractive one, and proceeded to have sex with the camel.

On the way back to the camp, the officer asked, "Sergeant, do the men actually enjoy sex with the camels?"

The sergeant looked at the officer in astonishment and exclaimed, "I don't know! They use them to ride into town to where the girls are."

What should Iraq get for its air defense system? A refund.

The soldier serving overseas and far from home was annoyed and upset when his girl wrote breaking off their engagement and asking for her photograph back.

He went out and collected from his friends all the unwanted photographs of women that he could find, bundled them all together and sent them to her with a note: "Regret can not remember which one is you. Please keep your photo and return the others."

A knight and his men return to their castle after a long hard day of fighting. "How are we faring?" asks the king.

"Sire," replies the knight, "I have been robbing and pillaging on your behalf all day, burning the towns of your enemies in the west."

"What?" shrieks the king. "I don't have any enemies to the west!"

"Oh," says the knight. "Well, you do now."

There was an Englishman, a Scotsman and a Frenchman who had been taken prisoner by the Germans and were about to be whipped.

The German officer said that he would allow them any one thing on their back to ease the pain. The Scotsman went first and had vinegar on his back, as he heard it helped. Next was the Frenchman who asked for garlic hoping that the smell would remind him of home and distract from the pain.

Then last came the Englishman who when asked said, "I'll have the Frenchman!"

How many members of the American Force Against Terrorism does it take to screw in a light bulb? We are not prepared to comment on specific numbers at this time."

"Who likes music?" asks a commander.

Two soldiers step forward. "OK you two. I bought a piano. Take it to my apartment on the fourth floor."

A soldier requested a two-day leave, as he was to become a father in the near future. When he returned to the base, a sergeant asked, "Was it a boy or girl?"

"I don't know yet. I'll let you know in about nine months."

The captain called the Sergeant in, "Sarge, I just got a telegram that Private Jones' mother died yesterday. Better go tell him and send him in to see me."

So the sergeant calls for his morning formation and lines up all the troops.

"Listen up, men," says the sergeant. "Johnson, step out and report to the mess hall for Hoskins, step out and report for guard duty. Jones, step out and report to personnel, your mother is dead. The rest of you are to report to the motor pool for maintenance."

Later that day the Captain called the Sergeant into his office. "Sergeant, that was a pretty cold way to inform Jones his mother died. Could you be a bit more tactful, next time, please?"

"Yes, sir," answered the sergeant.

A few months later, the captain called the sergeant in again. "Sarge, I just got a telegram that Private McGrath's mother died. You'd better go tell him, and then send him in to see me. This time, please be more tactful."

So the sergeant calls for his morning formation. "OK, men, fall in and listen up. Everybody with a mother, take two steps forward. Not so fast, McGrath ...!"

An army major visits the sick soldiers, goes up to one private and asks, "What's your problem, soldier?"

"Chronic syphilis, sir!"

"What treatment are you getting?"

"Five minutes with the wire brush each day, sir!"

"What's your ambition?"

"To get back to the front lines, sir!"

"Good man!" says the major.

He goes to the next bed. "What's your problem, soldier?"

"Chronic piles, sir!"

"What treatment are you getting?"

"Five minutes with the wire brush each day, sir!"

"What's your ambition?"

"To get back to the front lines, sir!"

"Good man!" says the major.

He goes to the next bed. "What's your problem, soldier?"

"Chronic gum disease, sir!"

"What treatment are you getting?"

"Five minutes with the wire brush each day, sir!"

"What's your ambition?"

"To get to the front of the line and get the wire brush before the other two, sir!"

The company commander and the sergeant were in the field.

As they hit the sack for the night, the sergeant said: "Sir, look up into the sky and tell me what you see."

The commander said, "I see millions of stars."

"And what does that tell you, sir?"

"Astronomically, it tells me that there are millions of galaxies and potentially billions of planets. Theologically, it tells me that God is great and that we are small and insignificant. Meteorologically, it tells me that we will have a beautiful day tomorrow. What does it tell you, sergeant?"

"Well sir, it tells me that somebody stole our tent …"

A soldier tips a mug upside down on the table in front of him and says to the sergeant, "I can't drink from this mug. It has no opening."
The sergeant picks it up and examines the mug and says, "You are right. And besides, it has no bottom."

"What do you think about the coming battle, general?"
"God knows it will be lost."
"Then why should we go into it?"
"It would be good to find out who is the loser, sir!"

At the height of the arms race, the Americans and Russians realized that if they continued in the usual manner they were going to blow up the whole world.

They decided to settle the whole dispute with one dog fight.

They'd have five years to breed the best fighting dog in the world and whichever side's dog won would be entitled to dominate the world. The losing side would have to lay down its arms.

The Russians found the biggest, meanest doberman and the biggest, meanest rottweiler in the entire world and bred them with the biggest meanest Siberian wolves.

They selected only the biggest and strongest puppy from each litter, killed his siblings, and gave him all the milk.

They used steroids and trainers and after five years came up with the biggest meanest dog the world had ever seen.

Its cage needed steel bars that were 20cm thick and nobody could get near it.

When the day came for the fight, the Americans showed up with a strange animal. It was a nine-foot long dachshund.

Everyone felt sorry for the Americans because they knew there was no way that this dog could possibly last ten seconds with the Russian dog.

When the cages were opened up, the dachshund came out and wrapped itself around the outside of the ring.

It had the Russian dog almost completely surrounded.

When the Russian dog leaned over to bite the dachshund's neck, the Dachshund, in a snarling, vicious movement, reached out, opened up its enormous jaws, and consumed the Russian dog in one bite.

There was nothing left of the Russian dog.

The Russians shook their heads in disbelief, "We don't understand how this could have happened. We had our best people working for five years with the meanest doberman and rottweiler in the world and the biggest, meanest Siberian wolves," they lamented.

"We looked at the problem from a different angle," an American replied. "We had our best plastic surgeons working for five years to make an alligator look like a d dachshund."

One thing about the smart bombs, they actually know where Iraq and Afghanistan is – which is more than most college students can claim.

UNREAL ESTATE

Phrases and statements that hide the real truth of that charming little residence in the superb suburb you are convinced is a bargain.

1. ARCHITECT'S DELIGHT – Built to cut-down plans from a former chemical factory he had designed before the scheme fell through and he was de-registered.
2. BRILLIANT CONCEPT – A two-storey defoliating fir tree standing amid a 10 metre all glass dome, surrounding a by water-fall and a perfectly-formed scale version of the Sphinx.
3. CHARMING – It's the size of a broom cupboard.
4. QUAINT – It's the size of a broom cupboard – full of brooms.
5. COMPLETELY UPDATED – Stainless steel appliances, polished floorboards, paved court-yard, and not a smidgin of greenery in sight.
6. CONTEMPORARY – Cheaply slapped together in a hurry to take advantage of the 'First Home Buyers Grant'.
7. DARING DESIGN – Still a warehouse.
8. GARDEN OUTLOOK – You get a good view of the neighbour's garden.

9. MUCH POTENTIAL – No-one else has dared develop this, largely because the back yard sits on a disused mine shaft.

10. MUST SEE TO BELIEVE – Unless you saw it, you'd *never* believe it

11. ONE-OF-A-KIND – Ugly as sin. Nothing quite like it still standing.

12. CERTIFIED – Actually, the architect has been certified

13. NATIONAL TRUST DESIGNATED – Look closer, and it actually reads "National Truss". This was a former geriatric accommodation unit, and you can still smell the wee.

14. RENOVATOR'S DELIGHT – A shit-heap.

15. SEA GLIMPSES – Take a chair into the bathroom, place it next to the toilet, get up on it, stand on your tippy-toes, crane your head to the left, and there – no, just there – is a flash of blue.

16. SOPHISTICATED – Black walls, flat roof, no windows. See "Architect's Delight."

17. ON COMPACT LOT – If you stretch your arms out, you will touch both fences at once.

18. UNIQUE CITY HOME – Was a former pasta sauce factory; walls are concrete, roof is cold steel; smells of pepperoni.

19. STEEPED IN HISTORY – There's mould on the walls.

20. YOU'LL LOVE IT – No, on second thoughts, you won't.

HEY, MUM!

Hey, Mum! What's an orgasm?
I don't know dear, ask your father.

Hey, Mum! If the stork brings the babies, who f...s the stork?

Hey, Mum! What's a nymphomaniac?
Shut up and help me get Grandma off the doorknob!

Hey, Mum! Why are we pushing the car off the cliff?
Shut up son, you'll wake your father.

Hey, Mum! The milk man is here. Have you got the money or should I go out and play?

Hey, Mum! Why's everybody running?
Shut up and reload.

Hey, Mum! Daddy's running down the street!
Shut up and step on the go pedal!

Come upstairs, son, like a good boy.
No, Mummy, you'll only throw me down again.

Hey, Mum! My head hurts!
Shut up and get away from the dart board!

Hey, Mum! Where did your scabs go?
Shut up and eat your corn flakes!

Hey, Mum! It's dark down here!
Shut up or I'll flush it again!

Hey, Mum! I'm getting dizzy.
Shut up or I'll nail your other foot down!

Hey, Mum! Can I lick the bowl?
Shut up and flush the toilet!

Hey, Mum! I hate Daddy's guts.
Shut up, kid, and keep eating.

Hey, Mum! Can I play with Grandma?
Shut up kid, you dug her up twice last week!

Hey, Mum! Why am I so ugly?
Shut up and comb your face.

Hey, Mum! What's for dinner?
Shut up and get back in the oven!

Hey, Mum!! What's a lesbian?
Go ask your father, she'll know.

Hey, Mum! Can I wear a bra now? I'm 16.
Shut up, Albert …

Hey, Mum! I hate tomato soup!
Shut up son, we only have it once a month!

Hey, Mum! Sally won't come skipping with me.
Don't be cruel, dear, you know it makes her stumps bleed.

Hey, Mum! Daddy puked again!
Shut up and get a fork, before your sister gets all the big
chunks!

ORDERING A PIZZA CAN BE FUN

Try some of these next time you ring the pizza place to just make life interesting.

1. Ask how many dolphins were killed to make that pizza.
2. Ask if the pizza can safely consumed by someone suffering from dengue fever.
3. Ask if the pizza is organically grown.
4. Ask if you can rent a pizza.
5. Ask if you get to keep the pizza box. When they say yes, sigh, and say, "Thank God for that. I need something to put my crayons in."
6. Ask specifically for the person who took your order last time.
7. Ask to see a menu.
8. Ask what clothes the order taker is wearing.
9. Ask what their phone number is. Hang up, call them, and say, "Do I have the right number for pizza?"
10. Avoid saying the word pizza at all costs. If the order person says it, reply, "Please don't mention that word, you will send me into toxic shock."
11. Berate the order taker with little-known facts about Willy Nelson.
12. Do not name the toppings you want. Rather, spell them out, and ask them to spell them back.

13. Give them no address, exclaim "Oh, just surprise me!" and hang up.

14. Learn to play the basic blues riff on the bag-pipes, and stop talking at regular intervals to play it.

15. Make the first topping you order anchovies. Make the last thing you say "Definitely no anchovies, please, they make me fit." Hang up before they have a chance to respond.

16. Order a Big Mac Super-Value Chicken Meal.

17. Cancel that order, and instead order a steamed pizza.

18. Stutter on the letter "p".

19. Put the accent on the last syllable of pepperoni. Use the long "i" sound.

20. Tell the order taker a rival pizza place is on the other line and you're going with the lowest bidder.

21. Tell the order taker you're depressed, and have a bottle of sleeping pills next to the phone, and try and get him/her to cheer you up.

22. Tell them to put the crust on top this time.

23. Terminate the call with, "Remember, we never had this conversation."

24. Use expletives like, "Great Caesar's Ghost" and, "Jesus Joseph and Mary in Tinsel Town."

25. When all else fails, sing the entire order to the tune of "Achy-Breaky Heart."

MOTHER-IN-LAW

Is it possible to kill a mother-in-law with newspaper?
Yes, but only if you wrap an iron in it.

Anewlywed farmer and his wife were visited by her
mother. She immediately demanded an inspection of the
place. The farmer had genuinely tried to be friendly to his
new mother-in-law, hoping that their's would be a non-
antagonistic relationship.

All to no avail. She nagged them at every opportunity,
demanding changes, offering unwanted advice, and
generally making life unbearable to the farmer and his new
bride.

During a forced inspection of the barn, the farmer's mule
suddenly reared up and kicked the mother-in-law in the
head, killing her instantly.

It was a shock to all, no matter what were their feelings
toward her demanding ways.

At the funeral service a few days later, the farmer stood
near the casket and greeted folks as they walked by.

The pastor noticed that whenever a woman would
whisper something to the farmer, he would nod his head
yes and say something.

Whenever a man walked by and whispered to the

farmer, however, he would shake his head no, and mumble a reply.

Very curious as to this bizarre behaviour, the pastor later asked the farmer what that was all about.

The farmer replied, "The women would say, 'What a terrible tragedy' and I would nod my head and say 'Yes, it was.'

"The men would ask, 'Can I borrow that mule?' and I would shake my head and say, 'I can't. It's all booked up for a year.'"

Two cannibals are eating their dinner and one cannibal says to the other, "I don't like my mother-in-law much."

The other cannibal replies, "Well, just eat your chips then!"

A big-game hunter went on safari with his wife and mother-in-law. One evening, while still deep in the jungle, the wife awoke to find her mother gone. Rushing to her husband, she insisted on them both trying to find her mother.

The hunter picked up his rifle, took a swig of whiskey, and started to look for her. In a clearing not far from the camp, they came upon a chilling sight: the mother-in-law was backed up against a thick, impenetrable bush, and a large male lion stood facing her.

The wife cried, "What are we going to do?"

"Nothing," said the husband. "The lion got himself into this mess. Let him get himself out of it."

A man returned home from the night shift and went straight up to the bedroom. He found his wife with the sheet pulled over her head, fast asleep. Not to be denied, the horny husband crawled under the sheet and proceeded to make love to her.

Afterward, as he hurried downstairs for something to eat, he was startled to find breakfast on the table and his wife pouring coffee.

"How'd you get down here so fast?" he asked. "We were just making love!"

"Oh my God," his wife gasped, "that's my mother up there! She came over early and complained of having a headache. I told her to lie down for awhile."

Rushing upstairs, the wife ran to the bedroom.

"Mother, I can't believe this happened. Why didn't you say something?"

The mother-in-law huffed, "I haven't spoken to that jerk for fifteen years, and I wasn't about to start now!"

A MEDICAL DICTIONARY

ARTERY	The study of painting
BACTERIA	The back door of the cafeteria
BARIUM	What the doctors do when patients die
CAESARIAN SECTION	A neighborhood in Rome
CAT SCAN	Searching for a kitty
CAUTERIZE	Made eye contact with her
COLIC	A sheep dog
DILATE	To live long
ENEMA	Not a friend
FESTER	Quicker
G.I.SERIES	A soldiers ball game
IMPOTENT	Distinguished, well known
LABOR PAIN	Getting hurt at work
MEDICAL STAFF	A doctor's cane
MORBID	A higher offer
NITRATES	Cheaper than day rates
NODE	Was aware of
PAP SMEAR	A fatherhood test
PELVIS	A cousin to Elvis
POST OPERATIVE	A letter carrier
RECOVERY ROOM	A place to do re-upholstery
RECTUM	Dang near killed 'em
SEIZURE	A Roman emperor
TABLET	A small table

TERMINAL ILLNESS	Getting sick at the airport
TUMOR	More than one
URINE	Opposite of you're out
VARICOSE	Nearby

MUSIC AND MUSICIANS

When Beethoven passed away, he was buried in a churchyard.

A couple days later, the town drunk was walking through the cemetery and heard some strange noise coming from the area where Beethoven was buried.

Terrified, the drunk ran and got the priest to come and listen to it. The priest bent close to the grave and heard some faint, unrecognisable music coming from the grave.

Frightened, the priest ran and got the town magistrate.

When the magistrate arrived, he bent his ear to the grave, listened for a moment, and said, "Ah, yes, that's Beethoven's Ninth Symphony, being played backwards."

He listened a while longer, and said, "There's the Eighth Symphony, and it's backwards, too! Most puzzling."

So the magistrate kept listening, "There's the Seventh ... the Sixth ... the Fifth ..." Suddenly the realization of what was happening dawned him.

He stood up and announced to the crowd that had gathered in the cemetery, "My fellow citizens, there's nothing to worry about. It's just Beethoven decomposing."

Satan comes down to visit a famous, utterly ruthless Hollywood musical producer.

Satan says, "Look, I have a business proposition for you.

I can get you any deal you want, with anybody in the business, on any terms you like."

The producer's eyes light up, "Hmm, and what do you want from me?"

Satan smiles, "Your immortal soul."

The producer sits back and ponders, stroking his goatee. "I don't get it. Where's the catch?"

Q.   What's the difference between a bull and an orchestra?
A.   The bull has the horns in the front and the asshole in the back.

Q.   Why are conductor's hearts so coveted for transplants?
A.   They've had so little use.

Q.   Why is a conductor like a condom?
A.   It's safer with one, but more fun without.

Q.   What's the difference between God and a conductor?
A.   God knows He's not a conductor.

Q.   How do you get a guitar player to play softer?
A.   Give him some sheet music.

Q.   What's a guy that hangs out with musicians called?
A.   A drummer.

Q. How can you tell when a drummer is sitting up straight?

A. He dribbles out of both sides of his mouth!

Q. What is the difference between a drummer and a vacuum cleaner?

A. You have to plug one of them in before it sucks.

Q. Why is a drum machine better than a drummer?

A. Because it can keep a steady beat and won't sleep with your girlfriend.

Q. How can you tell when a drummer's at the door?

A. He doesn't know when to come in.

Q. What's the last thing a drummer says in a band?

A. "Hey, guys – why don't we try one of my songs?"

Q. What's the difference between a pizza and a drummer?

A. A pizza can feed a family of four.

Q. If a drummer and a bass guitarist caught a cab, which one would be the musician?

A. The cab driver.

Q. Why are so many violists dating drummers?

A. It makes them feel superior.

Q. How do you get two piccolo players to play in unison?

A. Shoot one.

Q.   What is the definition of perfect pitch in a piccolo?
A.   When you throw it in the toilet and it doesn't hit the rim.

Q.   What's the difference between a sax player and a lawn mower?
A.   One cuts grass and the other smokes it.

Q.   What would you do if you had all the bagpipe players on earth lined up end-to-end to the moon and back?
A.   Leave them there.

Q.   How is playing a bagpipe like throwing a javelin blindfolded?
A.   You don't have to be very good to get people's attention.

Q.   How can you tell if a bagpipe is out of tune?
A.   Someone is blowing into it.

Q.   What's the difference between the bagpipes and the piano accordion?
A.   The piano accordion sinks faster.

Q.   Which is better: electric guitar or harmonica?
A.   Electric guitar. You can't beat a harmonica player to death with a harmonica.

Q.   What do violists and Mike Tyson have in common?
A.   They both are hard on ears.

Q. Why is intermission only 20 minutes long?
A. So that the cellists don't have to be retrained.

Q. Why are harps like elderly parents?
A. They're both unforgiving and hard to get in and out of cars.

BASTARD OF A DAY

YOU KNOW IT'S GOING TO BE A BASTARD OF A DAY IF...

1.   Your wife says "Good morning Bill" and your name is
      Wally.

2.   You put your bra on backwards, and it fits better.

3.   You call Suicide Prevention, and they put you on
      hold.

4.   The car horn goes off accidentally, and remains stuck
      while you're following a group of Hell's Angels.

5.   Your birthday cake collapses from the weight of the
      candles.

6.   You wake face down on the footpath.

7.   You see a '60 Minutes' team waiting in your office.

8.   You want to put on clothes you wore home from the
      party, and there aren't any.

9.   You put on the news, and they're showing
      emergency routes out of the city.

10.   The boss tells you not to bother taking off your coat.

11.   The bird singing outside your window is a vulture.

12.   You walk to work and then find your dress is stuck in the back of your pantyhose (even more embarrassing if you're a woman!).

13.   You call your answering service, and they tell you it's none of your business.

14.   Your blind date turns out to be your wife.

15.   Your twin forgot your birthday.

16.   You put both contact lenses in the same eye.

17.   Your Income Tax cheque bounces.

OFFICE AND THE WORKPLACE

OFFICE PRAYER

Grant me the serenity to accept the things I cannot change, the courage to change the things I cannot accept, and the wisdom to hide the bodies of those people I had to kill today because they pissed me off. Also, help me to be careful of the toes I step on today, as they may be connected to the ass I have to kiss tomorrow

10 EXCELLENT EXCUSES WHEN YOU ARE CAUGHT NAPPING AT YOUR DESK

1. ... in the Lord Jesus' name, Amen.
2. They told me at the blood bank this might happen.
3. Damn! Why did you interrupt me? I had almost figured out a solution to our biggest problem.
4. I was doing Yoga exercises to relieve work-related stress.
5. Someone must've put decaf in the wrong pot...
6. I was testing my keyboard for drool resistance.
7. This is just a 15 minute power-nap as described in that time management course you sent me.
8. I wasn't sleeping! I was meditating on the mission statement and envisioning a new paradigm.

9. The coffee machine is broken...
10. Whew! Guess I left the top off the White-Out! You got here just in time!

Two car salesmen were sitting at the bar. One complained to the other, "Boy, business sucks. If I don't sell more cars this month, I'm going to lose my f...ing ass."

Then he noticed a beautiful blonde sitting two stools away.

Immediately, he apologized for his bad language.

"That's okay," she said, "If I don't sell more ass this month, I'm going to lose my f...ing car."

A site foreman had ten very lazy men working for him, so one day he decided to trick them into doing some work for a change.

"I've got a really easy job today for the laziest one among you," he announced. "Will the laziest man please put his hand up?"

Nine hands went up.

"Why didn't you put your hand up?" he asked the tenth man.

"Too much trouble," came the reply.

A shepherd was herding his flock in a remote pasture when suddenly a brand new Jeep Cherokee advanced out of a dust cloud towards him.

The driver, a young man in a Hugo Boss suit, Gucci

shoes, Ray Ban sunglasses and a YSL tie leans out of the window and says, "If I can tell you exactly how many sheep you have in your flock, will you give me one?"

The shepherd looks at the yuppie, then at his peacefully grazing flock and calmly answers, "Sure."

The yuppie parks the car, whips out his laptop, connects it to a mobile phone, surfs to a NASA page on the internet where he calls up a GPS satellite navigation system, scans the area, opens up a database and some 60 Excel spreadsheets with complex formulas. Finally he prints out a 150 page report on his hi-tech miniaturized printer, turns to the shepherd and says, "You have here exactly 1,586 sheep."

"This is correct, and as agreed you can take one of the sheep," says the shepherd.

He watches the yuppie make a selection and bundle it in to his Cherokee. Then he says, "If I can tell you exactly what your business is, will you give me my property back?"

"OK, why not," answers the yuppie.

"You are a consultant," says the shepherd.

"This is correct," says the yuppie. "How did you guess that?"

"Easy" answers the shepherd. "You turn up here although nobody invited you; you want to be paid for an answer to a question I never asked; and you gave me information I already knew. Besides you don't know jack-shit about my business."

"How do you come to that conclusion?"

"Because you took my dog …"

DO YOU BELONG TO A GLOBAL COMPANY?

If any three of the following ring a bell, then you certainly have been an intrinsic part of globalization.

- You sat at the same desk for four years and worked for three different companies.
- You worked for the same company for four years and sat at more than ten different desks.
- You've been in the same job for four years and have had ten different managers.
- You see a good looking person and know it is a visitor.
- You order your business cards in "half orders" instead of whole boxes.
- When someone asks about what you do for a living, you can't explain it in one sentence.
- You get really excited about a 2% pay raise.
- You use acronyms in your sentences.
- Art involves a white board.
- Your biggest loss from a system crash is that you lose your best jokes.
- You sit in a cubicle smaller than your bedroom closet.
- Weekends are those days your significant other makes you stay home.
- It's dark when you drive to and from work.
- Fun is when issues are assigned to someone else.
- The word "opportunity" makes you shiver in fear.
- Free food left over from meetings is your main staple.

- Being sick is defined as can't walk or you're in the hospital.
- You're already late on the assignment you just got.
- Dilbert cartoons hang outside every cube and are read by your co-workers only.
- Your boss' favorite lines are, "when you get a few minutes" or, "when you're freed up".
- You read this entire list and understood it.

A man was eating in a restaurant when he dropped his spoon.

The waiter was immediately at his table and took another spoon out of his pocket and gave it to the man. The man thanked him, and took a sip of his soup and then asked, "Excuse me, but why do all the waiters have spoons in their pockets?"

The waiter said, "Well sir, a time and motion survey in our restaurant showed that one in four customers drop their spoon just like you, so we always have a spare spoon on hand so we can give it to the customer so that he is not eating with the dirty one. It saves time as the waiter does not have to go back to the kitchen to retrieve a clean spoon. The management prides itself in the efficiency of the staff."

As the waiter is about to walk back to the kitchen, the man noticed that there was a string hanging from his fly and said, "Excuse me but why do you, and all the other waiters have a string hanging out of your flies?"

The waiter said, "Well sir, a survey in our restaurant

showed that the waiters can save time and serve more customers, if we do not wash our hands after using the toilet. So we use the string tied to our penises to pull it out of our trousers so we don't get our hands dirty."

Then the man took another sip of his soup and replied, "That's all very well, but how do you get it back in again?"

"Well I don't know about the others," replied the waiter, "But personally, I use the spoon."

A man walks up to a woman in his office and tells her that her hair smells nice.

The woman immediately goes into her supervisor's office and tells him that she wants to file a sexual harassment suit and explains why.

The supervisor is puzzled, "What's wrong with the co-worker telling you that your hair smells nice."

The woman replies, "He's a midget."

NOTICE TO ALL EMPLOYEES

It has been brought to the management's attention that some individuals have been using foul language. Due to complaints from some of the easily offended employees, this conduct will no longer be tolerated. The management does, however, realise the importance of each person being able to express feelings properly when communicating with fellow employees. Therefore, the management has compiled the following code phrases, in order that the proper exchange of ideas and information can continue.

OLD PHRASE	NEW PHRASE
Another f…ing meeting	Yes, we should discuss this.
Ask me if I give a f…	Of course I'm concerned.
Eat shit and die.	Excuse me?
Eat shit and die, F…wit.	Excuse me, sir?
Eat shit.	You don't say.
F… it, I'm on salary.	I'm a bit overloaded at the moment.
F… it, it won't work.	I'm not sure I can implement this.
F… you.	How nice! How very nice!
He's got his head up his ass.	He's not familiar with the problem.
I really don't give a shit.	I don't think it will be a problem.
It's not my f…ing problem.	I wasn't involved in that project.
Kiss my ass.	So you'd like my help with it?
No f…ing way!	I'm not certain that's feasible.
Shove it up your ass.	I don't think you understand.
Tell someone who gives a f…	Perhaps you should check.
This job sucks.	I love a challenge.
What the f…?	Interesting behaviour.
When the f… do you expect me to do this?	Perhaps I can work late.
Who the f… cares?	Are you sure it's a problem.
Who the hell died and made you boss?	You want me to take care of this??

The sexy housewife was built so well the TV repairman couldn't keep his eyes off her. Every time she came in the room, he'd nearly jerk his neck right out of joint looking at her.

When he'd finished she paid him and said, "I'm going to make an unusual request. But you have to first promise me you'll keep it a secret."

The repairman quickly agreed and she went on.

"Well, it's kind of embarrassing to talk about, but while my husband is a kind, decent man, he has a certain physical weakness. A certain disability. Now, I'm a woman and you're a man ..."

The repairman salivated in anticipation, "Yes, yes!"

"And since I've been wanting to, ever since you came in the door ..."

"Yes, yes!"

"Would you please help me move the refrigerator?"

One day an out-of-work mime is visiting the zoo and attempts to earn some money as a street performer.

As soon as he starts to draw a crowd, a zoo keeper grabs him and drags him into his office.

The zoo keeper explains to the mime that the zoo's most popular attraction, a gorilla, has died suddenly and the keeper fears that attendance at the zoo will fall off. He offers the mime a job to dress up as the gorilla until they can get another one. The mime accepts.

So the next morning the mime puts on the gorilla suit and enters the cage before the crowd comes.

He discovers that it's a great job. He can sleep all he wants, play and make fun of people and he draws bigger crowds than he ever did as a mime.

However, eventually the crowds tire of him, and he tires of just swinging on tyres. He begins to notice that the people are paying more attention to the lion in the cage next to his.

Not wanting to lose the attention of his audience, he climbs to the top of his cage, crawls across a partition, and dangles from the top to the lion's cage. Of course, this makes the lion furious, but the crowd loves it.

At the end of the day the zoo keeper comes and gives the mime a raise for being such a good attraction. This goes on for some time. The mime keeps taunting the lion, the crowds grow larger, and his salary keeps going up.

Then one terrible day when he is dangling over the furious lion, he slips and falls into the lion enclosure. The mime is terrified. The lion gathers itself and prepares to pounce.

The mime is so scared that he begins to run round and round the cage with the lion close behind. Finally, the mime starts screaming and yelling, "Help, Help me!", but the lion is quick and pounces.

The mime soon finds himself flat on his back looking up at the angry lion, "Shut up you idiot!" hisses the lion, "do you want to get us both fired?"

A blonde, a brunette, and a redhead all work at the same office for a female boss who always goes home early.

"Hey, girls," says the brunette, "Let's go home early tomorrow. She'll never know."

So the next day, they all leave right after the boss does.

The brunette gets some extra gardening done, the redhead goes to a bar, and the blonde goes home to find her husband having sex with the female boss!

She quietly sneaks out of the house and returns home at her normal time.

"That was fun," says the brunette the next day at work. "We should do it again sometime."

"No way," says the blonde, "I almost got caught."

10 WAYS TO IRRITATE EVERYONE AT YOUR WORKPLACE

1.	Page yourself over the intercom. Don't disguise your voice.
2.	Find out where your boss shops and buy exactly the same outfits. Wear them one day after your boss does. This is especially effective if your boss is of a different gender than you.
3.	Make up nicknames for all your co-workers and refer to them only by these names. "That's a good point, Sparky." "No, I'm sorry, but I'm going to have to disagree with you there, Cha-Cha."
4.	Hi-Lite your shoes. Tell people you haven't lost them as much since you did this.
5.	Hang mosquito netting around your cubicle. When you emerge to get coffee or a printout or whatever, slap yourself randomly the whole way.

6.   Put a chair facing a printer. Sit there all day and tell people you're waiting for your document.

7.   Every time someone asks you to do something, anything, ask them if they want fries with that.

8.   Encourage your colleagues to join you in a little synchronized chair-dancing.

9.   Feign an unnatural and hysterical fear of staplers.

10.   Send e-mail messages saying there's free pizza or cake in the lunchroom. When people drift back to work complaining that they found none, lean back, pat your stomach and say, "Oh you've got to be faster than that!"

IS YOUR ACCOUNTANT NUTS?

You know he needs a break from the job when he:

- Advises you to save postage by filing your taxes telepathically.
- Counts a family of possums living in your yard as dependents.
- Demands that you call him the "Una-Countant".
- He laughs at the demand for an audit.
- He's got a GST Form tattooed on his arm.
- In several places on your tax forms he's written, "Give or take a million dollars".
- Insists that there's no such number as four.
- Instead of a C.P.A. license, he's got a framed photo of a shirtless Peter Costello.
- Tells you to put all your money into British cattle futures.

- You notice that his "calculator" is just a broken VCR remote.

There was an engineer who had an exceptional gift for fixing all things mechanical. After serving his company loyally for over 30 years, he happily retired.

A few years later the company contacted him regarding an impossible problem they were having with one of their multi-million dollar machines. They had tried everything and everyone else to get the machine fixed, but to no avail.

In desperation, they called on the retired engineer who had solved so many of their problems in the past. The engineer reluctantly took the challenge.

He spent a day studying the huge machine. At the end of the day, he marked a small "x" in chalk on a particular component of the machine and proudly stated, "This is where your problem is".

The part was replaced and the machine worked perfectly again. The company received a bill for $50,000 from the engineer for his service. They demanded an itemized accounting of his charges. The engineer responded briefly:

One chalk mark: $1

Knowing where to put it: $49,999

It was paid in full and the engineer retired again in peace.

WANT TO BE AN ENGINEER?

You may have the potential if you meet the following criteria:

1. At Christmas, it goes without saying that you will be the one to find the burnt-out bulb in the string of Christmas lights.
2. For you, it becomes a moral dilemma to decide whether to buy flowers for your girlfriend or spend the money to upgrade the RAM on your computer.
3. On the Alaskan Cruise, everyone else is on deck peering at the scenery and you are still on a personal tour of the engine room.
4. In college, you thought the Summer break was metal fatigue failure.
5. The only jokes you receive are through e-mail.
6. The salespeople at Computers Are Us can't answer any of your questions.
7. You are always late to meetings.
8. At an air show you know how fast the skydivers are falling.
9. If you were on death row in a French prison and you find that the guillotine is not working properly, you would offer to fix it.
10. You bought your wife a new CD-ROM for her birthday.
11. You can quote scenes from any Monty Python movie.
12. You can type 70 words per minute but can't read your own handwriting.
13. You can't write unless the paper has both horizontal and vertical lines.

14. You comment to your wife that her straight hair is nice and parallel.
15. You never have matching socks on.
16. You save the power cords from a broken appliance.
17. You have more friends on the Internet than in real life.
18. You have never backed up your hard drive.
19. You have never bought any new underwear or socks for yourself since you got married.
20. You know what http:// stands for.
21. You look forward to Christmas only to put together the kids' toys.
22. You see a good design and still have to change it.
23. You still own a slide rule and you know how to use it.
24. Your laptop computer costs more than your car.
25. You think that when people around you yawn, it's because they didn't get enough sleep.

BALLS, BALLS, BALLS

Newton's Law of Balls: The size of one's balls is inversely related to the size of one's pay packet.
Thus the sport of choice for:

1. Unemployed or incarcerated people: basketball.
2. Maintenance level employees: bowling.
3. Blue-collar workers: football.
4. Supervisors: cricket.
5. Middle management: tennis.
6. Corporate officers: golf.

Conclusion: The higher you rise in the corporate structure, the smaller your balls become.

CORPORATE SPEAK

ASSMOSIS – The process by which some people seem to absorb success and advancement by kissing up to the boss rather than working hard.

BLAMESTORMING – Sitting around in a group, discussing why a deadline was missed or a project failed, and who was responsible.

CHAINSAW CONSULTANT – An outside expert brought in to reduce the employee headcount, leaving the top brass with clean hands.

CLM (Career Limiting Move) – Used among micro-serfs to describe ill-advised activity. Trashing your boss while he or she is within earshot is a serious CLM.

COMPANY NOTICE – Guidelines for use of restrooms.

CUBE FARM – An office filled with cubicles.

GENERICA – Features of the landscape that are exactly the same no matter where one is, such as fast food joints, strip malls, subdivisions. Used as in "We were so lost in generica that I forgot what city we were in."

MOUSE POTATO – The on-line, wired generation's answer to the couch potato.

OHNOSECOND – That minuscule fraction of time in which you realize that you have just made a *big* mistake.

PERCUSSIVE MAINTENANCE – The fine art of whacking the heck out of an electronic device to get it to work again.

PRAIRIE DOGGING – When someone yells or drops something loudly in a cube farm, and people's heads pop up over the walls to see what's going on.

SALMON DAY – The experience of spending an entire day swimming upstream only to get screwed and die in the end.

SEAGULL MANAGER – A manager who flies in, makes a lot of noise, craps on everything, and then leaves.

SQUIRT THE BIRD – To transmit a signal to a satellite.

STARTER MARRIAGE – A short-lived first marriage that ends in divorce with no kids, no property and no regrets.

SWIPED OUT – An ATM or credit card that has been rendered useless because the magnetic strip is worn away from extensive use.

XEROX SUBSIDY – Euphemism for swiping free photocopies from one's workplace.

RESTROOM TRIP POLICY

Notice to Employees:
A Restroom Trip Policy will be established to provide a more consistent method of accounting for each employee's restroom time and ensuring equal opportunity for all employees.

Under this policy a "Restroom Trip Bank" (RTB) will be established for each employee. The first day of each month, employees will be given twenty (20) RTB credits.

- These credits may be accumulated indefinitely.
- Within two weeks, the entrance doors to all restrooms will be equipped with personnel identification stations and computer-linked voice print recognition devices.
- Each employee must provide two copies of voice prints – one normal and one under stress.
- Employees should acquaint themselves with the stations during the initial introduction period.
- If an employee's RTB balance reaches zero, the doors to the restroom will not unlock for that employee's voice until the first of the next month.
- In addition, all restroom stalls are being equipped with timed paper roll retractors and pressure sensitive seats. If the stall is occupied for more than three minutes an alarm will sound. Thirty seconds after the sounding of the alarm, the roll of paper will retract into the wall, the toilet will automatically flush, and the stall door will open. If the stall remains occupied, your picture will be taken.

- The picture will then be posted on the bulletin board and the first of no more than two official warnings will be issued. If a person's picture appears for a third time, it will be grounds for immediate termination.
- All supervisors have received advanced training on this policy. If you have any questions, please ask your supervisor.

20 CONDOMS – WHICH TYPE ARE YOU?

The brand of condom you use is a great insight into the type of person you are. Which type of condom would you use?

1. Campbell's Soup Condoms: Mmm, mmm good ...

2. Coca Cola Condoms: The real thing.

3. Diet Pepsi Condoms: You got the right one, baby.

4. Double Mint: Double your pleasure, double your fun!

5. Energizer: It keeps going and going and going ...

6. Ford Condoms: The best never rest.

7. Hewlett Packard Condoms: Expanding possibilities.

8. KFC Condoms: Finger-licking good.

9. M&M condom: It melts in your mouth, not in your hands!

10.   Mars Bar Condoms: The quicker picker upper.

11.   Maxwell House: Good to the last drop!

12.   Microsoft: Where do you want to go today?

13.   Nikc Condoms: Just do it.

14.   Pringles Condoms: Once you pop, you can't stop.

15.   Taco Bell: Get some; make a run for the border.

16.   Tattslotto Condoms: Who's next?

17.   The Star Trek Condom: To boldly go where no man has gone before.

18.   Toyota Condoms: Oh what a feeling.

19.   United Airlines travel pack: Fly United.

20.   Yellow Pages Condoms: Aren't you glad you use it? Don't you wish everybody did?

DRUNKS ON DISPLAY

A group of loud and rowdy drunks was making a racket in the street.

It was in the wee small hours of the morning, and the lady of the house flung open a window and shouted at them to keep quiet.

"Is this where Frank lives?" one of the drunks asked.

"Yes, it is," the woman replied.

"Well then," said the drunk, "could you come and pick him out, so the rest of us can go home?"

13 SIGNS THAT YOU MIGHT BE SLIGHTLY PISSED

1. The parking lot seems to have moved while you were in the bar.
2. You lose arguments with inanimate objects.
3. You have to hold onto the lawn to keep from falling off the earth.
4. Your job is interfering with your drinking.
5. Your doctor finds traces of blood in your alcohol stream.
6. You sincerely believe alcohol to be the elusive 5th food group.
7. Mosquitoes catch a buzz after attacking you.

8. The back of your head keeps getting hit by the toilet seat.
9. That there are 24 hours in a day and 24 beers in a case is not a coincidence to you.
10. You can focus better with one eye closed.
11. Your twin sons are named Barley and Hops.
12. At AA meetings you begin, "Hi, my name is ... um, er ..."
13. The whole bar says "Hi" when you come in.

Every night, Frank would go down to the liquor store, get a six-pack, bring it home, and drink it while he watched TV.

One night, as he finished his last beer, the doorbell rang. He stumbled to the door and found a six-foot cockroach standing there. The bug grabbed him by the collar and threw him across the room, then left.

The next night, after he finished his fourth beer, the doorbell rang. He walked slowly to the door and found the same huge cockroach standing there. The big bug punched him in the stomach, then left.

The next night, after Frank finished his first beer, the doorbell rang again. The same six-foot cockroach was standing there. This time Frank was kneed in the groin and hit behind the ear as he doubled over in pain. Then the big bug left.

The fourth night Frank didn't drink at all. The doorbell rang. The cockroach was standing there. The bug beat the snot out of Frank and left him in a heap on the living room floor.

The following day, Frank went to see his doctor. He explained events of the preceding four nights. "I thought it might be the drink. But he belted me when I didn't have a beer. What can I do?" Frank pleaded.

"Not much," the doctor replied. "There's just a nasty bug going around."

"**S**haaayyyy, buddy, what's a 'Breathalyser'?" asked a drunk of his barman.

"That's a bag that tells you when you've drunk too much," answered the barman.

"Ah hell, whaddya know? I've been married to one of those for years."

Bob, a travelling salesman, arrives at a small town late in the day, walks into the local bar, sits down and orders up a beer.

After a few moments, someone stands up and shouts, "28!" and the entire bar bursts into hysterical laughter.

Bob thinks this is strange, but goes back to his beer.

A few moments later someone else stands up and yells, "33!" Once again, the bar bursts into fits of laughter. Some are rolling on the floor.

Bob shakes his head, and goes back to his beer.

Soon, a third man stands up and shouts, "4!" Again, everyone in the bar laughs, some uncontrollable in their mirth.

The completely confused Bob summons the bartender and asks what the hell all the laughing is about.

The bartender replies: "See, pal, we're such a small town that everyone knows everyone and all of their jokes. So, to make life easier we catalogued all of our gags. Instead of telling the whole joke, we just shout out its number and everyone knows what joke it is and we laugh."

Bob listens carefully, nods, and sits down. More people stand up and shout numbers, and eventually Bob cannot stand it any longer. Well-known as the life of the party back home, he has to join in.

Bob stands up and shouts, "41!" Nobody laughs. There is stony silence. Bob sits down, shamefaced and embarrassed. He summons up the bartender, and says, "What happened? No-one laughed."

The bartender shakes his head and says, "Buddy, it's not so much the joke, it's the way you tell it."

The priest was having a heart-to-heart talk with a lapsed member of his flock, whose drinking of cheap cask wine invariably led to quarrelling with his neighbours, and occasional shotgun blasts at some of them.

"Can't you see, Ben," intoned the parson, "that not one good thing comes out of this drinking?"

"Well, I sort of disagree there," replied the drunk. "It makes me miss the people I shoot at."

Aman goes into a bar with his dog and asks for a drink. The bartender says, "You can't bring that dog in here!" The bloke, without missing a beat, says, "This is my seeing-eye dog."

"Oh man, I'm sorry," the bartender says, "I didn't realise you were blind. Here, the first drink's on me." The man takes his drink and goes to a table near the door.

Another guy walks in the bar with a chihuahua. The first bloke sees him, stops him and says, "They don't allow dogs in here, so you won't get a drink unless you tell him it's a seeing-eye dog."

The second man graciously thanks the first man and continues to the bar. He asks for a drink. The bartender says, "Sorry, you can't bring that dog in here!"

The second man replies, "This is my seeing-eye dog."

The bartender peers over the edge and says, "No, I don't think so. They do not have chihuahuas as seeing-eye dogs."

The man pauses for a half-second and replies, "What?! They gave me a chihuahua?"

Apoliceman is walking his beat when he finds a totally drunk man collapsed against a building, weeping uncontrollably and holding his car keys in his hands. He's moaning something about 'They took my car!'

Seeing he is quite well dressed, the cop thinks he may have a real case of theft on his hands and proceeds to question the man.

"What are your car keys doing out?"

"My car, it was right on the end of my key, and those

bastards stole it! Please, Ossifer, get my Porsche back. My God, it was right on the end of my key! Where is it? They stole it and it was right here; right on my key!"

"OK, OK, stand up, let's get some more information." He stands the man up, and notices his penis is hanging out. Aw, shit, mister, your dick is hanging out, would you put that thing away!"

The man looks down, sees his prick hanging there and screams, "Oh my God, they stole my girlfriend!"

JUST ONE MORE WON'T HURT

Governments just can't help it. They try to regulate and control everything. Now they are considering warning everyone against the demon drink by putting warnings on the labels of alcoholic beverages. Let's be practical and tell it how it is.

Warning. Consumption of alcohol may:

- Make you think you are whispering when you are actually shouting loudly.
- Create the illusion that you are tougher, more handsome, smarter, talk better and fight harder than a really, really, really big bikie named "Ball-Masher."
- Cause obstruction to the time-space continuum, with small, and sometimes large, gaps of time disappearing from your memory bank.
- Wipe out the whole memory bank.

- Cause you to tell the managing director what you *really* think about him and his crappy little company while photocopying your bum at the staff Christmas party.
- Make you dance like a genuine jerk.
- Lead you to believe that your ex-girlfriend really wants you to telephone her at half past three in the morning.
- Cause you to tell the same indescribably boring story over and over again.
- Cause you to thay things like thish.
- Leave you wondering what the hell ever happened to your pants anyway.
- Cause you to roll over in the morning and see something really scary.
- Cause inexplicable rug burns on your forehead.
- Lead you to believe you are invisible.
- Lead you to think people are laughing *with* you …

Scientists for Health Canada suggest that drinking beer makes men act like women.

To test the theory, one hundred men were fed six pints of beer each, within a one hour period.

It was then observed that 100% of the men gained weight, talked excessively without making sense, became overly emotional, couldn't drive, failed to think rationally, argued over nothing, and refused to apologize when they were wrong.

A woman and a man are involved in a bad car accident. Both cars are written off, but thankfully neither are hurt.

After they crawl out of their cars, the woman says, "So you're a man; that's interesting. I'm a woman. Gee, just look at our cars! There's nothing left, but fortunately we are unhurt. This must be a sign from God that we should meet and be friends and live together for the rest of our days."

Flattered, the man replied, "Oh yes, I agree with you completely! This must be a sign from God!"

The woman continued, "And look at this, here's another miracle. My car is completely demolished but this bottle of wine didn't break. Surely God wants us to drink this wine and celebrate our good fortune."

Then she hands the bottle to the man. The man nods his head in agreement, opens it and drinks half the bottle and then hands it back to the woman. The woman takes the bottle, immediately puts the cap back on, and hands it back to the man.

The man asks, "Aren't you having any?"

The woman replies, "No. I think I'll just wait for the police."

DID YOU KNOW THAT . . .

- The average bra is designed to last 180 days?
- Star-fish have eight legs and each leg has an eye on it?
- The average caterpillar has 2000 muscles in his body? The average human has only 700.
- There are 178 sesame seeds on the average McDonalds sesame seed bun?
- Nine per cent of the world's ostriches suffer from an eating disorder?
- Kilogram for kilogram, hamburgers cost more than a new car?
- Nearly all boys grow at least as tall as their mother?
- The average male shaves off half a kilogram of hair every ten years?
- It's possible to lead a cow upstairs but not downstairs?

DOCTOR, DOCTOR!

A badly constipated man went to the doctors. The doctor prescribed suppositories, and told the man to take one once every four hours. The man left the doctor, happy that his problem would soon be gone.

When he got home, he took a suppository, swallowing it with a glass of water.

Four hours passed. Nothing happened.

But, he figured that these things take time, so he swallowed another one, hoping that he would reap the benefits very soon. After several days of taking the suppositories every four hours, he was still constipated, so he returned to the doctor.

When he explained that he took one every four hours, as prescribed, the doctor exclaimed, "What the hell are you doing? Swallowing them?"

The man replied, sarcastically, "No, I'm shovin' them up my arse!!!!"

D octor: "Ma'am, are you sexually active?"
Woman: "Well, sometimes I is … and sometimes I just lays there."

A doctor is going about his business, with a rectal thermometer tucked behind his ear. He goes into a staff meeting to discuss the day's activities, when a co-worker asks why he has a thermometer behind his ear. In a wild motion he grabs for the thermometer, looks at it and exclaims, "Damn, some asshole has my pen!"

A SHORT HISTORY OF MEDICINE:

"Doctor, I have a bad headache."

2000 B.C. – "Here, eat this compound of root."

100 A.D. – "Don't dare touch that root. It is the tool of the devil. Say this prayer."

1850 A.D. – "That prayer is pure superstition, drink this potion."

1940 A.D. – "Believe me, that potion is snake oil, swallow this pill."

1975 A.D. – "That pill is ineffective, you must take this antibiotic."

2000 A.D. – "That antibiotic is artificial. Here, eat this compound of root!"

J ock was enjoying his life and career, but as he got older he was increasingly hampered by incredible headaches.

After being referred from one specialist to another, he finally came across a doctor who solved the problem.

"The good news is I can cure your headaches," said the

doctor. "The bad news is that it will require castration. You have a very rare condition which causes your testicles to press up against the base of your spine. The pressure creates one hell of a headache. The only way to relieve the pressure is to remove the testicles."

Jock was shocked and depressed. He wondered if he had anything to live for. He couldn't concentrate long enough to answer, but decided he had no choice but to go under the knife.

When he left the hospital, his mind was clear, but he felt like he was missing an important part of himself.

As he walked down the street, he realized that he felt like a different person. He could make a new beginning and live a new life. He walked past a men's clothing store and thought, "That's what I need, a new suit. My wife buys a new hat when she is sad and that cheers her up."

He entered the shop and told the salesman, "I'd like a new suit."

The salesman eyed him briefly and said, "Let's see ... size 42 long."

Jock laughed, "That's right, how did you know?"

"It's my job."

Jock tried on the suit. It fitted perfectly. As Jock admired himself in the mirror, the salesman asked, "How about a new shirt?"

Jock thought for a moment and then said, "Sure ..."

The salesman eyed Jock and said, "Let's see ... 36 sleeve and ... 15 and a half neck"

Jock was surprised, "That's right, how did you know?"

"It's my job."

Jock tried on the shirt, and it fitted perfectly. As Jock

adjusted the collar in the mirror, the salesman asked, "How about new shoes?"

Jock was on a roll and said, "Sure ..."

The salesman eyed Jock's feet and said, "Let's see ... 9 and a half... narrow."

Jock was astonished, "That's right, how did you know?"

"It's my job."

Jock tried on the shoes and they fitted perfectly. Jock walked comfortably around the shop and the salesman asked, "How about a new hat?"

Without hesitating, Jock said, "Sure ..."

The salesman eyed Jock's head and said, "Let's see, 7 5/8."

Jock was incredulous, "That's right, how did you know?"

"It's my job."

The hat fitted perfectly. Jock was feeling great, when the salesman asked, "How about some new underwear?"

Jock thought for a second and said, "Sure .."

The salesman stepped back, eyed Jock's waist and said, "Let's see, size 36."

Jock laughed, "No, I've worn size 34 since I was 18 years old."

The salesman shook his head, "No, no, no. You can't wear a size 34. Not you, sir. It would press your testicles up against the base of your spine and give you the most incredible headaches ..."

D octor: "I have some bad news and some very bad news."
Patient: "Well, might as well give me the bad news first."

Doctor: "The lab called with your test results. They said you have 24 hours to live."

Patient: "Twenty-four hours! That's terrible!! What the f…
could be worse than that? What's the very bad news?"

Doctor: "Your mobile has been switched off, and I've
been trying to reach you since yesterday …"

"Doctor, doctor, will I be able to play the violin after the
operation?"

"Yes, of course."

"Great! I never could before!"

A man goes to the eye doctor. The receptionist asks him
why he is there.

The man complains, "I keep seeing spots in front of my
eyes."

The receptionist asks, "Have you ever seen a doctor?"

And the man replies, "No, just spots."

A fellow walked into a doctor's office and the receptionist
asked him what he had.

He said, "Shingles."

So she took down his name, address, medical insurance
number and told him to have a seat. A few minutes later a
nurse's aid came out and asked him what he had. He said,
"Shingles." So she took down his height, weight, a complete
medical history and told him to wait in the examining
room.

Ten minutes later a nurse came in and asked him what he had. He said, "Shingles." So she gave him a blood test, a blood pressure test, an electrocardiogram, told him to take off all his clothes and wait for the doctor.

Fifteen minutes later the doctor came in and asked him what he had. He said, "Shingles." The doctor said, "Where?"

And the bloke replied, "Outside in the truck. Where do you want them?"

A man goes to his doctor for a complete check-up. He hasn't been feeling well and wants to find out if he's ill.

After the check-up the doctor comes out with the results of the examination.

"I'm afraid I have some bad news. You're dying and you don't have much time," the doctor says.

"Oh no, that's terrible. How long have I got?" the man asks.

"Ten ..." says the doctor.

"Ten? Ten what? Months? Weeks? What?!"

"Ten, nine, eight, seven ..."

Then there was the distraught patient who phoned her doctor's office.

"Is it true," the woman wanted to know, "that the medication you prescribed has to be taken for the rest of my life?"

"Yes, I'm afraid so," the doctor told her.

There was a moment of silence before the woman continued, "I'm wondering, then, just how serious my condition is. This prescription is marked 'NO REFILLS'."

Most dentist's chairs go up and down, don't they? The one I was in went back and forwards.

I thought, "This is unusual."

The dentist said to me, "Mr Buxton, get out of the filing cabinet."

An Israeli doctor said, "Medicine in my country is so advanced, we can take a kidney out of one person, put it in another and have him looking for work in six weeks."

A German doctor said, "That's nothing! In Germany, we can take a lung out of one person, put it in another and have him looking for work in four weeks."

A Russian doctor said, "In my country, medicine is so advanced, we can take half a heart from one person, put it in another and have them both looking for work in two weeks."

The American doctor, not to be outdone, said, "Hah! We are about to take an asshole out of Texas, put him in the White House and half the country will be looking for work the next day."

Did you hear about the bloke who walks into a psychologist's office wearing only cling film pants? The psychologist says, "I can clearly see your nuts!"

John was a clerk in a small chemist shop but he was not much of a salesman. He could never find the item the customer wanted. Peter, the owner, had had about enough and warned John that the next sale he missed would be his last.

Just then a man came in coughing and he asked John for their best cough syrup. Try as he might John could not find the cough syrup.

Remembering Peter's warning he sold the man a box of laxative pills and told him to take them all at once. The customer did as John said and then walked outside and leaned against a lamp post.

Peter had seen the whole thing and came over to ask John what had happened.

"He wanted something for his cough but I couldn't find the cough syrup. So I substituted laxatives and told him to take them all at once," John said.

"Laxatives won't cure a cough," Peter shouted angrily.

"Sure they will," John said, pointing at the man leaning on the lamp post. "Look at him! He's afraid to cough ..."

I went to the Doctors the other day to get a mole removed from the end of my dick. That's the last time I f... one of them.

An 80-year-old man is having his annual check-up. The doctor asks him how he's feeling. "I've never been better!" he replies. "I've got an 18-year-old bride who's pregnant and having my child! What do you think about that?"

The doctor considers this for a moment, then he says, "Well, let me tell you a story. I know a guy who's an avid hunter. He never misses a season. But one day he's in a bit of a hurry and he accidentally grabs his umbrella instead of his gun.

"So he's in the woods and suddenly a grizzly bear appears in front of him! He raises up his umbrella, points it at the bear, and squeezes the handle. The bear drops dead in front of him suffering from a bullet wound in its chest."

"That's impossible! Someone else must have shot that bear," the man said.

"Exactly."

A man came hobbling into the doctor's waiting room, assisted by his wife.

The poor bloke could hardly move. He was bent over and grimacing with pain as he shuffled along, his hands like two rigid claws.

The receptionist looked on sympathetically.

"Oh, dear," she said. "Arthritis with complications?"

"No," said the bloke's wife. "Do-it-yourself with concrete blocks."

Then there was the bloke who came home from the doctor's after getting a new hearing aid – the latest miniature electronic model, complete with silicon chip and all the works, worth five grand.

He walked in the door and proudly showed his wife.

"It looks fine," she said.

And he said, "Half past seven …"

An old woman came into her doctor's office and confessed to an embarrassing problem. "I fart all the time, Doctor Johnson," she said. "But they're soundless, and they have no odour. In fact, since I've been here, I've farted no less than twenty times. What can I do?"

"Here's a prescription, Mrs. McConville. Take these pills three times a day for seven days and come back and see me in a week."

Next week an upset Mrs. McConville marched into Dr. Johnson's office. "Doctor, I don't know what was in those pills, but the problem is worse! I'm farting just as much, but now they smell terrible! What do you have to say for yourself?"

"Calm down, Mrs. Harris," said the doctor soothingly. "Now that we've fixed your sinuses, we'll work on your hearing!!!"

This guy goes to see his Doctor, "Doc," he says, "I've got a problem, every minute of every day I've got that old song, *Delilah*, running through my head. I catch myself humming it and sometimes singing it in public places. My wife even says I sing it in my sleep, it's driving her nuts. What is the matter with me?"

The Doctor replies, "Sounds like Tom Jones Syndrome to me."

"Is it a rare disorder?" the guy asks, to which the Doctor answers, "*It's Not Unusual* ..."

29 QUESTIONS TO MAKE YOU PONDER

1. If all those smart-arse psychics know the friggin' winning lottery numbers, then why are they still working?
2. Why do they sterilize needles for lethal injections?
3. If quitters never win, and winners never quit, what idiot came up with, "Quit while you're ahead?"
4. Whose idea was it to have an "s" in the word "lisp"?
5. If it's zero degrees outside today and it's supposed to be twice as cold tomorrow, how bloody cold is it going to be?
6. Why is it that when a door is open, it's ajar – but when a jar is open, it's not a door?
7. Is it possible to have a civil war?
8. If the black box flight recorder is never damaged during a plane crash, why isn't the whole airplane made out of the stuff?
9. Why is it when you open a can of evaporated milk it's still full?
10. Why do shops which are open 24/7 have locks on the doors?
11. Why is it called tourist season if we can't shoot at them?
12. If most car accidents occur within 10 km of home, why doesn't everyone just move 20 km away?

13. Employment application blanks always ask who is to be notified in case of an emergency. Why can't you just write, "A Good Doctor"?

14. Before they invented drawing boards, what did they go back to?

15. If all the world is a stage, where does the audience sit?

16. If you ate pasta and antipasto, would you still be hungry?

17. If you try to fail, and succeed, which have you done?

18. Is a castrated pig disgruntled?

19. Why is the alphabet in that order? Is it because of that song?

20. Why is there an expiration date on sour cream?

21. Light travels faster than sound, so is that why some people appear bright until you hear them speak?

22. Does the reverse side also have a reverse side?

23. Why is there only one monopolies commission?

24. Why arc there five syllables in the word "monosyllabic"?

25. How much deeper would the ocean be if sponges didn't grow in it?

26. Why is abbreviated such a long word?

27. Is the Leaning Tower of Pisa a listed building?

28. What if there were no hypothetical questions?

29. Why is a carrot more orange than an orange?

RELATIONSHIPS

Three married couples, aged 20, 30, and 40 years old, wish to join the Orthodox Church of Sexual Repression. Near the end of the interview, the priest informs them that before they can be accepted they will have to pass one small test. They will have to abstain from all sex for a month.

They agree to try. A month later, they are having their final interview with the cleric. He asks the 40-year-old couple how they went

"Well, it wasn't too hard. I spent a lot of time in the workshop and my partner has a garden, so we had plenty of other things to do. We did OK," the husband said.

"Very good, my children," said the priest. "You are welcome in the Church.

"And how well did you manage?" he asked the 30-year-old couple.

"It was pretty difficult," the husband answered. "We thought about it all the time. We had to sleep in different beds and we prayed a lot. But we were celibate for the entire month."

"Very good, my children, you also are welcome in the Church.

"And how about you?" he asked the 20-year-old couple.

"Not too good, I'm afraid, Father. We did OK for the first week," the man said sheepishly. "By the second week we were going crazy with lust. Then one day during the third week my wife dropped a head of lettuce, and when she bent over to pick it up, I weakened and took her right there."

"I'm sorry my son, you are not welcome in the Church"

"Yeah, and we're not too welcome in the Safeway supermarket anymore, either ..."

Three women are having lunch, discussing their husbands. The first says, "My husband is cheating on me, I just know it. I found a pair of stockings in his jacket pocket, and they weren't mine!"

The second says, "My husband is cheating on me, I just know it. I found a condom in his wallet, so I poked it full of holes with my sewing needle!"

The third woman fainted.

Women want a relationship without the complication of unnecessary sex. Men want sex without the complication of an unnecessary relationship.

After a horrible day at the office a man gets home from work. When he comes through the door his wife greets him and says, "Hi, Honey. Notice anything different about me?"

"Oh, I don't know. You got your hair done."

"Nope, try again."

"Oh, you bought a new dress."

"Nope, keep trying."

"You got your nails done."

"No, try again."

"I give up. I'm too tired to play twenty questions."

"I'm wearing a gas mask!"

A drug company has just invented a pill that combines the effects of Viagra and Prozac – Apparently if you don't get a f..., you don't give a f...!

Man says to God, "God, why did you make woman so beautiful?"

God says, "So you would love her."

"But God," the man says, "why did you make her so dumb?"

God replies, "So she would love you."

A bloke walks into a pub and orders six double vodkas. The barman says, "Bad day?"

To which the bloke replies, "Yes, I just found out my brother is gay!"

"Oh you'll get used to it," replies the barman.

The following day the man re-enters and again orders six double vodkas. "Not another bad day?" asks the barman.

"Yes," replies the man, "I just found out my other brother is gay, too."

"Have an extra one, on the house," offers the barman.

Two days later the man returns to the pub, looking more depressed than usual. He sits down and orders six double vodkas.

The barman asks, "For God's sake, does no one in your family like women?"

"Yes," replies the man, "my wife does!"

DICTIONARY OF RELATIONSHIPS

ATTRACTION	The act of associating horniness with a particular person.
BIRTH CONTROL	Avoiding pregnancy through such tactics as swallowing special pills, inserting a diaphragm, using a condom, and dating repulsive men.
DATING	The process of spending enormous amounts of money, time and energy to get better acquainted with a person whom you don't especially like in the present and will learn to like a lot less in the future.
EASY	A term used to describe a woman who has the sexual morals of a man.

EYE CONTACT   A method utilized by one person to indicate that they are interested in another. Despite being advised to do so, many men have difficulty looking a woman directly in the eyes, not necessarily due to shyness, but usually due to the fact that a woman's eyes are not located on her breasts.

FRIEND   A person in your acquaintance who has some flaw which makes sleeping with him/her totally unappealing.

INDIFFERENCE   A woman's feeling towards a man, which is interpreted by the man to be "playing hard to get".

INTERESTING   A word a man uses to describe a woman who lets him do all the talking.

IRRITATING HABIT   What the endearing little qualities, that initially attract two people to each other, turn into after a few months together.

LOVE AT FIRST SIGHT   What occurs when two extremely horny, but not entirely choosy people meet.

Kathleen came home from a Women's Liberation meeting, and told her husband, Mike that the meeting had been about free love.

Mike said, "Surely you don't believe in free love?"
She replied, "Have I ever sent you a bill?"

I t's clear that since there are more and more idiots in the world, there must be a large number of f…ing idiots.

WOMEN SEEKING MEN
The code for working out what is actually meant by what.

Code word	Actually Means
Adventurer	Has had more partners than you ever will.
Affectionate	Possessive.
Artist	Unreliable.
Athletic	Flat-chested.
Average looking	Ugly.
Beautiful	Pathological liar.
Commitment-minded	Pick out curtains, now!
Communication important	Just try to get a word in edgewise.
Contagious smile	Bring your anti-biotics.
Educated	College dropout.
Emotionally secure	Medicated.
Employed	Has part-time job stuffing envelopes at home.
Enjoys art and opera	Snob.
Forty-ish	48.

Financially secure	One pay cheque from the street.
Free spirit	Substance abuser.
Friendship first	Trying to live down reputation as slut.
Gentle	Comatose.
Good listener	Borderline Autistic.
Intuitive	Your opinion doesn't count.
Light drinker	Piss-pot.
Looks younger	If viewed from far away in bad light.
Loves travel	If you're paying.
New-age	All body hair, all the time.
Non-traditional	Ex-husband lives in basement with llama.
Old-fashioned	Lights out, missionary position only.
Open-minded	Desperate.
Poet	Depressive Schizophrenic.
Professional	Bitch.
Reliable	Frumpy.
Romantic	Looks better by light of 40 watt globe.
Spiritual	Involved with a cult.
Stable	Boring.
Tall, thin	Anorexic.
Tanned	Wrinkled.
Writer	Pompous.
Young at heart	Toothless crone.

MEN SEEKING WOMEN

The code for working out what is actually meant by what.

Code word	Actually Means
Artist	Delicate ego badly in need of massage.
Distinguished-looking	Fat, grey, and bald.
Educated	Will always treat you like an idiot.
Forty-ish	52 and looking for 25-yr-old.
Free spirit	Sleeps with your sister.
Good looking	Arrogant bastard.
Huggable	Overweight, more body hair than a gorilla.
Open-minded	Wants to sleep with your sister again.
Sensitive	Needy.
Spiritual	Once went to church with his grandmother.
Stable	Occasional stalker, but never arrested.
Thoughtful	Says please when demanding a beer.
Young at heart	How young is your sister?

Two strangers, a man and a woman, are sitting next to each other on a trans-Atlantic flight. Suddenly, the plane plummets out of control. In panic, the woman turns to the man, tears off her blouse and cries, "Make me feel like a woman one more time!"

Rising to the occasion, the man tears off his shirt and says, "Here, iron this."

Three blokes are waiting to get into heaven. One bloke asks another why he's there and he replies, "Well I suspected my wife of having an affair so I rushed home and ran up four flights of stairs to our flat as the lift is buggered, burst through the door, and found my wife naked in bed. But although I searched the flat upside down I couldn't find a man anywhere. All the time I was getting more and more frustrated and angry, so finally I picked up the wife's brand new fridge and threw it out the window. That was when I got a heart attack. I died before the ambulance men could get to me because of some disturbance in the street below. What about you?"

"Well," says the other man, "I was walking down the street when this fridge came whistling down and hit me on the head and killed me stone dead!"

He turns to the third man, "How about you pal?"

"Well," says he, "I was minding my own business, sitting in this fridge when suddenly ..."

A boy and his date were parked on a back road some distance from town, doing what boys and girls do on back roads some distance from town.

The girl stopped the boy.

"I really should have mentioned this earlier, but I'm

actually a hooker and I charge $20 for sex," she said.

The boy reluctantly paid her, and they did their thing.

After a cigarette, the boy just sat in the driver's seat looking out the window.

"Why aren't we going anywhere?" asked the girl.

"Well, I should have mentioned this before, but I'm actually a taxi driver, and the fare back to town is $25."

A couple was told to individually write a sentence using the words 'sex' and 'love.' The woman wrote, "When two people love each other very much, like Bob and I do, it is morally acceptable for them to engage in sex"

Bob wrote, "I love sex"'

THE BEFORE AND AFTER OF FALLING IN LOVE

Before – Passion.
After – Ration.

Before – Don't stop.
After – Don't start.

Before – Turbocharged.
After – Jump-start.

Before – Twice a night.
After – Twice a month.

Before – Saturday Night Fever.
After – Monday Night Football.

Before – Idol.
After – Idle.

Before – Oysters.
After – Fishsticks.

Before – Is that all you're having?
After – Maybe you should have just a salad, honey.

Before – It's like I'm living in a dream.
After – It's like he lives in a dorm.

Before – We agree on everything.
After – Doesn't she have a mind of her own?

Before – Charming and noble.
After – Chernobyl.

Before – I love a woman with curves.
After – I never said you were fat!

Before – He's completely lost without me.
After – Why won't he ever ask for directions?

Before – You look so seductive in black.
After – Your clothes are so depressing.

Before – She says she loves the way I take control of a
            situation.

After – She calls me a controlling, manipulative
       egomaniacal prick.

Before – You take my breath away.
After – I feel like I'm suffocating.

Before – I can hardly believe we found each other.
After – I can't believe I ended up with someone like you.

Before – Time stood still.
After – This relationship is going nowhere.

Before – Once upon a time.
After – The end.

A gay man, finally deciding he could no longer hide his sexuality from his parents, went over to their house, and found his mother in the kitchen cooking dinner. He sat down at the kitchen table, let out a big sigh, and said, "Mom, I have something to tell you: I'm gay."

His mother made no reply or gave any response, and the guy was about to repeat it to make sure she'd heard him, when she turned away from the pot she was stirring and said calmly, "You're gay. Doesn't that mean you put other men's penises in your mouth?

"The guy said nervously, "Uh, yeah, Mom, that's right."

His mother went back to stirring the pot, then suddenly whirled around, whacked him over the head with her spoon and said, "Don't you *ever* complain about my cooking again!!"

What do you do if a bird shits on your car? You never take her out again.

THE ULTIMATE DATING CHECKLIST

I had a wonderful time last night.	Who the hell are you?
Did you come?	Because I didn't.
You're so mature.	I hope you're eighteen.
Is there something wrong?	Is it supposed to be this soft?
Was it good for you?	I'm insecure about my manhood.
It's never been like this before.	It's my first time.
I have something to tell you.	Get tested.
It's time to express our love for each other again.	Give me a blow-job.
I love you.	You're a good root.
I never meant to hurt you.	I thought you weren't a virgin.
I think we should see other people.	I have been seeing other people.
I still think about you.	I miss the sex.
I want to make love to you.	Let's f….
I've been thinking a lot.	You're not as attractive as when I was pissed.
Trust me.	I'm cheating on you.
We need to talk.	I'm pregnant.
I've learned a lot from you.	Next!

The young mechanic came to pick up his girlfriend with a pair of jumper-leads holding up his pants in lieu of a belt.

"Don't you start anything" she warned.

AH, THIS IS ISLAND LIFE

A group of bureaucrats from the European Economic
Union set out on a convention on a chartered luxury
liner through the Pacific.

A storm blows up, the cruiser starts to sink, and
everyone abandons ship. By a quirk of fate, the only
survivors are two men and one woman from each of the
EEU countries.

They stagger onto the shore of a beautiful desert island.

Three months pass, by which time:

One Italian man has killed the other Italian man in a fight
over the Italian woman.

The two French men and the French woman are enjoying a
threesome, but complain bitterly about the multitude of
foreigners on their island.

The two English men are waiting patiently for someone to
introduce them to the English woman.

The German men have a strict, weekly alternating sex-
schedule; the woman gets weekends off.

The Belgian men have realized that the Belgian woman is, in fact, a seven year old boy and are mighty ashamed of the whole thing.

The Dutch men are fully prepared, in general, to share the woman. However, they are still debating how to ensure that both will have an exactly equal share, how to reduce supervision cost, and how to guarantee the woman equal rights. They are writing to the Hague.

The Luxembourg men are still recovering from the shock of seeing half the population of Luxembourg stranded on the island. But they will soon start collecting sea-shells on the beach.

The Finnish men took one look at the endless ocean, one look at the Finnish woman, and started swimming.

They were soon overtaken by the Portuguese men.

The Danish trio embarked on a search for people to join them in an orgy. They gladly accepted the participation of the Finnish woman, and are still vainly trying to persuade the Portuguese woman.

The Spanish men are protecting the virginity of the Spanish woman and are constantly and suspiciously spying on one another. Meanwhile, she dances flamenco.

The Austrian men initiated a yodelling contest for the woman. The loser immediately started learning flamenco, as well as Portuguese, Finnish and Danish.

The Greek men are sleeping with each other and the Greek woman is cleaning and cooking for them.

The Swedish woman keeps on bitching about female exploitation while the men are sunbathing and waiting for her to tell them what to do.

The Irish began by setting up a distillery for which they expect to receive a substantial EU subsidy. They don't recall if sex is in the picture, because it gets sort of foggy after the first few rounds of coconut whiskey. But they're happy that, at least, the English aren't getting any …

I've decided to take anti-histamine tablets with my Viagra. That way I achieve an erection that's not to be sneezed at.

A man walks up to a farmer's house and knocks on the door.

When a woman opens the door, the man asks if she knows how to have sex. Not amused, she slams the door.

Again, the man knocks, and again, asks the same question. Still not amused, she screams at the man to go away.

Later, she tells her husband of the incident.

He offers to stay home the following day, just in case. Sure enough, the next day the same man returns. The husband hides with his gun while the lady answers the door.

She is asked again if she knows how to have sex.

She answers, "Yes."

The man replies, "Great! Give some to your husband the next time you see him, and tell him to keep away from my wife."

POLITICALLY CORRECT TERMS OF ENDEARMENT

Amphibian Person – *frog*.

Aquatically Challenged – *drowning*.

Biologically Challenged – *dead*.

Caucasian Culturally-Disadvantaged – *white trash*.

Certified Astrological Consultant – *crackpot*.

Certified Crystal Therapist – *crackpot*.

Certified Past-Life Regression Hypnotist – *crackpot*.

Chronologically-Gifted – *old*.

Co-Dependent – *finger-pointer*.

Creatively Re-Dyed – *blonde*.

Differently-Organized – *messy*.

Differently-Brained – *stupid*.

Energy-Efficient – *off*.

Environmentally-Correct Human – *dead*.

Facially-Challenged – *ugly*.

Factually-Unencumbered – *ignorant*.

Financially Inept – *poor*.

Folically Independent – *bald*.

Genetically Discriminating – *racist*.

Gravitationally-Challenged – *fat*.

Horizontally-Challenged – *thin*.

Horizontally-Gifted – *fat*.

In Denial – *unaware that forgetting something obviously proves it happened*.

In Recovery – *drunk/junkie*.

Intellectually-Impaired – *stupid*.

Living-Impaired – *dead*.

Metabolically-Challenged – *dead*.

Monetarily-Challenged – *poor*.

Morally-Challenged – *a crook*.

Morally-Handicapped – *someone who has no other reason to park in a handicapped zone*.

Motivationally-Challenged – *lazy*.

Musically-Delayed – *tone deaf*.

Nasally-Disadvantaged – *really big nose*.

Nasally-Gifted – *large nose*.

Outdoor Urban Dwellers – *homeless*.

Persons Living With Entropy – *dead*.

Petroleum Transfer Technician – *gas station attendant*.

Sanitation Engineer – *garbage man*.

Sexually-Focused Chronologically-Gifted Individual – *dirty old man*.

Socially-Challenged – *geek, nerd*.

Spatially-Perplexed – *drunk*.

Uniquely-Coordinated – *clumsy*.

Vertically-Challenged – *short*.

Visually-Challenged – *blind*.

"Have you ever met a man whose touch makes you tremble?"

"Yes."

"Wow, who was he?"

"A dentist."

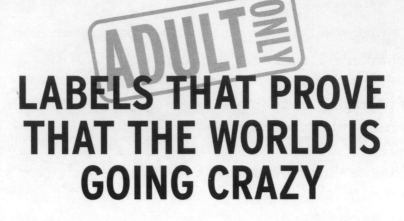

LABELS THAT PROVE THAT THE WORLD IS GOING CRAZY

On a child's superman costume:
Wearing of this garment does not enable you to fly.

On a bar of Dial soap:
Directions: Use like regular soap.

On Sears hairdryer:
Do not use while sleeping.

On a bag of Fritos:
You could be a winner! No purchase necessary. Details inside.

On some Swann frozen dinners:
Serving suggestion: Defrost.

On a hotel provided shower cap in a box:
Fits one head.

On Tesco's Tiramisu dessert:
(printed on bottom of the box) Do not turn upside down.

On Marks & Spencer Bread Pudding:
Product will be hot after heating.

On packaging for an iron:
Do not iron clothes on body.

On Boot's Children's cough medicine:
Do not drive car or operate machinery.

On sleep aid:
Warning: may cause drowsiness.

On a Korean kitchen knife:
Warning keep out of children.

On a string of Chinese-made Christmas lights:
For indoor or outdoor use only.

On a Japanese food processor:
Not to be used for the other use.

On Sainsbury's peanuts:
Warning: contains nuts.

On an American Airlines packet of nuts:
Instructions: open packet, eat nuts.

On a Swedish chain saw:
Do not attempt to stop chain with your hands or genitals.

RELIGION

Moses, returning from the mountain, spoke to his people, "The good news is we got them down to ten. The bad news is that adultery is still one of them."

Jesus came across an adulteress crouching in a corner with a crowd around her preparing to stone her to death.

Jesus stopped them and said, "Let he who is without sin cast the first stone."

Suddenly a woman at the back of the crowd fired off a stone at the adulteress. At which point Jesus looked over and said, "Mother! Sometimes you really piss me off!"

There were three nuns driving down a highway one day when they lost control of their car and plunged off a cliff. They awoke and found themselves standing before the pearly gates.

St. Peter walked toward them and, after greeting them, told them that they would have to answer one question each before they were admitted to the Kingdom of Heaven.

This made the nuns very nervous. They had never heard of this requirement before. Finally, one nun stepped forward and said, "St. Peter, I'm ready for my question."

St. Peter replied, "Your question is: Who was the first Man on Earth?"

The nun breathed a huge sigh of relief, and said, "Why, it was Adam."

The lights flashed, the bells tolled, and the gates of Heaven opened. It was a cause of great relief to the others. The second stepped forward without hesitation.

St. Peter said, "And you must tell me who the first Woman on Earth was."

Another great sigh of relief, "Eve" the nun replied. The lights flashed, the bells tolled, and the gates of Heaven opened.

The third was brimming with excitement. "I'm ready St. Peter!"

St. Peter said, "All right, what was the first thing Eve said to Adam?"

The nun was shocked, "My goodness, that's a hard one." The lights flashed, the bells tolled, and the gates of Heaven opened ...

Jesus walks into a Holiday Inn, tosses three nails on the counter and asks, "Can you put me up for the night?"

The Pope arrives in New York for a United Nations Conference He is running late. As he comes out of the airline terminal he hails a cab.

He says to the cabbie, "I have to be at the UN building in ten minutes."

"Ten minutes! It takes at least forty minutes! I can't do it!"

"Well, you get out and let me drive," says the Pope.

The cabbie was a bit taken back by this, but it was the Pope, so he jumped into the back seat while the Pope drove.

The Pope was enjoying the experience, flying along, dodging in and out of traffic, when he zoomed past a New York policeman. The cop jumped on his motorbike and pursued the speeding vehicle.

Finally, he caught up with it, pulled it over, and asked the driver to wind down the window. He saw who was driving and got on his radio for assistance. "This is road patrol to base I need some help," said the policeman.

"What's up?" asked headquarters.

"Well I've pulled someone over for speeding and he is very big. What should I do?"

"How big is he? A local politician?" asked headquarters.

"No, bigger than that."

"The Mayor of New York?"

"No, bigger than that."

"A movie star?"

"No, bigger than that."

"Hell, not the President?"

"No, bigger than that"

"Bigger than that?" asked headquarters in a bewildered tone, "Who the hell is it?"

"I don't know" replied the cop, "but he's got the Pope driving him around."

Mortal: "What is a million years like to you?"
God: "Like one second."
Mortal: "What is a million dollars like to you?"
God: "Like one penny".
Mortal: "Can I have a penny?"
God: "Just a second ..."

Two Irish lads had been out shacking up with their girl friends. One felt guilty and decided he should stop at the church and confess.

He went into the confessional booth and told the priest, "Father, I have sinned. I have committed fornication with a lady. Please forgive me."

The Father said, "Tell me who the lady was."

The young man said he couldn't do that and the priest said he couldn't grant him forgiveness unless he did.

"Was it Mollie O'Grady?" asked the Father.

"No."

"Was it Rosie Kelly?"

"No."

"Was it that little red-headed wench Tessie O'Malley?"

"No."

"Well then," said the Father, "You'll not be forgiven."

When the lad met his friend outside the friend asked, "So, did you find forgiveness?"

"No," said the other, "but I picked up three good prospects!"

Two nuns are ordered to paint a room that is going to be redecorated in the convent for a visit by the Pope.

The last instruction from Mother Superior is that they must not get so much as a drop of paint on their habits.

After conferring about this for a while, the two nuns decide to lock the door of the room, strip off their habits, and paint in the nude.

In the middle of the project, there comes a knock at the door. "Who is it?" calls one of the nuns.

"It's the blind man," replies a voice from the other side of the door.

The two nuns look at each other and shrug, deciding that no harm can come from letting a blind man into the room. They open the door.

"Nice tits," says the man, "where do you want the blinds?"

Mr. Johnson, a business-man, went on a business trip to Kuala Lumpur. Upon arrival he immediately sent an e-mail back home to his wife, Jean.

Unfortunately, he mis-typed one character and the e-mail ended up going to a Mrs Joan Johnson, the wife of a minister who had just passed away that morning. The vicar's wife took one look at the e-mail and promptly fainted.

When she was finally revived, she nervously pointed to the message, which read: *"Arrived safely, but it sure is hot down here."*

A man sick of the outside world joins a temple in Tibet. One of the stipulations upon entry to this most holy order was that he was only permitted to say two words every five years.

The first five years he eats rice, he sleeps on a wooden bed, and has only one blanket with holes in it. He tends to the fields and looks after livestock everyday.

After five years the head monk comes to him and says he can use his two words to which he replies, "More blankets."

Now the man is warm at night on his wooden bed with all his blankets but still only eats rice and tends to the fields and livestock everyday.

Another five years passes and the head monk comes to him again and says that he can use two more words.

He replies, "More food."

He now sleeps on his wooden bed with all his blankets and eats gourmet food everyday but he still has to tend to the fields and livestock.

Another five years passes and the head monk comes again to him and says, "You may use two words."

The man replies, "I'm leaving."

"Good," said the head monk, "all you've done is f...ing complain since you got here."

God is tired, worn out. He speaks to St. Peter, "I need a vacation," he says "Got any suggestions where I should go?"

St. Peter begins to think, nods his head, then says, "How about Jupiter? It's nice and warm there at this time of the year."

God shakes His head, saying, "No. Too much gravity. You know how that hurts my back."

St. Peter reflects, "Well, how about Mercury?"

"No way!" God replies. "It's way too hot for me there!"

"I've got it," St. Peter says, his face lighting up. "How about going down to Earth for your vacation?"

"Are you winding me up?" God replies. "Two thousand years ago I went there, had an affair with some nice Jewish girl, and they're still going on about it!"

A group of eminent scientists got together and decided that Man had come such a long way that they no longer needed God.

God was redundant, they decided. So they went to God and said, "We can clone people and do many wondrous things. We really don't need you any more and we think that you should retire."

God listened patiently. "OK," he said, "But first let us both make a man just like I did with Adam, and we can compare our work."

"Yes, let's do that!" replied the scientists, as one bent down to scoop up a handful of dirt from the ground.

"Oh, no, you don't," scolded God. "Go and get your own dirt."

There were three priests who were put into a group by the archbishop, purely for the purpose of debriefing and having time out from parish duties. As they didn't know each other, they decided that the best thing to do was to bare their souls and to confess to each other their innermost secrets.

The first priest said, "I'm addicted to gambling. Each Saturday night I take exactly half the takings from the previous Sunday's plate and gamble it on the horses."

The second minister said, "I am an alcoholic. I drink everything in sight. If there is nothing else around, I even drink the altar wine."

"Well, I'm a dreadful gossip," said the third, "and I can't wait to get out of here to tell everybody."

The church service was under way and they passed around the collection plate.

When the preacher saw a $100 bill in the plate, he was so surprised that he stopped the service and asked, "Will who ever put the $100 bill in the plate, please stand up?"

A young, gay man in the congregation stood up.

The preacher told him, "I am so impressed that you would donate such a large sum. Since you put that money in the plate I think that it is only fair that you should choose three hymns."

Excitedly, the gay guy looked around, and said, "Well, I'll take him and him and him."

Four Catholic mothers are sitting around bragging about their sons, each of whom is a priest.

First mother says, "My son is a monsignor, and when he walks in the room, people greet him with, 'Good morning, Monsignor.'"

The second mother says, "Well, my son is a bishop, and people greet him 'Good morning, Your Grace.'"

The third mother says, "Well, my son is a cardinal, and people greet him 'Good morning, Your Eminence.'"

The fourth mother pauses, and finally says, "My son is six feet, ten inches tall and is 300 pounds of pure muscle. When he walks in the room, people greet him by saying, 'Oh, My God!'"

A monastery was perched high on an isolated cliff, and the only way to reach it was to ride in a basket which was hauled to the top by a team of monks.

The ride up was not for the faint-hearted, and one visitor was looking exceedingly pale by the time he reached the summit. As he stepped trembling from the basket, he couldn't help noticing that the rope was old and frayed.

"How often do you change that rope?" he asked one of the monks.

The monk thought for a moment, then replied, "Whenever it breaks."

The Pope and one of his top cardinals were taking a long train ride one day. The Pope was doing a crossword puzzle, and the cardinal was reading the Bible. Suddenly the Pope asked the cardinal, "What's a four letter word for 'woman' ending in u, n, t?"

The startled cardinal stammered for a bit, then said, "Uh, er, aunt! Yes, aunt!"

"Oh, of course," said the Pope, "Got an eraser?"

God is talking to one of his angels. He says, "Boy, I just created a twenty four hour period of alternating light and darkness on Earth."

The angel says, "What are you going to do now?"

God says, "Call it a day."

An Amish family went to New York and visited all the massive multi-storey department stores. They had never left their home before and were spellbound by what they saw.

The father and his son visited a particular store and were fascinated by the lifts, although they did not know what they were or what they did.

"What are those silver things with doors?" said the son.

"I don't know – let's stand here and watch for a while," said the father.

Shortly an old lady on a zimmer frame struggled up to the lift door, pressed the call button and went in.

Thirty seconds later the door opened and out stepped a gorgeous 24 year old blonde, with legs up to her armpits, wearing a micro-micro-mini skirt.

"Quick!" said the father to his son, "Go and get your mother!"

A sanctimonious man sat listening to flood warnings on his radio on a stormy night. He was a religious man so he did not worry. He had lived a good life. God would protect him.

The storms came; the rains came; the rains continued and slowly the waters began to rise. It continued raining, and the waters now flooded his ground floor. Indeed, the whole town was flooded.

The emergency services began evacuating the residents. Rescuers in a boat knocked at his door and urged him to jump into the boat and to be taken to a place of safety. He steadfastly refused.

"God will save me, rescue others whose need is greater than mine," he said. The rescuers left. The rains continued unabated. The waters continued to rise.

By now the flood waters were three metres high and the man was forced to go upstairs. He was kneeling and praying when he heard a banging on the window.

"Come on, get into the boat and we will take you to higher ground," the rescuers shouted.

"No! I'm OK, I have faith in God, he will save me," said the man. "Go and rescue others who are in more need."

The rescuers left. The storms continued into the night

and so the flood waters continued rising.

By now the waters had risen to six metres and the man was forced to climb onto the roof of his house. He clung desperately onto the chimney-stack.

He was dazzled by a search light from above, and a voice from a loud-hailer urged him to climb the ladder and board the helicopter to be taken to a place of safety.

He still refused, insisting that his God would save him. The helicopter left. The storm raged on and the waters continued to rise. Sadly, the man eventually drowned. He died and went to Heaven.

As he arrived at the pearly gates, he had to ask God one question. "You know that I've always been a religious man and have lived a righteous life," he said. "What I can't understand is, why didn't you save me from the floods?"

God replied, "I don't quite understand it myself. I did my best. I sent two boats and a helicopter, but still you weren't saved."

Colonel Sanders of Kentucky Fried Chicken fame was exploring new ways to advertise. He phoned Vatican City and asked to speak to the Pope, indicating that he would like to make a sizable donation.

"Hello, my son," said the Pope.

"Hello, your Holiness," said the Colonel. "I am calling because I would like to make a sizable donation to the Roman Catholic Church."

"How nice! Why don't you send it in the mail?"

"Would you like me to send one hundred million dollars in the mail?"

"One hundred million dollars! Bless you, my son. Why no, of course. My representative can visit you at your convenience!"

"But there is one little string attached."

"Oh?"

"You know that part in the Lord's Prayer where you say 'Give us this day our daily bread'? I'd like that changed to 'Give us this day our daily chicken'."

"Oh, I see ..."

The Pope covers the telephone and yells to the cardinal attending him, "How long do we still have on that Hi-Fibre Bread Contract?"

Three men of the cloth from the country were having lunch in a diner.

One said, "You know, since summer started I've been having trouble with bats in my loft and attic at church. I've tried everything – noise, spray, cats – nothing seems to scare them away."

Another said, "Yes, me too. I've got hundreds living in my belfry and in the attic. I've even had the place fumigated, and they won't go away."

The third said, "I baptized all mine, and made them members of the church. Haven't seen one back since!"

A huge crowd had gathered as Jesus was nailed to the cross. As Jesus surveyed the crowd he saw St. Peter at the back. He strained to call to him, "Peter, Peter".

Peter tried to get through the crowd, pushing people as he went.

Still Jesus cried, "Peter, Peter".

"I'm coming Lord," shouted Peter as he worked his way through the crowd. Eventually he reached the foot of Jesus' cross, and asked, "What is it, Lord?"

And Jesus said, "I can see your house from here!"

"**S**ometimes I want to ask God why He allows injustice, violence and evil, when he could do something about it," said one man to his friend.

"So, why don't you ask him?" the friend responded.

"I don't like to," answered the first, "because he might ask me the same thing."

A man who smelled like a distillery flopped on a subway seat next to a priest. The man's tie was stained, his face was plastered with red lipstick, and a half-empty bottle of gin was sticking out of his torn coat pocket.

He opened his newspaper and began reading.

After a few minutes the dishevelled guy turned to the priest and asked, "Say, Father, what causes arthritis?"

"Mister, it's caused by loose living, being with cheap, wicked, women, too much alcohol, and a contempt for your fellow man."

"Well, I'll be damned," the drunk muttered, returning to his paper.

The priest, thinking about what he had said, nudged the man and apologized, "I'm very sorry, I didn't mean to come on so strong. How long have you had arthritis?"

"I don't have it, Father. I was just reading here that the Pope does."

Someone asks a guide in hell, "Why does Hitler stand up to his neck in shit, while Stalin is only up to his waist?"

He answers, "Because Stalin is standing on Lenin's shoulders."

A gentleman had been trying for years to meet the Pope. Finally, his wish was granted. When the gentleman approached the Pope he said, "Your Holiness, I am so happy to be given this chance to speak with you and I would like to tell you a joke before I start."

The Pope replied, "Of course my son. Go ahead and tell your joke."

The gentleman continued, "There were these two Polacks and ..."

The Pope interrupted, "My son, do you realize that I am Polish?"

"I'm sorry, Your Holiness. I'll speak slower ..."

Poor old Larry dies and finds himself in hell. He is wallowing in despair when he has his first meeting with the Devil ...
Devil: Why so miserable?

Larry: What do you think? I'm in Hell.

Devil: Hell's not so bad. We actually have a lot of fun down here ... you like a drink, Larry?

Larry: Sure, I like a drink.

Devil: Well you're going to love Mondays then. On Mondays that's all we do is drink. Beer, whiskey, tequila, Guinness, wine coolers, diet tab ... we drink till we throw up and then we drink some more!

Larry: Gee that sounds great.

Devil: You a smoker?

Larry: You better believe it! Love smoking.

Devil: OK!! You're going to love Tuesdays. We get the finest Cuban cigars, and smoke our lungs out. If you get cancer – no problem – you're already dead, remember?

Larry: Wow. That's awesome!

Devil: I bet you like to gamble.

Larry: Why, yes, as a matter of fact, I do. Love the gambling.

Devil: 'Cause Wednesday you can gamble all you want. blackjack, roulette, poker, slots, craps, whatever. If you go bankrupt – who cares, you're dead anyhow. You into drugs?

Larry: Are you kidding? Love drugs! You don't mean ...

Devil: I do! Thursday is drug day. Help yourself to a great big bowl of crack. Or smack. Smoke a bong the size of a submarine. You can do all the drugs you want and if you overdose, that's okay – you're dead – so, who cares! O.D. as much as you like!

Larry: Gee whiz, I never realized that Hell was such a great place!!

Devil: See, now you're getting the hang of it! Now Larry, tell me, are you gay?

Larry: Ah, no.

Devil: Ooooh, Larry, you're really gonna hate Fridays!

One day Mrs. Jones went to have a talk with the minister at the local church.

"Reverend," she said, "I have a problem, my husband keeps falling asleep during your sermons. It's very embarrassing. What should I do?"

"I have an idea," said the minister. "Take this hat-pin with you. I will be able to tell when Mr. Jones is sleeping, and I will motion to you at specific times. When I motion, you give him a good poke in the leg."

In church the following Sunday, Mr. Jones dozed off. Noticing this, the preacher put his plan to work.

"And who made the ultimate sacrifice for you?" he said, nodding to Mrs. Jones.

"Jesus!" Jones cried, as his wife jabbed him the leg with the hat-pin.

"Yes, you are right, Mr. Jones," said the minister.

Soon, Mr. Jones nodded off again.

Again, the minister noticed. "Who is your redeemer?" he asked the congregation, motioning towards Mrs. Jones.

"God!" Mr. Jones cried out, as he was stuck again with the hat-pin.

"Right again," said the minister, smiling.

Before long, Mr. Jones again winked off. However, this time the minister did not notice. As he picked up the tempo of his sermon, he made a few motions that Mrs. Jones mistook as signals to bayonet her husband with the hat-pin again. The minister asked, "And what did Eve say to Adam after she bore him his 99th son?"

Mrs. Jones poked her husband, who yelled, "You stick that goddamned thing in me one more time and I'll break it in half and shove it up your ass!"

A new priest was so nervous at his first Mass that he could hardly speak. After Mass he asked the monsignor how he had done.

The monsignor replied, "When I am worried about getting nervous on the pulpit, I put a glass of vodka next to the water glass."

So the next Sunday, he took the monsignor's advice. At the beginning of the sermon, he got nervous and took a drink.

He proceeded to talk up a storm.

Upon his return to his office after Mass, he found the following note on the door:

To Our New Curate – A Few Tips.
- Sip the vodka, don't gulp it.
- There are 10 commandments, not 12.
- There are 12 disciples, not 10.
- Jesus was consecrated, not constipated.
- Jacob wagered his donkey; he did not bet his ass.
- We do not refer to Jesus Christ as the late JC.
- The Father, Son and the Holy Ghost are not referred to as Daddy, Junior and the Spook.
- David slew Goliath; he did not kick the shit out of him.

- When David was hit by a rock and knocked off his donkey, don't say he was stoned off his ass.
- We do not refer to the cross as the "Big T."
- When Jesus broke the bread at the Last Supper he said, "Take this and eat it for it is my body." He did not say, "Eat me."
- The Virgin Mary is not called "Mary with the Cherry."
- The recommended grace before a meal is not, "Rub-A-Dub-Dub, Thanks for the grub, yeah God."
- Next Sunday, there will be a taffy pulling contest at St. Peter's, not a peter pulling contest at St. Taffy's.

A Jewish man, Moses, had dedicated his life to circumcising young boys Moses was getting on a bit and decided to retire, so he took his huge sackful of foreskins to the shop and asked the shopkeeper to make him a retirement present with the foreskins.

The shopkeeper agreed and told him to come back the next day. The next day Moses went back and asked the shopkeeper what he had made.

The shopkeeper gave him a nice wallet. Moses agreed but said, "It's nice but it's not much for a whole sackful is it?"

The shopkeeper replied, "Yeah, but if you stroke it, it turns into a briefcase!"

R ussian leader Brezhnev asks the Pope, "Why do people believe in your paradise in heaven, but refuse to believe in the communist paradise?"

"That's because," says the Pope, "we never show ours to anybody."

A young boy had just gained his driving permit. He asked his father, who was a minister, if they could discuss the use of the car.

His father took him to his study and said to him, "I'll make a deal with you. You bring your grades up, study your Bible a little and get your hair cut and we'll talk about it."

After about a month the boy came back and again asked his father if they could discuss use of the car.

They again went to the father's study where his father said, "Son, I've been real proud of you. You have brought your grades up, you've studied your Bible diligently, but you didn't get your hair cut!"

The young man waited a moment and replied, "You know Dad, I've been thinking about that. You know, Samson had long hair, Moses had long hair, Noah had long hair, and even Jesus had long hair."

To which his father replied, "Yes, and they walked every where they went!"

W hat do you get when you cross a Jehovah's Witness and a skinhead?

Someone who comes knocking on your door at 8 am on a Sunday and tells you to f… off.

Six of the seven dwarfs are sitting around the house one day when Sleepy rushes in and says, "Guess what guys, I've won us a trip to see the Pope!"

They all become very excited and dance around the room chanting, "We finally get to ask him, we finally get to ask him!"

Eventually, they are standing before the Pope. Dopey is out in front of the other six. They start pushing Dopey and saying, "Go ahead, Dopey, ask him, ask him!"

The Pope looks at Dopey and asks, "Do you have a question to ask me, young man?"

Dopey looks up shyly and says, "Well, yes."

The Pope tells him to go ahead and ask.

Dopey asks, "Well, do ... do they have nuns in Alaska?"

The Pope replies, "Well, yes, I'm sure we have nuns in Alaska."

The others continue to nudge Dopey and chant, "Ask him the rest, Dopey, ask him the rest!"

The Pope asks Dopey if there's more to his question.

Dopey continues, "Well, uh, do they have, uh, black nuns in Alaska?"

To which the Pope replies, "Well, my son, I think there must be a few black nuns in Alaska, yes."

Still not satisfied, the others continue, "Ask him the last part, Dopey, ask him the last part!"

The Pope asks Dopey, "Is there still more to your question?"

Dopey replies, "Well, uh, yeah ... are there, uh, are there any midget black nuns in Alaska?"

The startled Pope replies, "Well, no, my son, I really don't think there are any midget black nuns in Alaska."

Dopey turns all kinds of colors, and the others start laughing, and yelling, "Dopey screwed a penguin, Dopey screwed a penguin!"

A man wonders if having sex on the Sabbath is a sin because he is not sure if sex is work or play. He asks a priest for his opinion on this question.

The priest says, after consulting the Bible, "My son, after an exhaustive search I am positive sex is work and is not permitted on Sundays."

The man thinks, "What does a priest know of sex?"

He goes to a minister, a married man, experienced, for the answer. He queries the minister and receives the same reply, "Sex is work and not for the Sabbath!"

Not pleased with the reply, he seeks out the ultimate authority, a man of thousands of years of tradition and knowledge - a Rabbi.

The Rabbi ponders the question and states, "My son, sex is definitely play."

The man replies, "Rabbi, how can you be so sure when so many others tell me sex is work?"

The Rabbi softly speaks, "If sex were work, my wife would have the maid do it!"

A local preacher was dissatisfied with the small amount in the collection plates each Sunday. Someone suggested to him that perhaps he might be able to hypnotize the congregation into giving more.

"And just how would I go about doing that?" he asked.

"It is very simple. First you turn up the air conditioner so that the auditorium is warmer than usual. Then you preach in a monotone. Meanwhile, you dangle a watch on a chain and swing it in a slow arc above the lectern and suggest they put twenty dollars in the collection plate."

So the very next Sunday, the reverend did as suggested, and lo and behold the plates were full of twenty-dollar bills.

Now, the preacher did not want to take advantage of this technique each and every Sunday. So he waited for a couple of weeks and then tried his mass hypnosis again.

Just as the last of the congregation was becoming mesmerized, the chain on the watch broke and the watch hit the lectern with a loud thud and springs and parts flew everywhere.

"Shit!" exclaimed the pastor.

It took them a week to clean up the church.

Bush asks God, "When will unemployment go down in the US?"

God answers, "In 20 years time."

"That's too bad that it won't happen during my lifetime," regrets Bush.

Putin asks, "When will the Russian people get a happy life?"

"Not during my lifetime," says God.

In a rural area, on a Sunday morning, the church is packed and the Devil decides to pay a visit.

The doors burst open, and a rolling black cloud rolls in with the Devil in it. People jump out of the pews and run outdoors, screaming.

There are only two people left in the church. One is the Pastor, the other is an elderly farmer. Satan is a bit perplexed.

He points to the Pastor and says, "You! I can understand why you didn't run away, you are in your Lord's house, you preach against me everyday and you aren't afraid of me. But, you," he says, pointing to the farmer, "Why didn't you run away like everyone else?"

The farmer crosses one leg over the other and drawls, "Why, I'm surprised you don't recognize me. I've been married to your sister for thirty six years!"

Abraham: "What will you do if you violate one of the Ten Commandments?"

Cain: "Nothing. I'll still have nine left."

One day God calls down to Noah and says, "Noah, I want you to make me a new Ark."

Noah replies, "No problem God, anything you want. After all you're the boss."

God then adds, "I want twenty decks, one on top of the other."

"Twenty decks!" screams Noah, "That's a lot of decks.

Shall I fill it up with animals just like the last time?"

"No. This time I want you to fill it up with fish," God answers.

"Fish?" queried Noah, stunned. "Fish?"

"Yes Noah, I want wall to wall, floor to ceiling – carp!"

Noah looks to the skies, "Let me get this right. You want a new Ark and you want it full of carp. Is that right? But why?" asks the perplexed Noah.

"I just fancied," said God, "a Multi-Storey Carp Ark!!!"

Forrest Gump dies and goes to Heaven. The gates are closed, however, and Forrest approaches the gatekeeper. It is St Peter himself.

"Well, Forrest, it's certainly good to see you. We have heard a lot about you. It's now our policy to administer an entrance examination which you must pass before you can get into Heaven."

"Nobody ever told me about any entrance exams," says Forrest. "Sure hope the test ain't too hard; life was a big enough test as it was. But the test will be like a box of chocolates – you never know until you bite into it. So dish her up to me now. I'm a-ready, St. Pete."

"The test I have for you is only three questions. The first one is, what days of the week begin with the letter 'T'?

"Second, how many seconds are there in a year?

"Third, what is God's first name?

"Take your time, think about it and come back to me when you reckon that you have the answers."

Forrest goes away to think the questions over.

He returns the next day.

St. Peter waves him up and asks, "Now that you have had a chance to think the questions over, tell me your answers."

Forrest says, "Well, the first one, how many days of the week begin with the letter 'T'? Shucks, that one's easy; that'd be Today and Tomorrow!"

The saint's eyes open wide and he exclaims, "Forrest! That's not what I was thinking, but, you do have a point though, and I guess I didn't specify, so I give you credit for that answer."

"How about the next one," says St. Peter, "How many seconds in a year?"

"Now that one's harder," says Forest. "But, I thunk and thunk about that, and I guess the only answer can be twelve."

Astounded, St. Peter says, "Twelve! Twelve! Forrest, how in Heaven's name could you come up with twelve seconds in a year?"

Forrest says, "Shucks, there gotta be twelve: January second, February second, March second ..."

"Hold it," interrupts St. Peter. "I see where you're going with it. And I guess I see your point, though that wasn't quite what I had in mind, but I'll give you credit for that one too."

"Let's go on with the next and final question," says St. Peter. "Can you tell me God's first name?"

Forrest says, "Well sure, I know God's first name. Everybody probably knows it. It's Howard."

"Howard?" asks St. Peter. "What makes you think it's 'Howard'?"

Forrest answers, "It's in the prayer."

"The prayer?" asks St. Peter. "Which prayer?"

"The Lord's Prayer," responds Forest. "Our Father, who art in heaven, Howard be thy name …"

A visitor to the Vatican needs to relieve himself. Imagine his surprise when in the rest rooms he sees the Pope sitting on a toilet masturbating.

As this was a sight few people saw, he quickly took a few photos.

The Pope recovers his composure and buys the camera for $100,000.

As it was a nice camera, the Pope decided to keep it and use it on his travels.

One of his entourage sees it and asks how much it cost.

"$100,000" says the Pope.

"Wow! That guy must have seen you coming!"

Two nuns go out of the convent to sell cookies. One of them is known as Sister Mathematical (S.M.), the other is known as Sister Logical (S.L.). It is getting dark and they are still far away for the convent.

S.L: Have you noticed a man that has been following us for the past half an hour?

S.M: Yes, I wonder what he wants

S.L: It's logical. It's logical. He wants to rape us.

S.M: On no! At this pace he will reach us in 15 minutes at the most. What can we do?

S.L: The only logical thing to do of course, we'll have to start walking faster

S.M: It is not working

S.L: Of course it is not working. The man did the only logical thing to do. He also started to walk faster.

S.M: So what shall we do? At this pace, he will reach us in less than one minute.

S.L: The only logical thing we can do is to split. You go that way and I will go this way. He can't follow both of us. So, the man decides to go after Sister Logical. Sister Mathematical arrives at the convent and is worried because Sister Logical has not arrived yet. Finally, Sister Logical arrives.

S.M: Sister Logical! Thank God you are here. Tell us what happened?

S.L: The only logical thing happened. The man could not follow both of us, so he decided to go after me.

S.M: So, what happened? Please tell us.

S.L: The only logical thing to happen. I started to run as fast as I could.

S.M: So what happened?

S.L: The only logical thing to happen. The man also started to run as fast as I could.

S.M: And what else?

S.L: The only logical thing to happen. He reached me.

S.M: Oh no. what did you do then?

S.L: The only logical thing to do. I took my dress up.

S.M: Oh Sister! What did the man do?

S.L: The logical thing to do. He pulled down his pants.

S.M: Oh no, what happened then?

S.L: Isn't it logical Sister? A nun with her dress up runs faster than a man with his pants down.

HEAVEN IS A PLACE WHERE:
>   The lovers are Italian
>   The cooks are French
>   The mechanics are German
>   The police are English
>   The government is run by the Swiss

HELL IS A PLACE WHERE:
>   The lovers are Swiss
>   The cooks are English
>   The mechanics are French
>   The police are German
>   The government is run by the Italians

GOING DOWN IN STYLE

Failing your final exam can actually be an amusing experience. Try these to keep the exam room giggling, or at least perplexed:

- Walk in, get the exam, sit down. About five minutes into it, loudly say to the instructor, "I don't understand *any* of this!"
- Bring a pillow. Fall asleep (or pretend to) until the last 15 minutes. Wake up, and say, "Oh Jeez, better get cracking!"
- Talk the entire way through the exam. Read questions aloud, debate your answers with yourself out loud. If asked to stop, yell out, "I'm so sure you can hear me thinking."
- Arrive wearing a black cloak. After about 30 minutes, put on a white mask and start yelling, "I'm here, the phantom of the opera," until they drag you away.
- After you get the exam, call the instructor over, point to a question, and ask for the answer.
- Try to get people in the room to do the Mexican Wave

- Get a copy of the exam paper, run down the hall screaming, "Dr. Evil, Dr. Evil, I've got the secret documents!!"
- If it is a maths/science exam, answer in essay form. If it is a long answer/essay exam, answer with numbers and symbols.
- Make paper aeroplanes out of the examination paper. Aim them at the instructor's left nostril.
- Bring a Game Boy and play with the volume at maximum level.
- Come down with a bad case of Tourette's syndrome during the exam. The louder with the "involuntary" sounds, the better.
- On the answer sheet find a new, interesting way to refuse to answer every question. For example, I refuse to answer this question on the grounds that it conflicts with my religious beliefs.
- Fifteen minutes into the exam, stand up, rip up all the papers into very small pieces, and throw them into the air. Then calmly ask for another copy of the exam.
- Twenty minutes into it, throw your papers down violently, scream out, "Screw this!" And walk out triumphantly.
- Every five minutes, stand up, collect all your things, move to another seat, and continue with the exam.
- Turn in the exam approximately 30 minutes into it. As you walk out, start saying loudly, "Easy, easy!"

POLITICS

Why did Reagan pick Bush for Vice President of the United States? Here is the true story:

Ronald Reagan asked his wife, Nancy how he should make a choice. Nancy gave him a riddle to use as a test, saying that if one of the contenders is able to answer it, then he should have the job.

Reagan asks Bush, "Who is it who is your father's son, but not your brother?"

Bush replies, "Golly gee, Mr. Reagan, That's difficult. I'll need to go and think about that one for a while."

That evening Bush returns and happily shouts, "I got it, Ron! I figured it out! It's me! It's me!"

Reagan then presents the same riddle to the other hopeful.

"That's a tough one Mr. Reagan. I'll get back to you on that."

That evening he returns and says, "Try as I might, I just couldn't figure that one out. Who is it?"

Reagan answers, "It's George Bush, but I'm not exactly sure why."

Late one night, a mugger wearing a ski mask jumped into the path of a well-dressed man and stuck a gun in his ribs.

"Give me your money," he demanded.

Indignant, the affluent man replied, "You can't do this – I'm a United States Congressman!"

"In that case," replied the mugger, "give me *my* money."

Official: So you see, comrade, this is the way that Marx explained it, 'From each according to his abilities, to each according to his needs.' You understand?

Farmer: (confused) Not really.

Official: OK. It is like this. Say a comrade has two cows. We take one cow from him and give it to comrade who has no cow. That is socialism. You see?

Farmer: Yes, yes, this is good.

Official: And if a comrade has two tractors, we take one of his tractors and give to man who has no tractors. Yes?

Farmer: Yes, yes that is very good.

Official: And if a comrade has two chickens, we give one chicken to man who has no chickens.

Farmer: No. That is not good!

Official: Why?

Farmer: Because I have two chickens.

A speaker explains the advantages of communism to the residents of a lunatic asylum.

Everybody applauds except for one guy standing at a distance.

"Why aren't you clapping?" asks the speaker.

"I'm a nurse," he answers, "not a madman."

The USA and France yelled, "Charge!" and waved their rifles. Japan and Germany yelled, "Charge!" and waved their credit cards.

The American ambassador visited the Romanian president. In the waiting room he talked with two of the ministers for five minutes.

When he entered he said to the Romanian president, "I really don't want to bother you but I talked with two of your ministers, and my gold watch has disappeared."

So the president answered, "OK. I'll take care of it."

He left the room and came back two minutes later with the watch.

The ambassador said, "Thank you very much. I hope that I didn't cause any crisis between you and them."

"That's OK," said the president. "They did not notice."

Al Gore and the Clintons are flying on Air Force One. Bill looks at Al, chuckles, and says, "You know, I could throw a $100 bill out the window right now and make someone very happy."

Al shrugs his stiff shoulders and says, "Well, I could throw ten $10 bills out the window and make 10 people very happy."

Hillary tosses her perfectly hair-sprayed hair and says, "I could throw one hundred $1 bills out the window and make a hundred people very happy."

Chelsea rolls her eyes, looks at all of them and says, "I could throw all three of you out the window and make the whole country happy!"

During a surgeon's conference in Harare, Zimbabwe, three of the surgeons go out for a drink one evening. The first is American, the second English and the third Zimbabwean. They start boasting about their surgical abilities.

The American says, "Two years ago a man fell into a giant meat mixer, and all that was left of him was his leg. We took him into our lab, created another artificial leg, arms, a body, head, everything. Six months later he went back to work and he was so efficient, he put three people out of work!"

"That's nothing," says the English surgeon. "A while back a worker fell into a nuclear reactor. All that was left was his right hand. So we built on an arm, a body, legs, a head, everything. When he went back to work six months later, he was so efficient he put 10 people out of work."

The Zimbabwean Surgeon looks at his colleagues, "You

guys are just amateurs. Twenty years ago I was walking down the street and I smelled a fart. I caught it in a jar and took it back to the lab. There, we built an arsehole around it, a torso, and finally a complete body. We called him Robert Mugabe, and he's put the whole bloody country out of work!"

Saddam Hussein, curious to see how his newly implemented decree allowing Iraqis to travel abroad for the first time in years, heads down to the passport office.

Once there he joins the line. One after another, the passport seekers ahead of him insist that President Saddam take their place.

Very quickly he has moved to the head of the line and he is dealing with the clerk. The clerk issues President Saddam his passport with lightning speed.

The president thanks the clerk, and then turns around to discover that all those in line behind him have vanished without a trace.

Saddam turns back to the clerk and asks what has happened.

"Simple," says the clerk, "if you leave Iraq, no one else has to."

Einstein dies and goes to heaven. At the Pearly Gates, Saint Peter tells him, "You look like Einstein, but you have no idea the lengths that some people will go to in order to sneak into Heaven. Can you prove who you really are?"

Einstein ponders for a few seconds and asks, "Could I have a blackboard and some chalk?"

Saint Peter snaps his fingers and a blackboard and chalk instantly appear. Einstein proceeds to describe with arcane mathematics and symbols his Theory of Relativity.

Saint Peter is suitably impressed, "You really are Einstein!" he says. "Welcome to Heaven!"

The next to arrive is Picasso. Once again, Saint Peter asks for credentials.

Picasso asks, "Mind if I use that blackboard and chalk?"

Saint Peter says, "Go ahead."

Picasso erases Einstein's equations and sketches a truly stunning mural with just a few strokes of chalk.

Saint Peter claps, "Surely you are the great artist you claim to be!" he says. "Come on in!"

Then Saint Peter looks up and sees George W. Bush. Saint Peter scratches his head and says, "Einstein and Picasso both managed to prove their identity. How can you prove yours?"

George W. looks bewildered and says, "Who are Einstein and Picasso?"

Saint Peter sighs and says, "Come on in, George."

Brezhnev gives his radio address to the Russian people, "Comrades! I have two important announcements for you – one, good news and one, bad news.

"I shall give you the bad news first.

"For the next three years we'll be eating nothing but shit.

"The good news is that there will be an abundance of it."

A five year old little boy asked his dad to explain the government to him.

The father said, "Okay, son I'll explain it the best way I can.

"See, me, I'm like the government, because everything has to come through me in order for this house to work smoothly.

"Your mother is like the people, because she has some say, but I can override it.

"The maid is the working class, because she works for us.

"Your baby brother is the future."

Needless to say the little boy was very confused.

That night after he went to bed he happened to wake up because he heard his little brother crying.

He went to his parents' room to get his mom but when he opened the door his mother was asleep, and his dad wasn't there.

So, he went to get the maid, but when he opened her door, he saw his dad and the maid, in a lather of sweat and screwing madly. He went to check on his brother himself. He opened his diaper to find that it was full of shit.

The next morning he went up to his dad and said, "Dad, I think I understand the government."

His dad replied, "Oh, really, tell me."

So the little boy said, "While the people are sleeping, the government is busy screwing the working class. And the future is full of shit!"

THINGS THAT THEY SAY:

George Bush Senior, during his first Presidential campaign: "I want to make sure everybody who has a job wants a job"

Richard Nixon, while attending Charles De Gaulle's funeral: "This is a great day for France!"

George Bush, talking about drug abuse to a group of students: "Now, like, I'm President. It would be pretty hard for some drug guy to come into the White House and start offering it up, you know? ... I bet if they did, I hope I would say, 'Hey, get lost. We don't want any of that.'"

George Bush Senior: "For seven and a half years I've worked alongside President Reagan. We've had triumphs. Made some mistakes. We've had some sex ... uh ... setbacks."

Ronald Reagan, about to go on the air for a radio broadcast, unaware that the microphone was already on: "My fellow Americans, I've signed legislation that will outlaw Russia forever. We begin bombing in five minutes."

Dan Quayle: "Mars is essentially in the same orbit. Mars is somewhat the same distance from the sun, which is very important. We have seen pictures where there are canals, we believe, and water. If there is water, that means there is oxygen. If oxygen, that means we can breathe."

The president of a certain country went to the interior of that country – where there was no electricity, poor roads, and no form of telecommunication – to give his campaign speech.

The people spoke a different dialect to the native one.

"We, the ruling party," said the president, "promise to provide electricity for the entire district."

Upon hearing the president's words, the people cheered, "Fombre!"

The president continued, "Not only will we provide electricity to the community, but we will also be installing telephones and telephone lines, and this will commence shortly."

Again, shrieks of "Fombre" were heard, as the president anxiously awaited the resumption of his speech.

"We have given careful thought to the repair of the roadways so as to facilitate better means of transportation and have allotted sufficient finances for the successful execution of this venture."

Shouts of "Fombre!" filled the air, as the president continued to lay it down with his words.

After the speech, the president, with a content grin on his face, walked through the grassy terrain with his bodyguards, his interpreter, and a few of the officials.

One of the officials, seeing a pile of horse's dung in front of the president, cried out, "Mr. President, watch out for the Fombre!"

Revised judicial oath: "I solemnly swear to tell the truth as I know it, the whole truth as I believe it to be, and nothing but what I think you need to know."

Politicians and diapers have one thing in common. They should both be changed regularly, and for the same reason.

COINCIDENCE?

Here are some of extraordinary co-incidences between the lives of John F. Kennedy and. Abraham Lincoln:

Abraham Lincoln was elected to Congress in 1846.
John F. Kennedy was elected to Congress in 1946.

Abraham Lincoln was elected President in 1860.
John F. Kennedy was elected President in 1960.

Lincoln's secretary was named Kennedy.
Kennedy's secretary was named Lincoln.

Both Presidents were shot in the head.
Southerners assassinated both.
Southerners succeeded both.

John Wilkes Booth, who assassinated Lincoln, was born in 1839.
Lee Harvey Oswald, who allegedly assassinated Kennedy, was born in 1939.

Lincoln was shot at the theatre named "Kennedy".
Kennedy was shot in a car called a "Lincoln".

Both assassins were known by their three names.
Both names are comprised of fifteen letters.

Booth ran from the theatre and was caught in a warehouse.
Oswald ran from a warehouse and was caught in a theatre.
Booth and Oswald were assassinated before their trials.

Both successors were named Johnson.
Andrew Johnson, who succeeded Lincoln, was born in 1808.
Lyndon Johnson, who succeeded Kennedy, was born in 1908.

The names Lincoln and Kennedy each contain seven letters.
Both were particularly concerned with civil rights.
Both wives lost their children while living in the White House.

TELL ME AGAIN, WHO'S THERE?

Knock, knock.
Who's there?
Hutch.
Hutch who?
God bless you!

Knock, knock.
Who's there?
Ben.
Ben who?
Ben waiting, what took you so long?

Knock, knock.
Who's there?
Lettuce.
Lettuce, who?
Lettuce in, it's cold out here!

Knock, knock.
Who's there?
Little old lady.
Little old lady who?
I didn't know you could yodel!

Knock, knock.
Who's there?
Atch.
Atch who?
Bless you!

Knock, knock.
Who's there?
Dishes.
Dishes, who?
Dishes the stupidest knock-knock joke ever!

Knock, knock.
Who's there?
Doris.
Doris who?
Doris closed, that's why I'm knocking.

Knock, knock.
Who's there!
Acid!
Acid who?
Acid sit down and be quiet!

Knock, knock.
Who's there!
Ada!
Ada who?
Ada burger for lunch!

Knock, knock.
Who's there!
Adair!
Adair who?
Adair once but I'm bald now!

Knock, knock.
Who's there!
Adolf!
Adolf who?
Adolf ball hit me in the mouth!

Knock, knock.
Who's there!
Alaska!
Alaska who?
Alaska my friend the question then!

Knock, knock.
Who's there!
Aida!
Aida who?
Aida lot of sweets and now I've got tummy ache!

Knock, knock.
Who's there!
Aladdin!
Aladdin who?
Aladdin the street wants a word with you!

Knock, knock.
Who's there!
Alba!
Alba who?
Alba in the kitchen if you need me!

Knock, knock.
Who's there!
Alec!
Alec who?
Alec-tricity. Isn't that a shock!

Knock, knock.
Who's there!
Alexia!
Alexia who?
Alexia again to open this door!

Knock, knock.
Who's there!
Alfalfa!
Alfalfa who?
Alfalfa you, if you give me a kiss!

Knock, knock.
Who's there?
Alfie!
Alfie who?
Alfie terrible if you leave!

Knock, knock.
Who's there!
Alfred!
Alfred who!
Alfred the needle if you sew!

Knock, knock.
Who's there!
Allied!
Allied who?
Allied, so sue me!

Knock, knock.
Who's there!
Alma!
Alma who?
Alma-ny knock knock jokes can you take!

Knock, knock.
Who's there!
Amana!
Amana who?
Amana bad mood!

Knock, knock.
Who's there!
Ammonia!
Ammonia who?
Ammonia little kid!

Knock, knock.
Who's there!
Amory!
Amory who?
Amory Christmas and a Happy New Year!

Knock, knock.
Who's there!
Amy!
Amy who?
Amy fraid I've forgotten!

Knock, knock.
Who's there!
Annetta!
Annetta who?
Annetta wisecrack and you're out of here!

Knock, knock.
Who's there!
Augusta!
Augusta who?
Augusta go home now!

Knock, knock.
Who's there!
Boo!
Boo who?
Don't cry it's only a joke!

Knock, knock.
Who's there!
Button!
Button who?
Button in is not polite!

Knock, knock.
Who's there!
Carl!
Carl who?
Carl get you there quicker than if you walk!

Knock, knock.
Who's there!
Cash!
Cash who?
I knew you were nuts!

Knock, knock.
Who's there!
Cassie!
Cassie who?
Cassie the forest for the trees!

Knock, knock.
Who's there!
Celeste!
Celeste who?
Celeste time I'm going to tell you this!

Knock, knock.
Who's there!
Cereal!
Cereal who?
Cereal pleasure to meet you!

Knock, knock.
Who's there!
Colleen!
Colleen who?
Colleen up this mess!

Knock, knock.
Who's there?
Cologne!
Cologne who?
Cologne me names won't help!

Knock, knock.
Who's there?
Cosy!
Cosy who?
Cosy who's knocking!

Knock, knock.
Who's there?
Collier!
Collier who?
Collier big brother see if I care!

Knock, knock.
Who's there!
Congo!
Congo who?
Congo out, I'm grounded!

Knock, knock.
Who's there?
Lettuce
Lettuce who?
Lettuce pray!!!

WOMEN, WOMEN, WOMEN . . .

HOW IT ALL BEGAN

And God created Woman, and gave her three breasts.

God spoke, saying to her, "I have created thee as I see fit. Is there anything about thee that thou would prefer differently?"

And Woman spoke, saying, "Lord, I am not made to birth whole litters. I need but two breasts."

And God said, "Thou speak wisely, as I have created thee with wisdom."

There was a crack of lightning and a lingering odor of ozone, and it was done, and God stood holding the surplus breast in his hands.

"What are you going to do with that useless boob?" Woman exclaimed.

And so it was, God created Man.

10 SEMINARS FOR FEMALES

1. Gaining Five Pounds. Is it the End of the World?
2. Elementary Map Reading.
3. How to Program your VCR.

4. Football: Not a Game. A Religion.
5. PMS: It's Your Problem, Not Mine.
6. Your Mate – Selfish Bastard, or Victimized Sensitive Man?
7. Makeup and Driving: It's as Simple as Oil and Water.
8. Earning Your Own Money.
9. Lowering the Toilet Seat all by Yourself.
10. You, Too, Can Fill Up at a Self Serve Station.

THE MEANING OF LIFE …

If a man says something in the woods, and there is no woman around … is he still wrong?

INSIDE KNOWLEDGE FOR BLOKES

The 13 most innocuous, common words, phrases and sounds, and what they *really* mean when a woman says them.

1. *Fine:* This is the word we use at the end of any argument that we feel we are right about, but need to shut you up. Never use "fine" to describe how a woman looks. This will cause you to have one of those very arguments.
2. *Five minutes:* This is, in fact, half an hour. It is equivalent to the five minutes that your football

gamc is going to last before you take out the trash, so it's an cven trade.

3. *Nothing:* This actually means "something" and you should be on your toes. "Nothing" is usually used to describe the feeling a woman has when she doesn't expect that you even want to understand. It is not worth even beginning to tell you what is wrong. "Nothing" usually signifies an argument that will last "Five Minutes" and end up with the word "Fine".

4. *Go Ahead (with raised eyebrows):* This is a dare. One that will result in a woman getting upset over "Nothing", and will end with the word "Fine".

5. *Go Ahead (with normal eyebrows):* This means "I give up" or, "You do what you want, because I don't care". You will get a raised-eyebrows "Go ahead" in just a few minutes, followed by "Nothing" and a "Fine", and she will talk to you in about "Five Minutes" when she cools off.

6. *Loud Sigh:* Not actually a word, but still often a verbal statement vcry misunderstood by men. A "Loud Sigh" means she thinks you are an idiot at that moment and wonders why she is wasting her time standing here and arguing with you over "Nothing".

7. *Soft Sigh:* Another verbal statement. "Soft Sighs" are one of the few things that you can actually understand. She is content. Your best bet is to not move, or breathe, or do anything to flag your existence, and she will stay content.

8. *Oh:* This word, followed by any given statement, mean trouble. Example: "Oh, let me get that". Or, "Oh, I talked to so and so about what you were doing last

night." If she says "Oh" before a statement, run, do not walk, to the nearest exit.

9. *Oh (upward exclamation, beginning of a sentence):* Usually signifies that you are caught in a lie. Do not try to lie any more to get out of it, or you will get a raised-eyebrows "Go ahead", and then you are really are in the fertilizer.

10. *That's Okay:* This is one of the most dangerous statements that a woman can make. "That's Okay" means that she wants to think long and hard about whatever it is that you have done. "That's Okay" is often used with the word "Fine" and in conjunction with a raised-eyebrows "Go ahead". At some point in the near future when she has plotted and planned, you are going to be in big trouble.

11. *Please Do:* This is an offer, not a statement. A woman is giving you the chance to come up with whatever excuse or reason you have for doing whatever it is that you have done.

12. *Thanks:* A woman is thanking you. Do not faint; just say "My pleasure," or "You're welcome."

13. *Thanks a lot:* This is vastly different from "Thanks". A woman will say, "Thanks a lot," when she is really having a go at you, especially with a heavy emphasis on the word "lot". It signifies that you have hurt her in some callous way. You can bet on it – it will be followed by the "Loud Sigh".

What do bullet-proof vests, fire escapes, windshield wipers and laser printers all have in common?

All invented by women.

GREAT FEMALE COMEBACKS

"I'd like to call you. What's your number?"
"It's in the phone book."
"But I don't know your name."
"That's in the phone book too."

"Haven't we met before?"
"Yes, I'm the receptionist at the VD Clinic."

"Your place or mine?"
"Both. You go to yours and I'll go to mine."

"Is this seat empty?"
"Yes, and this one will be, too, if you sit down."

"I'm here to fulfil your every sexual fantasy."
"You mean you've got both a donkey and a Great Dane?"

"I know how to please a woman."
"Then please leave me alone."

"So what do you do for a living?"
"I'm a female impersonator."

"Hey, come on, we're both here at this bar for the same reason"
"Yeah! Let's pick up some chicks!"

"Hey, baby, what's your sign?"
"Do Not Enter."

"If I could see you naked, I'd die happy."
"Yeah, but if I saw you naked, I'd probably die laughing."

How do you like your eggs in the morning?"
"Unfertilised!"

"I'd go through anything for you."
"Good! Let's start with your bank account."

"I would go to the end of the world for you."
"Yes, but would you stay there?"

10 RULES THAT BLOKES WISH WOMEN KNEW

1. Never cut your hair. Ever. It only causes arguments when I comment on it.
2. Wear anything you want. It's fine. Really.
3. If you want some dessert after a meal, please order some. You don't have to finish it. I order mine because I would like to eat it myself.
4. Shopping is not a sport to me. Please don't make me go.

5. What makes you think I'd be any good at choosing which, out of thirty-seven pairs of shoes, would look good with that dress? Most blokes only own two or three pairs of shoes, some of which actually match.

6. I'm sure you have plenty to catch up with that school chum from 20 years ago that we have just met right here in the fish market, but it's been two hours now ...

7. Pissing standing up is more difficult than pissing from point blank range. We're bound to miss sometimes.

8. They're called foreign films because that is what they are. Foreign films are best left to foreigners.

9. Please learn to check your oil. That's the long stick thing you pull it out. Oil is an essential part of the car.

10. The male models with the great bodies you see in magazines are all gay.

A WOMAN'S VIEW ON MEN

Men are just like ...

- Copiers. You need them in reproduction but that's about it.
- Bike helmets. They're good in emergencies but usually just look silly.
- Mini skirts. If you're not careful they'll creep up your legs.
- Handguns. Keep one around long enough and you arc going to want to shoot it.
- Placemats. They only show up when there's food on the table.

- Mascara. They usually run at the first sign of emotion.
- Government bonds. They take so long to mature.
- Lava lamps. Fun to look at it but not all that bright.
- Bank accounts. Without a lot of money they don't generate a lot of interest.
- High heels. They're easy to walk on once you get the hang of it.
- Curling irons. They're always hot and always in your hair.

A SPECIAL SET OF RULES FOR MEN

1. The Female always makes The Rules.
2. The Rules are subject to change at any time without prior notification.
3. No Male can possibly know all The Rules.
4. If the Female suspects the Male is making some sense of The Rules, she will immediately change some or all of The Rules.
5. The Female is never wrong.
6. If the Female says or does something that could be interpreted as being wrong, it is because of a flagrant misunderstanding which was a direct result of something the Male did or said wrong.
7. If Rule 6 applies, the Male must apologize immediately for causing the misunderstanding.
8. The Female can change her mind at any given point in time.
9. The Male must never change his mind without express written consent from the Female.

10. The Female has every right to be angry or upset at any time.
11. The Male must remain calm at all times, unless the Female wants him to be angry or upset.
12. The Female must under no circumstances let the Male know whether or not she wants him to be angry or upset.
13. The Male is expected to mind read at all times.
14. The Male who doesn't abide by The Rules, obviously can't take the heat, lacks a backbone, and is a wimp.
15. It is the job of The Female to regularly remind the Male that he obviously can't take the heat, lacks a backbone, and is a wimp.
16. Any attempt by The Male to document The Rules could result in bodily harm.
17. At no time can the Male make such comments as "Insignificant" and "Is that all?" when the Female is complaining.

SPECIAL RULE: If the Female has PMS, all Rules are null and void ...

Syd had been acting strangely, saying odd things to his wife, and undergoing mood swings. One day he comes home absolutely ashen.

His wife could see at once that something was seriously wrong. "What's wrong, Syd?" she asked.

"Do you remember that I told you how I had this tremendous urge to put my penis in the pickle slicer?"

"Oh, Syd, you didn't."

"Yes, I did."

"My God, Syd, what happened?"

"I got fired."

"No, Syd. I mean, what happened with the pickle-slicer?"

"She got fired too."

Why do men snore? Because their balls hang over their arses and they vapour lock.

A young man and his manager go down to the red light district of town. The manager is betting every person he meets that his young friend can screw and satisfy one hundred women in a row, without pausing. Bets are made and they agree that they'll meet the next day to complete the arrangement.

The next day, one hundred women are lined up! The young Romeo drops his pants and begins the task at hand.

True to his word, he moves from one to the next, satisfying each one without pausing: 1 ... 2 ... 3 ... on and on he goes: 49 ... 50 ... 51. He slows down somewhat: 83..... 84..... 85........ but he is still moving from one to the next and the women are still satisfied: 97............ 98.............. 99................

Then catastrophe strikes. Before he can get to the last woman he has a heart attack and dies!

The manager scratches his head and says, "I don't understand it! It went perfectly at practice this morning!"

Married men revealed that they perform the following act twice as often as single men.

Change their underwear.

15 POLITICALLY CORRECT WAYS OF TALKING ABOUT A MAN

1.   He is not short; he is *vertically challenged.*
2.   He is not balding; he is in *advanced follicle regression.*
3.   He does not have a whopping great beer belly; he has developed a *portable liquid malt and hops storage facility.*

4. He is not quiet; he is a *conversational minimalist*.
5. He is not stupid; he suffers from *minimal cranial development*.
6. He is not a cradle snatcher; he prefers *generationally differential relationships*.
7. He does not get lost; he *discovers alternative destinations*.
8. He does not act like a total arse-hole; he inadvertently develops a case of RCI – *Rectal-Cranial Inversion*.
9. He does not get falling-down drunk; he becomes *involuntarily horizontal*.
10. He does not hog the blankets; he is *thermally unappreciative*.
11. He does not constantly talk about cars; he has a *vehicular addiction*.
12. He is not unsophisticated; he is suffering from *distinct social malformation*.
13. He is not a male chauvinist pig; he has *grunt-hog empathy*.
14. He does not eat like a pig; he suffers from *reverse bulimia*.
15. He doesn't have a dirty mind; he has *introspective pornographic experiences*.

Q & As THAT INDICATE HE MAY BE STILL BE A LITTLE BIT CHAUVINIST

Q.   What's worse than a Male Chauvinist Pig?
A.   A woman that won't do what she's told.

Q.   What do you call a woman with two brain cells?
A.   Pregnant.

Q.   How many men does it take to open a beer?
A.   None. It should be open by the time she brings it.

Q.   Why is a laundromat a really bad place to pick up a woman?
A.   Because a woman who can't even afford a washing machine will never be able to support you.

Q.   Why do women have smaller feet than men?
A.   So they can stand closer to the kitchen sink.

Q.   How do you know when a woman's about to say something smart?
A.   She starts her sentence with "A man once told me ..."

Q.   How do you fix a woman's watch?
A.   You don't. There's a clock on the oven!

Q.   Why do men pass gas more than women?
A.   Because women won't shut up long enough to build up pressure.

Q.   Why were shopping carts invented?

A.   To teach women to walk on their hind legs.

Q.   If your dog is barking at the back door and your wife is yelling at the front door, who do you let in first?

A.   The dog, of course . . . at least he'll shut up after you let him in.

Q.   How many women does it take to paint a wall?

A.   It depends on how hard you throw them.

Q.   What do you call a woman who has lost 95% of her intelligence?

A.   Divorced.

Q.   Which food diminishes a woman's sex drive.

A.   Wedding cake.

THE 5 TOP BLOKEY ONE LINERS ABOUT WOMEN

1.   I married Miss Right. I just didn't know her first name was Always.

2.   Marriage is a three ring circus: engagement ring, wedding ring, and suffering.

3.   I haven't spoken to my wife for 18 months – I don't like to interrupt her.

4.   All wives are alike, but they have different faces so you can tell them apart.

5.   Bigamy is having one wife too many. Some say monogamy is the same.

Did you hear that the first consignment of Viagra to be imported into Britain was stolen?

Police are looking for hardened criminals in possession of swollen goods.

WHAT MEN ARE REALLY THINKING ...

Men say one thing, but their mind is operating in entirely another direction. Here's what guys say, but what they really mean.

"It's a guy thing."
Really means ...
"There is no rational thought pattern connected with it, and you have no chance at all of making it logical."

"Sure, honey," or "Yes, dear."
Really means ...
Absolutely nothing. It's a conditioned response like Pavlov's dog drooling.

"My wife doesn't understand me."
Really means ...
"She's heard all my stories before, and is tired of them."

"It would take too long to explain."
Really means ...
"I have no idea how it works."

"I'm getting more exercise lately."
Really means ...
"The batteries in the remote are dead."

"Take a break, honey, you're working too hard."
Really means ...
"I can't hear the game over the vacuum cleaner."

"That's interesting, dear."
Really means ...
"Are you still talking?"

"You expect too much of me."
Really means ...
"You want me to stay awake."

"That's women's work."
Really means ...
"It's difficult, dirty, and thankless."

"Will you marry me?"
Really means ...
"Both my roommates have moved out, I can't find the washer, and there is no more peanut butter."

"I do help around the house."
Really means ...
"I once put a dirty towel in the laundry basket."

"I can't find it."
Really means ...
"It didn't fall into my outstretched hands, so I'm completely clueless."

"What did I do this time?"
Really means ...
"What did you catch me at?"

"She's one of those rabid feminists."
Really means ...
"She refused to make my coffee."

"I'm going to stop off for a quick one with the guys."
Really means ...
"I am planning on drinking myself into a vegetative stupor with my chest-pounding, mouth-breathing, pre-evolutionary companions."

"You know I could never love anyone else."
Really means ...
"I am used to the way you yell at me, and realize it could be worse."

"You look terrific."
Really means ...
"Oh, God, please don't try on one more outfit. I'm starving."

"I missed you."
Really means ...
"I can't find my sock drawer, the kids are hungry and we are out of toilet paper."

"I'm not lost. I know exactly where we are."
Really means ...
"No one will ever see us alive again."

"We share the housework."
Really means ...
"I make the messes, she cleans them up."

"This relationship is getting too serious."
Really means ...
"I like you more than my truck."

"I recycle."
Really means ...
"We could pay the rent with the money from my empties."

"I don't need to read the instructions."
Really means ...
"I am perfectly capable of screwing it up without printed help."

"I broke up with her."
Really means ...
"She dumped me."

THE TAXING OF THE TOCKLEY

The only thing that the Taxation Department has not taxed yet is the male penis. This is due to the fact that:

40% of the time it is hanging around unemployed,

30% of the time it is hard up,

20% of the time it is pissed off

10% of the time it is in the hole.

On top of that, it has two dependents and they are both nuts.

The penis will soon be taxed according to size

10 - 12"	Luxury Tax $30.00
8 - 10"	Pole Tax $25.00
5 - 8"	Privilege Tax $15.00
4 - 5"	Nuisance Tax $3.00

Males exceeding 12 inches must file under capital gains.

Anyone who measures under 4 inches is eligible for a refund.

Please, do not ask for an extension!

As of next week Viagra will only be available through the chemists by its chemical name. Please ask for mycoxafloppin.

10 REASONS FOR MEN!   VIVA LA DIFFERENCE!

1.   A man will pay $2 for a $1 item he wants. A woman will pay $1 for a $2 item that she doesn't want.

2.   A woman worries about the future until she gets a husband. A man never worries about the future until he gets a wife.

3.   A successful man is one who makes more money than his wife can spend. A successful woman is one who can find such a man.

4.   To be happy with a man you must understand him a lot and love him a little. To be happy with a woman you must love her a lot and not try to understand her at all.

5.   Married men love longer than single men – but married men are a lot more willing to die.

6.   Any married man should forget his mistakes – there's no use in two people remembering the same thing.

7.   Men wake up as good-looking as they went to bed. Women somehow deteriorate during the night.

8.   A woman marries a man expecting he will change, but he doesn't. A man marries a woman expecting that she won't change and she does.

9.   A woman has the last word in any argument. Anything a man says after that is the beginning of a new argument.

10. There are two times when a man doesn't understand a woman – before marriage and after marriage.

FIVE ESSENTIAL SEMINARS FOR MEN

1. You Can Do the Housework, Too.
2. Understanding the Female Response to You and Barry Staggering in Pissed at 4 a.m.
3. Parenting – Participation doesn't End with the Root.
4. Get A Life – Learn to Cook.
5. Effective Laundry Techniques (formerly called Don't Wash my Silk Knickers with your Boiler Suit Again).

HONEST,
IT HAPPENED . . .

These are explanations taken from actual insurance claims:

1. The guy was all over the road. I had to swerve several times before I hit him.

2. Coming home I drove into the wrong house and collided with a tree I don't have.

3. The other car collided with mine without giving me warning of its intention.

4. I thought my window was down, but I found it was up when I put my head through it.

5. I collided with a stationary truck coming the other way.

6. In an attempt to kill a fly, I drove into a telephone pole.

7. A pedestrian hit me and went under my car.

8. I pulled away from the side of the road, glanced at my mother in law and headed over the embankment.

9. I had been shopping for a plant all day and was on my way home. As I reached an inter-section a hedge sprang up, obscuring my vision and I did not see the other car.

10. I had been driving for 40 years when I fell asleep at the wheel and had an accident.

11. As I approached the intersection a sign appeared in a place where no stop sign had ever appeared before. I was unable to stop in time to avoid the accident.

12. I was on the way to the doctor with rear end trouble when my universal joint gave way causing me to have an accident and damage my big end.

13. The pedestrian had no idea which direction to run. So I ran over him.

14. I saw a slow moving, sad faced, old gentleman as he bounced off the roof of my car.

15. To avoid hitting the bumper of the car in front I struck a pedestrian.

16. My car was legally parked as it backed into another vehicle.

17. An invisible car came out of nowhere, struck my car and vanished.

18. I told the police that I was not injured, but on removing my hat I found that I had a fractured skull.

19. I was sure the old fellow would never make it to the other side of the road when I struck him.

20. The telephone pole was approaching. I was attempting to swerve out the way when I struck the front end.

21. The accident was caused by me waving to the man I hit last week.

22. I knocked over a man, he admitted it was his fault as he'd been knocked over before.

23. The indirect cause of the accident was a little guy in a small car with a big mouth.

24. I was thrown from my car as it left the road. I was later found in a ditch by some stray cows.

GODDAM GOLF

Golf – a good walk spoiled, and an infuriating game that brings out the worst and very worst in people. Why was it called golf? Simply because all the other four letter words were taken …

Two Scottish golfers are just about to putt out on the 16th green, which is adjacent to a road, when suddenly a funeral procession passes by.

As the hearse draws near, one of the golfers, Mr. McTavish, interrupts his putting, takes off his hat and bows to the procession.

His partner says, "That was really gentlemanly of you – paying your respects like that!"

McTavish replies, "Well, she *was* my wife for 25 years …"

Three golfers, Ted, Bill, and Hank are looking for a fourth. Bill mentions that his friend George is a pretty good golfer, so they decide to invite him for the following match.

"Sure, I'd love to play," says George, "but I may be about ten minutes late, so wait for me."

So the day rolls around and the three mates arrive promptly at 9:00, and find George already waiting for them.

He plays right-handed, and beats them all. Quite pleased with their new fourth, they ask him if he'd like to play again the following Saturday.

"Yeah, sounds great," says George. "But I may be about ten minutes late, so wait for me."

The following Saturday, again, all four golfers show up on time, but this time George plays left-handed, and beats them all.

As they're getting ready to leave, George says, "See you next Saturday. But I may be about ten minutes late, so wait for me."

Every week, George is right on time, and plays great with whichever hand he decides to use. And every week, he departs with the same message.

After a couple months, Ted is pretty tired of this routine, so he says, "Wait a minute, George. Every week you say you may be about ten minutes late, but you're right on time. And you beat us either left-handed or right-handed. What's the story?"

"Well," George says, "I'm kind of superstitious. When I get up in the morning, I look at my wife. If she's sleeping on her left side, I play left-handed. And if she's sleeping on her right side, I play right-handed."

"So what do you do if she's sleeping on her back?" Bill asks.

"Then I'm about ten minutes late," George answers.

It is Good Friday, the holiest day of the religious calendar. An angel peers off a cloud, looking far down below onto a golf course, and he sees a rabbi playing golf.

"Lord there's a priest down there playing golf on the holiest day of the year," the angel tells his God. "You must do something. What will you do?"

"Oh, I'll fix him, watch this!" cackles the Lord.

So the angel watches the priest as he lifts his golf club high over his shoulder and prepares to tee off. He hits the ball with a loud thump. Up into the air it goes, it rockets along the fairway, lands, bounces three times, runs on the green, rolls up to the hole, and drops in. A hole in one.

"Hey, I thought you were going to punish him. He just got a hole in one!" complains the angel.

"You don't understand," replies God, "... who can he tell?"

Old golfers never die, they just lose their balls.

It was a sunny Saturday morning on the course and he was beginning his pre-shot routine, visualizing his upcoming shot, when a voice came over the clubhouse loudspeaker, "Would the gentleman on the woman's tee please go back up to the men's tee."

He was still deep into his routine, seemingly impervious to the interruption.

Again the announcement, "Would the *man* on the *women's* tee kindly go back up to the men's tee."

He simply ignored the voice and kept concentrating.

Once more the man yelled, "Would the man on the woman's tee back up to the men's tee, please!"

He finally stopped, turned, looked through the clubhouse window directly at the person with the mike and shouted back, "Would the person in the clubhouse kindly shut the hell up and let me play my second shot?"

Studies have shown that single gentlemen who play golf are thinner than married club members.

The way this fact was determined was as follows: the single golfer goes out and plays his round of golf, has a refreshment at the 19th hole, goes home and goes to his refrigerator, finds nothing decent there, so he goes to bed.

The married golfer goes out and plays his round of golf, has a refreshment at the 19th hole, goes home and goes to bed, finds nothing decent there, so he goes to his refrigerator.

"You fool! You almost hit my wife with that shot!" "Sorry old chap! Here, take a shot at mine!"

One day Moses and Jesus were playing golf. They were at the tee of a beautiful par 3, with a lake right in the middle of the fairway.

Moses selects a 5 iron, tees-up his ball and swings.

His ball sails very high and lands in the middle of the lake. He mutters to himself and tees-up a second ball, this time selecting a 4 iron. This shot was perfect; landing right in the middle of the green.

Jesus pauses for a moment to ponder his club selection. "Hmmmm ... Tiger Woods would use this," he says as he picks up a 5 iron.

"But, Jesus. My 5 iron shot ended up in the lake. You should use a 4 iron!"

"Nope. Tiger would use a 5," insisted Jesus.

So, Jesus swings hard and, alas, his shot ends up in the middle of the lake. Jesus strolls over to the lake and walks out on the water to retrieve his ball.

As Jesus is walking on the water, a foursome comes up to the tee. One of them, spotting the man walking on the water, exclaims, "Who does he think he is? Jesus Christ?"

"No," explains Moses, "He thinks he's Tiger Woods ..."

We all know what a Birdie (1 under) and a Bogey (one over) are. Now there's a Lewinsky. It's when the shot lands three feet from the hole.

A businessman, while out of town, felt he should play a little golf after a short work day. He did not know any golfers in this town so he decided to go out to the course and get paired up there.

When he arrived there were no guys ready to play, but there was a very nice looking lady waiting for a foursome. At the suggestion of the club, he decided to pair up with the lady.

While playing the first 17 holes the two got to be friendly, but were shooting as poor a game as either had seen in years. They were both getting very frustrated.

On the 18th, a par 4, the game was about to finish on a good note as they both were on in two. When they arrived on the green, they saw that this was the worst green that either had ever seen. The green slopped away from the cup with a very rolling surface.

He was about twenty-nine feet away and she twenty-six. He looked over the green and was very frustrated.

He said, "If I make this shot I'll buy us dinner tonight."

He hit and the ball rolled over the bump down through the grove, around the short hill, and up past the cup and slowed. Just as it looked as though he had missed the putt, the slope of the green helped, and the ball rolled back into the cup. He made a great shot.

Not to be outdone the lady tried to line up her shot.

She said, "If I make this putt I'll invite you to my place for drinks after dinner, and we can have hot spa in my tub, and drink French champagne, and who knows what the night will bring. But only if I make this putt."

The guy says, "Wait! Let me help you line up the shot."

And walking over to the ball, he grabs it, picks it up and says, "That's a gimme if I ever saw one ..."

An avid, yet average, golfer was out playing one day, when his ball went into a sand trap. As he entered the trap to play his shot, he noticed a shiny object.

Upon digging it up, he noticed it was a lamp. He rubbed

the lamp, and to his amazement, a genie appeared, "Since you have released me from my lamp, I will grant you anything you wish, but I must warn you, your sex life will suffer for one year."

The golfer thought for a moment, then replied, "That's okay, I can handle it. I want to be the world's greatest golfer."

"OK," said the genie, "you're now the world's greatest golfer," and he disappeared back into the lamp.

The golfer took his sand shot, and to his amazement, it went in the hole. For the next year, he was, as the genie had said, the world's greatest golfer.

A year later, the man was playing the same course again, and the ball again went into the sand trap. As he entered the trap, he again noticed the lamp, so he picked it up and rubbed it. Sure enough, the genie appeared.

He looked at the golfer and asked, "You were here last year, weren't you. No one has ever come back a second time. Tell me, did your sex life really suffer?"

"Well," said the golfer, "I did only have sex five times last year. But that's not too bad for a priest from a small parish ..."

"Did you hear that the board fined me $50 for hitting my wife with a 9-iron?"

"Really, for conduct unbecoming a gentleman?"

"No, for using the wrong club."

Four married guys go golfing.

First Guy, "You have no idea what I had to do to be able

to come out golfing this weekend. I had to promise my wife that I will paint every room in the house next weekend."

Second Guy, "That's nothing, I had to promise my wife that I will build her a new deck for the pool."

Third Guy, "Man, you both have it easy! I had to promise my wife that I will remodel the kitchen for her."

They continue to play the hole when they realize that the fourth guy has not said a word. So they ask him, "You haven't said anything about what you had to do to be able to come golfing this weekend. What's the deal?"

Fourth Guy, "I just set my alarm for 5:30am. When it goes off, I shut off my alarm, give the wife a nudge and say, 'Golf course or intercourse?' and she says, 'Wear your sweater.'"

It was the wedding night for a young couple and the groom wanted everything to be just perfect.

He arranged to stay in the Honeymoon Suite of a plush hotel, and he and his new bride eagerly jumped into the heart-shaped bed to make love.

After making wild and passionate love for a considerate length of time, they both reached the climactic moment simultaneously, slipping into a state of utmost relaxation. At this point, the groom reaches for the telephone.

"What on earth do you think you are doing?" asks the young bride

"Well, I want everything to be perfect, so I thought I should call room service for a bottle of their finest champagne," came the reply.

"Well," says the bride, "I used to date Arnold Palmer, and

when Arnold and I finished making love we would wait 10 minutes and make love again."

"If that's what you are used to, I will be glad to comply."

And 10 minutes or so later the young couple was making wild and passionate love again. At the culmination of this second lovemaking session, the young groom reaches for the phone once again.

"What on earth do you think you are doing?" asks the young bride.

"Like I said before, I want this to be a special occasion, so I was going to call room service for that bottle of champagne."

"Well, Arnold and I used to relax for 15 minutes or so, and then make love a third time," came her reply.

So, once again, not wanting to disappoint his young bride, the groom relaxed a bit and finally was capable of making love a third time.

After this third wild and passionate session, the couple finally reaches the climactic moment and returns to a relaxed state. Once again, the groom reaches for the phone.

"What on earth do you think you are doing?" asks the young bride.

"Calling Arnold to find out what's par for this hole!"

"Bless me Father, for I have sinned. This morning, on the golf course I used the F-word."

"Tell me, my son, what were the circumstances that provoked you to such an extent."

"Father, I drove my tee shot three hundred metres, but

the wind caught it and it landed in the rough."

"I am a golfer myself so I appreciate your disappointment and using the F-word."

"No, it was okay father, I didn't use it then. I hit a beautiful shot out of the rough. But it nipped the edge of the sand trap and rolled back into it."

"Now I can really understand you using that word."

"No, that was okay, too, Father. I pulled out my wedge and hit the perfect shot onto the green. The ball hit the pin and landed ten centimetres from the hole."

"Is that when you used the F-word?"

"No, Father."

"Jesus, don't tell me you missed the f...ing putt?"

A professional golfer in his Porsche picked up a young Irish backpacker who was hitchhiking around Australia.

He had all of his golfing gear sitting on the back seat.

She picked up the tees, looked inquiringly at them and asked, "What are these."

"They are tees. I rest my balls on them when I drive."

"Wow!" exclaimed the girl, "What will those car makers think of next?"

THE RULES OF BEDROOM GOLF

Bedroom Golf is a game that has been played since time immemorial. However, because of the way layouts vary from course to course, interpretation of local rules can be confusing, and uncertainties in terms of protocol, games can sometime end in dispute.

In order to promote harmony, the Bedroom Golf Sub-Committee of the Royal and Ancient Club of St Randy's has developed the following rules:

1. Each player shall furnish his own equipment for play, normally one club and two balls.

2. Play on course must be approved by the owner of the hole.

3. Unlike outdoor golf, the object is to get the club in the hole and keep the balls out.

4. For most effective play, the club should have a firm shaft. Course owners are permitted to check staff stiffness before play begins.

5. Course owners reserve the right to restrict club length to avoid damage to the hole.

6. Again, unlike outdoor golf, the object is to take as many strokes as necessary, until the owner is satisfied play is complete. Failure to do so may result in being denied other course privileges and permission to play again.

7. It is considered bad form to begin playing the hole immediately upon arrival. Experienced players will normally take time to admire the entire course, paying special attention to well formed mounds and bunkers.

8. Players are cautioned not to mention other courses they have played, or are currently playing, to the owner of the course being played. Upset owners have been known to damage a player's equipment for this reason, or ban the player from the course for life.

9. Players are encouraged to have proper rain gear on hand, just in case.

10. Players should not assume that the course is in shape to play at all times. Players may be embarrassed if they find the course temporarily under repair. Players are advised to be extremely tactful in this situation. More advanced players will find alternate means of play when this is the case.

11. Players should assume their match has been properly scheduled, particularly when playing a new course for the first time. Previous players have been known to become irate if they discover someone else is playing what they considered a private course.

12. The owner of the course is responsible for the pruning of any bushes, which may reduce the visibility of the hole.

13. Players are strongly advised to get the owner's permission before attempting to play the backside.

14. Slow play is, in fact, encouraged, however, players should be prepared to proceed at a quicker pace at the owner's request.

15. It is considered an outstanding performance, time permitting, to play the same hole several times in one match.

Two blokes are playing golf, and are being held up by a pair of women playing very slowly ahead. As the day drags on, they get increasingly frustrated, and one of them says, "I'm going to go up there, and ask them to either hurry up, or if we can play through."

The bloke goes up, but comes back a few minutes later, looking very sheepish.

"You'll never believe this, when I got up closer, I realised that one is my wife, and the other is my lover! So I took off before they saw me, and came back."

The other bloke says, "Oh, well, I'll go up there and hurry them up."

He heads off, and comes back a few minutes later, looking very sheepish, too.

"Gee," he says, "it's a small world isn't it?"

NOT TO PUT TOO FINE A POINT ON IT . . .

ADULT ONLY

Let's face it, there are a lot of dumb people out there. Not you and me, of course! Here's 30 ways of saying it without giving offence:

1.   The wheel's spinning, but the hamster's dead.
2.   The cheese slid off his cracker.
3.   As smart as bait.
4.   The chimney's clogged.
5.   Doesn't have all his dogs on one leash.
6.   The elevator doesn't go all the way to the top floor.
7.   Forgot to pay his brain bill.
8.   Her sewing machine is out of thread.
9.   A few beers short of a six-pack.
10. His antenna doesn't pick up all channels.
11. If he had another brain, it would be lonely.
12. Missing a few buttons on his remote control.
13. Proof that evolution *can* go in reverse.
14. Receiver is off the hook.
15. Several nuts short of a full pouch.
16. Skylight leaks a little.
17. Too much yardage between the goal posts.
18. No grain in the silo.
19. A few clowns short of a circus.

20.   A few fries short of a Happy Meal.

21.   A sandwich short of a picnic.

22.   One fruit loop shy of a full bowl.

23.   A few feathers short of a whole duck.

24.   All foam, no beer.

25.   He fell out of the stupid tree and hit every branch on the way down.

26.   Not the sharpest knife in the drawer.

27.   A few peas short of a casserole.

28.   The lights are on, but nobody's home.

29.   His belt doesn't go through all the loops.

30.   A few bricks shy of a full load.

STORIES FROM THE
BACK OF BEYOND

A city boy went duck hunting in the country, and shot a duck which fell on the property of a farmer.

The boy crawled over the fence to claim his kill. But, the farmer, seeing what had happened, rushed out with his shotgun and yelled, "See here! That duck belongs to me!"

The city boy replies, "But I shot the duck, therefore it belongs to me!"

The farmer says, "It fell on my property so it belongs to me!"

They continue to argue. After awhile the farmer says, "We should settle this the old-fashioned way."

The city boy asks, "What is the 'old-fashioned way'?"

The farmer explains, "First, I kick you in the groin. Then, you kick me in the groin and we continue in this fashion until one of us gives up. The one who wins gets the duck."

The city boy, willing to do anything to get his duck and leave, agrees to the contest.

The farmer draws back his leg and kicks the city boy in the groin with all his might. The city boy, in horrible pain, falls to the ground moaning and groaning.

Ten minutes of this passes and the city boy stands up shakily and croaks, "It's my turn now."

"Oh, you can have the duck," says the farmer and he leaves.

Then there's the little outback town that's so small it doesn't have a jail. When someone commits a crime, they have to stand in the corner.

A farmer's rooster is getting on in years and just not producing enough; he decides that he should get a new, younger one to replace it.

When the new rooster arrives he moves the old one to the rear corner of the henhouse. Once he has left the new rooster starts having a good time.

The old rooster looks on and finally can take no more – he starts a fight with the young one.

Soon the fight moves outdoors and with a great deal of squawking the old rooster is being chased around the henhouse by the young one.

All of a sudden the young rooster falls dead with a bullet through his head. The farmer saunters over, all the while cursing, "Damn it! That's the third gay rooster that I've bought in the past month!"

TOP 10 COUNTRY MUSIC SONGS

1. Her Teeth Was Stained, But Her Heart Was Pure
2. I Don't Know What Came Over Me (When I Came All Over You)
3. I'm Just A Bug On The Windshield Of Life
4. You're The Reason Our Kids Are So Ugly

5.   My Wife Ran Off With My Best Friend, And I Sure Do Miss Him

6.   Get Your Tongue Outta My Mouth 'Cause I'm Kissing You Goodbye

7.   How Can I Miss You If You Won't Go Away?

8.   I'd Rather Have A Bottle In Front Of Me Than A Frontal Lobotomy

9.   I Hate Every Bone In Your Body Except Mine

10.   If She Puts Lipstick On My Dipstick, I'll Fall In Love

A young ventriloquist is touring the outback and stops to entertain at a bar at the back of beyond.

He's going through his usual country bumpkin jokes, when a big, burly guy in the audience stands up and says, "I've heard just about enough of your smart arse jokes. We ain't all stupid here, you know."

Flustered, the ventriloquist begins to apologize.

But the big guy cuts him off, "You just stay out of this mister, I'm talking to the little smart arse that's sitting on your knee!"

I rang up my local swimming baths. I said, "Is that the local swimming baths?"

The man said, "It depends where you're calling from."

In the local pub, a farmer was boasting that one of his hired hands could eat a sheep a day. Nobody believed him, of course, and it wasn't long before a lot of bets were being laid.

A sheep was provided to test the claim, and the publican got his cook to use up all the meat on the sheep and make it into pies.

On the appointed day for the great challenge, the farmer arrived with his hired hand. The bloke took a seat, and the pies were served up to him, tray after tray.

And tray after tray was cleaned up, the bloke wolfing down the pies until there were only two left.

He sighed, belched, then pushed the two remaining pies away, stood up, and made for the door. The farmer stood to lose a bundle if his man didn't finish. He grabbed him and pushed him back down in his seat.

"Come on, lad, only two to go," he urged.

The bloke shook his head. "Fair go, boss," he said, "No more bloody pies. I've got a bloody sheep to eat today."

A passerby asks a farmer, "Do your pigs smoke?"
"No!"
"Then I think your pigsty is on fire."

Two farmhands went to a country dance. One of the hands, Jimmy, had a false eye and was very self-conscious about it.

Jimmy told the other guy, Mick, that he was worried about someone saying something about his false eye. Mick told him not to worry because it was a good eye and most people couldn't tell it from a real eye.

Mick danced nearly every dance with all the farm girls. Jimmy didn't dance at all. Finally, Mick went over to Jimmy and asked if he had danced with any of the girls.

Jimmy told him that he hadn't because he was concerned about them saying something about his false eye. Mick told him again not to worry about it.

Mick pointed to a girl sitting across the room and told Jimmy, "See that good-looking girl over there? She's got a hare-lip and hasn't danced but once or twice. I danced with her once and she's an excellent dancer and real polite. Go over there and ask her to dance. She won't say anything about your false eye."

So Jimmy had a couple of more snorts of courage and went over to the girl and asked, "Do you want to dance?"

To which she replied in a high-pitched hare-lipped voice, "Would I, Would I!!!"

To which Jimmy replied, "Hare-lip, hare-lip!!!!"

The man gets out of the car, walks all the way out to the farmer and asks him, "Ah excuse me mister, but what are you doing?"

The farmer replies, "I'm trying to win a Nobel Prize."

"How?" asks the man, puzzled.

"Well I heard they give the Nobel Prize to people who are out standing in their field."

Two tall trees are growing in the woods. A small tree begins to grow between them. One tree says to the other, "Is that a son of a beech or a son of a birch?"

The woodpecker takes a taste of the small tree. He replies, "It is neither a son of a beech nor a son of a birch. That, my friends, is the best piece of ash I have ever put my pecker in."

You know that your mum and dad wasted their time sending you to that fancy finishing school when you still take a leak in the swimming pool.

From the high board …

19 WAYS TO BE A SHOPPER FROM HELL

1. As the cashier runs your purchases over the scanner, look astounded and say, "That is just magic!"
2. Sample all the spray fresheners until the aisle reeks of the smell.
3. Re-dress the mannequins as you see fit.
4. Take shopping carts for the express purpose of filling them and stranding them at strategic locations.
5. Set all the alarm clocks to go off at ten minute intervals throughout the day.
6. Nonchalantly "test" the brushes and combs in cosmetics.
7. Ride a display bicycle through the store; claim you're taking it for a "test drive."
8. Challenge other customers to duels with tubes of gift wrap.
9. Tune all the radios to a hard rock station then turn them all off and turn the volumes to "10".
10. When someone steps away from their trolley to look at something, quickly make off with it without saying a word.
11. Play with the calculators so that they all spell "hello" upside down.
12. When someone asks if you need help, begin to cry and ask, "Why won't you people just leave me alone?"

13. Settle down in front of the biggest of the big TV's on display to watch an entire five-day Test cricket match.

14. Ride those little electronic cars at the front of the store.

15. Rearrange the CD's by color-coding them.

16. Relax in the patio furniture until you get kicked out.

17. During announcements over the PA, assume the foetal position and scream, "No, no! It's those voices again!"

18. Drag a lounge chair on display over to the magazines and relax.

19. Have a bit of fun with the McDonalds schoolkid who serves you by asking for last month's specials.

NO WAY TO FLY

The plane of White Knuckle Airways was taxiing down the tarmac for take-off, when it suddenly stopped, turned around and returned to the gate.

After a hour and a quarter wait, it finally took off.

A worried passenger asked the flight attendant, "What was the problem?"

"The pilot was bothered by a noise he heard in the engine," explained the flight attendant, "and it took us a while to find a new pilot ..."

Michael Jackson, Bill Clinton and Nelson Mandela are in a jet with 20 kids. The plane suffers an irreparable electronics failure and is doomed to crash. As smoke billows though the plane, it becomes apparent that the plane has only 20 parachutes.

Nelson Mandela, as a great humanitarian says that the children should have them.

Bill Clinton gets panicky and shouts, "Screw the children!"

Michael Jackson whispers, "Do we have enough time?"

They left home and arrived at the airport laden with luggage, most of it hers. They managed to cart the seven suit cases, triple-deck make-up case, and five bags of hand luggage to the check-in counter by which time the husband mournfully mumbled, "God, I wish I'd brought the piano with me!"

"No need to be sarcastic," she snapped.

"No, really," he replied, "I left the plane tickets on top of it ..."

A flight dispatcher watches a plane somehow manage to spin on the tarmac and land tail end forward. "Flight Tango Victor Foxtrot, what the hell is going on?" he shouts into the microphone, "Let me speak to the captain!"

"The c ... c ... the captain is drunk," comes the reply.

"Then give me the second pilot."

"He, he's d ... d ... d ... drunk too."

"Well, and who's talking?"

"A ... auto ... p ... p ... p ... pilot.."

After a holiday on the Sunshine coast a young man boarded the aeroplane for the flight home with a parcel of freshly caught crabs for his girlfriend to eat with a bottle of champagne that night.

The hostess took them from him and put them in the fridge for safe keeping. The plane landed, the passengers were asked to remain seated until the plane came to a halt.

"And will the gentleman who gave me the crabs in Cairns, please come forward."

On reaching his plane seat a man is surprised to see a parrot strapped in next to him. He asks the stewardess for a coffee where upon the parrot squawks, "And get me a whisky, you cow!"

The stewardess, flustered, brings back a whisky for the parrot and forgets the man's coffee. When this is pointed out to her, the parrot drains its glass and bawls: "And get me another whisky, you idiot". Upset, the stewardess comes back shaking with another whisky – but still no coffee.

By now in desperate need of his coffee, the man tries the parrot's style, "I've asked you twice for a coffee, go and get it now, you moron."

Before they know it, two burly flight stewards storm down the aisle, grab the parrot and the man, yank them out of their seats, and throw out of the emergency exit.

Plunging downwards the parrot turns to the man and says, "For someone who can't fly, you sure complain too much!"

Then there were the two paratrooper recruits in an aeroplane.

"Are you crazy, Doug?" says one, "You're going to jump without a parachute?"

"Is it mandatory to wear one?"

"Sure. It's raining outside."

A young lady was conducting a study on human sexual behavior. She came to the conclusion that the best place to find participants for the survey would be at the airport.

After three hours of questioning passengers, she sees a pilot walking to his gate. Having heard of the reputation of pilots she stops him. "Excuse me, Captain" she says, "I am doing a survey on human sexuality. I was wondering if you could answer a few questions?"

The pilot agrees, and the young lady starts questioning him. After three questions, she asks him, "And when was the last time you had sex?"

Straight away, without having to think, the Captain replies, "1959."

The girl was shocked. She looks at the captain and asks "1959? Isn't that a long time ago?"

"Oh," the pilot replies, "I guess so, but it's only 2015 now …"

C ruising at 32,000 feet, the aeroplane suddenly shuddered and an anxious passenger looked out the window.

"Heaven help us!," he screamed, "One of the engines just blew up!"

Scared passengers left their seats and came running over. While they were looking, the aircraft was rocked by a second blast, as an engine exploded on the other side.

The passengers went into wild panic, not even the stewardesses being able to maintain order. Just then, standing tall and smiling confidently, the pilot strode from the cockpit.

"There is nothing to worry about," he assured everyone.

His tranquil demeanour made everyone feel better, and

they sat down, as he calmly walked to the door of the aircraft. He took several packages from under the seats and began handing them to the flight attendants. Each crewmember attached the package to their backs.

"Hey, wait a minute, aren't those parachutes?" asked an alert passenger.

"Yes, they are," said the pilot calmly.

"But I thought you said there was nothing to worry about?"

"There isn't," replied the pilot as a third engine exploded, "We're going to get help …"

Flying can get a bit boring at times. Airline attendants occasionally make an effort to make announcements and in-flight safety lectures more entertaining. These are just some of genuine examples that have been heard or reported over the years:

- "To operate your seatbelt, insert the metal tab into the buckle, and pull tight. It works just like every other seatbelt. If you don't know how to operate one, you probably shouldn't be out in public unsupervised."
- "As you exit the plane, make sure to gather all of your belongings. Anything left behind will be distributed evenly among the flight attendants. Please do not leave children or spouses."
- "There may be 50 ways to leave your lover, but there are only four ways out of this aeroplane."

- When a plane finally came to a halt, "We ask you to please remain seated as Captain Kangaroo bounces us to the terminal."
- "Thank you for flying Delta Business Express. We hope you enjoyed giving us the business as much as we enjoyed taking you for a ride."
- As the plane landed and was coming to a stop, a lone voice came over the loudspeaker, "Whoa, big fella. WHOA!"
- After a particularly rough landing during thunderstorms, a flight attendant flight announced, "Please take care when opening the overhead compartments because, after a landing like that, sure as heck, everything has shifted."
- "In the event of a sudden loss of cabin pressure margarine cups will descend from the ceiling. Stop screaming, grab the mask, and pull it over your face. If you have a small child travelling with you, secure your mask before assisting with theirs. If you are travelling with more than one small child, then pick your favorite."
- "Weather at our destination is 50 degrees with some broken clouds, but we'll try to have them fixed for you before we arrive."
- "Thank you, and remember, nobody loves you, or your money, more than Arrow Airlines."
- "Your seat cushions can be used for flotation, and in the event of an emergency water landing, please paddle to shore and take them with our complements."
- From a passenger, after a series of noises and shuddering bumps during arrival, "Did we land, or were we shot down?"

- "Should the cabin lose pressure, oxygen masks will drop from the overhead area. Please place the bag over your own mouth and nose before assisting children or other adults acting like children."
- "Last one off the plane must clean it."
- And from the pilot during his welcome message, "We are pleased to have some of the best flight attendants in the industry. Unfortunately, none of them are on this flight!"
- After a particularly windy and bumpy final approach, "Ladies and Gentlemen, please remain in your seats with your seatbelts fastened while the Captain taxis what's left of our aeroplane to the gate!"
- "Ladies and Gentlemen, please remain in your seats until Captain Braveheart and his magnificent crew have brought the aircraft to a screeching halt against the gate. And, once the tyre smoke has cleared and the warning bells are silenced, we'll open the door and you can pick your way through the wreckage to the terminal."

An obviously gay male flight attendant bounced over and announced, "The Captain has asked me to announce that he will be landing the big scary plane shortly, so if you could just put up your trays, that would be great."

A woman sitting on the aisle did not do as she was asked. The flight attendant came back and said to her, "Ma'am, perhaps you couldn't hear me over the big scary engine, but I asked you to please put up your tray so that the captain can land the plane." She still wouldn't comply. He was getting angry and asked her again to put up the tray. She calmly turned to him and said, "In my country, I am called a princess. I take orders from no one."

The flight attendant replied, "Oh yeah? Well in *my* country, I'm called a queen and I outrank you, so put the tray up!"

15 PROFOUND THINGS THAT CONFUSCIOUS SAYS

ADULT ONLY

1. Crowded elevator smells different to midget.
2. Man who fight with wife all day get no piece at night.
3. War doesn't determine who is right, war determines who is left.
4. Man with one chopstick go hungry.
5. Man with hand in pocket feel cocky all day.
6. Virginity like bubble, one prick all gone.
7. Passionate kiss like spider's web, soon lead to undoing of fly.
8. Man who run in front of car get tired.
9. Man who run behind car get exhausted.
10. Man who fishes in other man's well often catches crabs.
11. Man who drive like hell bound to get there.
12. Man who scratches ass should not bite fingernails.
13. Man who eat many prunes get good run for money.
14. It take many nails to build crib but one screw to fill it.
15. Man who stand on toilet is high on pot.

FAVORITE PET STORIES

Did you hear about my dog? I called him Stay. It was great fun, "Come here, Stay! Come here, Stay!" He went insane.

A veterinarian had a tough day. However, when he got home from tending to a waiting room full of sick animals his wife was ready with a long cool drink and a romantic candle-lit dinner. Then they had a few more drinks and went happily to bed. Then the phone rang ...

"Is this the vet?" asked an elderly lady's voice.

"Yes, it is," replied the vet, "Is this an emergency?"

"Well, yes, sort of," said the elderly lady, "there's a whole bunch of cats on the roof outside making a terrible noise mating and I can't get to sleep. What can I do about it?"

The vet drew a long breath, shook his head and patiently replied, "Open the window and tell them they're wanted on the phone"

"Really?" said the elderly lady, "Will that stop them?"

"Should do," said the vet, "it stopped me!"

Donald Duck had split up with Daisy, and after several days could not control himself anymore and headed off to a brothel.

"I want sex," he told the Madam.

"You've come to the right place," she said. "But before we go any further, I have to tell you that we have a policy, in this brothel that you must wear a condom."

"Okay," said Donald.

"We charge $1.00 extra for that. Shall I stick it on your bill?"

"What sort of duck do you think I am?"

I had a dog once. I named him Spot. Unfortunately, I accidentally spilled spot remover on him, and now he's disappeared.

A man buys a parrot, but after several weeks of trying, is unable to get it to speak a single word. In desperation he takes the bird to the vet.

The vet tells him that the parrot has too long a beak, and that is stopping him from talking.

"I just need to file it down a bit, and he should be allright," he says.

The man says that is OK, and the vet replies, "It will cost a hundred dollars."

"A hundred bucks!" says the owner.

The vet tells him that it is a very delicate procedure. If he does not file enough, the bird still will not be able to talk, but if he files too much, the bird will drown while drinking his water. The man decides to think it over and leaves with his parrot.

The next day, he comes back into the vet's shop, looking both sad and puzzled.

"What happened?" said the vet.

"Well I just couldn't afford the hundred dollars, so I took him into my tool-shed, and did the filing myself."

"And?"

"And now he's dead."

"Dead? What happened?"

"That's what I came to ask you about. I used a medium-grade file, and got the beak down to what I thought was the right length, so that he could talk but not drown while he was drinking his water."

"Sounds good so far, then what happened?"

"And then I took his head out of the vice, and ..."

A snake and a rabbit, both blind from birth, meet in the forest one day.

The rabbit does not know what a snake looks like, but decides he can trust him and asks, "Would you mind running your hands over my body and telling me what kind of an animal I am? I'm too embarrassed to ask my sighted friends because I'm afraid they'll make fun of me."

The snake says, "OK," and proceeds to wind himself around the rabbit from one end to the other. "Well," the snake says, "You're kind of warm, with soft fur and two very long, furry ears."

The rabbit thinks for a moment and then exclaims, "Wow! I must be a bunny!" And he hops around in a little circle, and starts hopping away.

"Wait!" shouts the snake, "What about me? Come back here and do the same thing for me!"

The rabbit hops over and with his fury little paws, pats the snake from one end to the other and then back again. He sits down without saying a word.

"Well?" asks the snake, "What kind of animal am I?"

"I'm not really sure," says the rabbit, "You're kind of cold and slimy, and for the life of me, I can't tell your head from your arse."

The snake thinks and thinks about this, then exclaims with delight, "Wow! I must be a lawyer!"

Donald Duck wanted a divorce from Daisy and he was talking to his Lawyer.

"I don't understand," said Donald, "Daisy's not insane!"

"I didn't say that she was insane," replied the lawyer, "I said that she was f...ing Goofy."

Then there was this bloke who had a parrot that knew only one sentence, which was, "Let's make love."

The parrot said it all the time, embarrassing the owner to no end. Finally, the owner went to his parish priest and told him of his parrot problem.

The priest replied, "I have a parrot who also only knows one sentence. He always says, 'Let us pray.' You bring your parrot over Sunday after Mass, and I'm sure your parrot will be praying by the end of the day."

So the owner brings the parrot over to the rectory after mass. The parrot, spying the priest's parrot, opens his mouth and blurts, "Let's make love."

The priest's parrot closes his eyes, looks up at heaven and says, "My prayers have been answered ..."

Did you hear about the two nude statues, man and woman, standing across from each other in a secluded park? A few hundred years after they've been put in place, an angel flutters down to them. With a wave of his hand, the statues are given flesh, and they step down from their pedestals.

The angel says, "I have been sent to grant the mutual request you both have made after hundreds of years of standing across from each other, unable to move. But be quick, you only have fifteen minutes until you must become statues again."

The man looks at the woman, and they both flush, and giggle, and run off into some bushes in the park. Some loud rustling noises come from the bushes, and seven minutes later, they both come back to the angel, obviously satisfied. The angel smiles at the couple, "That was only seven minutes. Why not go back and do it again?"

The former statues look at each other for a minute, and then the woman says, "Why not? But let's reverse it this time – you hold down the pigeon, and it's my turn to shit on it ..."

My dog is named "Sex." He has caused me a great deal of embarrassment.

When I went to the city hall to renew his dog license, I told the clerk I would like a license for Sex. He said, "I'd like one too."

Then I said, "But this is a dog." He said he didn't care what she looked like. Then I said, "You don't understand, I've had Sex since I was nine years old."

He winked and said, "You must have been quite a kid."

When I got married and went on my honeymoon, I took the dog with me. I told the motel clerk that I wanted a room for my wife and me and a special room for Sex.

He said, "You don't need a special room. As long as you pay your bill we don't care what you do."

I said, "Look, you don't seem to understand, Sex keeps me awake at night."

The clerk said, "Funny, I have the same problem."

One day I entered Sex in a contest, but before the competition began the dog ran away. Another contestant asked me why I was just standing there, looking disappointed. I told him I had planned to have Sex in the contest. He told me I should have sold my own tickets. "But you don't understand," I said, "I had hoped to have Sex on TV."

He said, "Now that cable is all over the place it's no big deal anymore."

When my wife and I separated, we went to court to fight for custody of the dog. I said, "Your honor, I had Sex before I was married."

The judge said, "The courtroom isn't a confessional. Stick to the case, please."

Then I told him that after I was married, Sex left me. He

said, "Me, too."

Last night Sex ran off again. I spent hours looking around town for him. A cop came over to me and asked, "What are you doing in this alley at 4 o'clock in the morning?" I told him that I was looking for Sex.

My case comes up Friday.

So there's this magician working on a small cruise ship. He's been doing his routines every night for a year or two now.

The audiences appreciate him, and they change over often enough that he doesn't have to worry too much about new tricks. However, there's this parrot which sits in the back row and watches him night after night, year after year. Finally, the parrot figures out how the tricks work, and starts giving it away for the audience. When the magician makes a bouquet of flowers disappear, the parrot squawks, "Behind his back! Behind his back!"

The magician gets really annoyed at this, but he doesn't know what to do. The parrot belongs to the Captain, so he can't just kill it.

One day, the ship springs a leak and sinks. The magician manages to swim to a plank of wood floating by and grabs on. The parrot is sitting on the other end of the plank. They just stare at each other and drift. They drift for three days, and still don't speak. On the morning of the fourth day, the parrot looks over at the magician and says, "OK, I give up. Where did you hide the ship?"

I had a dog once. Some dogs are afraid of heights. Not him, he was afraid of widths. I took him for walks around my building ... on the ledge.

A preacher was trying to raise money for his parish and he found out there was a great deal of money to be made in the horse racing business. However, at the horse auction, the prices of horses were too much and all he could afford was a donkey, which he bought.

Determined to make money for his parish, he entered his donkey in a race and to everyone's surprise it finished third. The next day, the newspaper headline read: PREACHER'S ASS SHOWS.

The following week the preacher again entered the race and this time won! The newspaper headline read: PREACHER'S ASS OUT IN FRONT.

Annoyed by this kind of publicity, the preacher's Bishop suggested that the preacher not continue this activity. The headline read: BISHOP SCRATCHES PREACHER'S ASS.

The Bishop then demanded that the preacher get rid of the donkey. The preacher gave the donkey to a Nun in the local convent. The headlines read: NUN HAS BEST ASS IN TOWN.

When he recovered from the shock, the Bishop ordered the nun to sell the donkey. When it was discovered that the Nun sold the donkey to a farmer for $10.00 the headline read: NUN PEDDLES ASS FOR TEN BUCKS.

A zoo acquired a very rare species of gorilla. Within a few weeks, the gorilla, a female, became very horny and difficult to handle.

Upon examination, a veterinarian determined the problem: she was in heat.

What to do? There was no male of this species available.

While reflecting on their problem, the zoo administrators noticed Burl, an employee responsible for cleaning the animals' cages. Now Burl was rumoured to possess ample ability to satisfy any female, and he wasn't very bright.

So the zoo administrators thought they might entice Burl to satisfy the female gorilla. They approached him with a proposition: would he be willing to have sex with the gorilla for $500?

Burl suggested that he might be interested, but he needed time to think it over. The following day he entered the zoo administrators' office.

"I accept your offer, but with three conditions," he said.

"Firstly, I don't want to have to kiss her. Two, I want nothing to do with any offspring that may result."

The zoo administration nodded and agreed to these conditions, but inquired about the third condition?

"Well, you'll have to give me another week to come up with the $500."

SMART ANSWERING MACHINE ANSWERS

Want to beef up your message on the answering machine? Here's some to try:

- A is for academics, B is for beer. One of those reasons is why we're not here. So, leave a message.
- Hello. This is Ralph: If you are the phone company, I already sent the money. If you are my parents, please send money. If you are my financial aid institution, you didn't lend me enough money. If you are my friends, you owe me money. If you are a female, don't worry, I have plenty of money.
- Hi. Now you say something.
- I'm not home right now, but my answering machine is, so you can talk to it instead. Wait for the beep.
- Hello. I am Stan's answering machine. What are you?
- If you leave a message, I'll call you soon. If you leave a sexy message, I'll call sooner!
- Hi! Fred's answering machine is broken. This is his refrigerator, speaking. Please speak very slowly, and I'll stick your message to myself with one of these magnets.
- Hello, you are talking to a machine. I am capable of receiving messages. My owners do not need

aluminium cladding, double-glazing, or a hot tub, and their carpets are clean. They give to charity through their office and do not need their picture taken. If you're still with me, leave your name and number and they will get back to you.

- This is not an answering machine. This is a telepathic thought-recording device. After the tone, do not say anything. Simply think about your name, your number and your reason for calling, and I'll think about returning your call.

- Hi. I'm probably home. I'm just avoiding someone I don't like. Leave me a message, and if I don't call back, it's you.

- Hi, this is Frank. I'm sorry I can't answer the phone right now. Leave a message and then wait by your phone until I call you back.

- If you are a burglar, then we're sitting in this house right now, cleaning our weapons, and can't come to the phone. Otherwise, we probably aren't home, and it's safe to leave a message.

- Please leave a message. However, you have the right to remain silent. Everything you say will be recorded and will be used by us.

- Hello, who am I, again ?

A MATTER OF RACIAL IN DIFFERENCE

It is not widely known that Adolf Hitler was very keen on the occult. He went to a fortune-teller hoping that the woman could tell him how long he would live.

After careful charting, she said, "I can't predict the exact date of your death, but I do know that you will die on a Jewish holiday."

"And which holiday will this be?" he asked.

"It does not matter," she replied. "Any day that you die will be a Jewish holiday ..."

A tourist arrived in Auckland, hired a car and then set off to explore the country. He was surprised to see a bloke having sex with a sheep in the middle of an open paddock.

He was so horrified that he felt the need to pull into the next pub he saw and to order a stiff scotch. He was just about to throw it back when he noticed a one legged bloke masturbating furiously at the bar next to him.

"What the Hell is it with place?" he cried out.

"I've only been here for a couple of hours and I have seen a bloke shagging a sheep in the paddock, and now there's some bloke wanking himself off in the bar next to me."

"Go easy, mate, calm down," the bartender said. "You can't expect a man with only one leg to catch a sheep."

How do the Greeks separate the men from the boys? With a crowbar.

Did you hear about the Chinaman who went to the toilet? He wiped the chain and pulled himself.

Telephone rings.

Maid:	Hello
Tough Mafioso:	Put my wife on the phone.
Maid:	Just a moment. (Maid comes back after a minute). I'm sorry but she's indisposed in the bathroom.
Tough Mafioso:	I said put her on the phone. Now!
Maid stutters:	She can't come to the phone right now.
Tough Mafioso:	If you don't get her on the phone in two seconds I'm gonna come over there and pull your jaw from your face.
Maid stutters:	You, you don't understand, she's in there with another man.
Tough Mafioso:	What!?!
Maid:	Yeah.

Tough Mafioso:	Listen, this is what I want you to do, I want you to shoot them both dead and then get rid of the gun.
Maid stutters:	I, I can't do that, I can't shoot anybody.
Tough Mafioso:	You do it! Now!
Maid stutters:	I, I can't!
Tough Mafioso:	If you don't do it right now I'm gonna kill you and your whole family. Go do it now! I wanna hear the shots.
Maid:	OK.
(The tough Mafioso hears two loud shots over the phone.)	
Maid stutters:	I did it.
Tough Mafioso:	Good. Whad'ya you do with the gun?
Maid stutters:	I threw it in the pool.
Tough Mafioso:	Pool? What pool? We don't have a pool!

It's Saturday morning and Pete's just about to set off on a round of golf, when he realizes that he forgot to tell his wife that the bloke who fixes the washing machine is coming around at noon.

So Pete heads back to the clubhouse and phones home.

"Hello?" says a little girl's voice.

"Hi, honey, it's Daddy," says Pete. "Is Mommy near the phone?"

"No, Daddy. She's upstairs in the bedroom with Uncle Frank."

After a brief pause, Pete says, "But you haven't got an Uncle Frank, honey!"

"Yes, I do, and he's upstairs in the bedroom with Mommy!"

"Okay, then. Here's what I want you do. Put down the phone, run upstairs and knock on the bedroom door and shout in to Mommy and Uncle Frank that my car has just pulled up outside the house."

"Okay, Daddy!" A few minutes later, the little girl comes back to the phone. "Well, I did what you said, Daddy."

"And what happened?"

"Well, Mommy jumped out of bed with no clothes on and ran around screaming, then she tripped over the rug and fell right out the front window and now she's all dead."

"Oh, my God! What about Uncle Frank?"

"He jumped out of bed with no clothes on too, and he was all scared and he jumped out the back window into the swimming pool. But he must have forgot that last week you took out all the water to clean it, so he hit the bottom of the swimming pool and now he's dead too."

There is a long pause.

"Swimming pool? Is this 278-9872?"

How can you tell when an Italian woman is embarrassed about her long black hair? When she wears gloves to cover up.

There once was this white fella who was feeling lonely because his wife-to-be, Wanda, was on vacation.

He wanted to do something for her that would both impress her as well as proclaim his undying ever-enduring love for her.

After much contemplation he thought what better way than to have her name, "Wanda," actually tattooed onto his body.

Further consideration of his idea resulted in his deciding to have her name tattooed right onto his penis. So he went to a tattoo parlor and had it done immediately.

Well, because of the nature of the terrain, the tattoo usually said, "WA." But he knew she would be surprised and delighted to see her whole name on his penis once it became erect. He could hardly wait for her return.

The scabs wore off just in time too, as she was due home from her vacation. He went to meet her at the airport, beaming to himself as he imagined her pleasure at discovering his surprise.

He could hardly even contain himself. While he was waiting for her plane, he went into the washroom to have a pee. He marched right up the urinal next to a tall black fella who was just shaking it off.

The white fella looks down and says, "Hey wow!!! You've got a WA on *your* penis too! What a coincidence!" The black fella looks at him.

"I just had mine done, it really says 'Wanda'," beamed the white fella, "What does yours say?"

The black fella looks down at him, gives a big wide smile and says warmly, "Mine says, 'Welcome to beautiful, sunny Jamaica'."

What do Japanese men do when they have erections? They vote.

A Jew and a Chinese are traveling on a train together. The Jew stands up, and gives the Chinaman a tremendous slap.

"What are you doing?" says the stricken Chinaman.

"That's for Pearl-Harbor" says the Jew.

"But I am Chinese! The Japanese were responsible for that!" says the Chinaman.

"Japanese, Chinaman – all the same."

They resume their seats. Time passes. The Chinaman gets up, and kicks the Jew.

"Hey! What's going on?"

"That's for the Titanic!" says the Chinaman.

"But the Titanic was hit by an Iceberg!"

"Iceberg, Weissberg – all the same."

A bar customer asked the bartender if he wanted to hear a Polack joke.

The bartender pointed to a large, muscled man at the end of the bar and said, "See that big guy over there? He's Polish."

Then the bartender pointed to a burly policeman near the door and repeated, "And him, the one carrying the night-stick, he's Polish."

The bartender finished, "I'm Polish, too. Now, if I was you, I would think very carefully about whether you want to tell that joke."

The customer replied, "I guess I won't tell that joke after all. I'd have to explain it three times."

Why is the Mexican Olympic Team so unsuccessful? Because anyone who can run, jump or swim is in America by now.

A priest, a minister and a rabbi are out in a field. The priest says, "Let's draw a circle on the ground and throw our money into the air. Whatever lands outside the circle, we keep; whatever lands inside the circle, we give to God."

The minister says, "I have a better idea: we only keep what lands *inside* the circle."

The Rabbi says, "Tell you what: let's just throw the money up, and whatever God wants, he can keep."

Three construction contractors, died and went to Heaven – a Black, a Jew, and an Italian. When they got there, St Peter welcomed them warmly and asked if they could do him a favor before they entered Heaven.

It seems that the Pearly Gates were in need of some repair, and he wanted some estimates.

The Black contractor looked the job over carefully and estimated the job at $600. When asked how he came up with that figure, he said, "$200 materials, $200 labor, and $200 profit."

St. Peter then asked the Jewish contractor for an estimate. After careful inspection the Jew answered, "$3000 – $1000 materials, $1000 labor, and $1000 profit."

When St. Peter asked the Italian for an estimate, he

answered immediately, without looking over the job at all, "$2600."

When asked how he came up with that figure he answered, "Simple, $1000 for you, $1000 for me, and $600 to get the lowest bidder over there to do the work."

A kilted Scotsman was walking down a country path after finishing off a considerable amount of whisky at a local pub. As he staggered down the road, he felt quite sleepy and decided to take a nap, with his back against a tree.

As he slept, two young lasses walked down the road and heard the Scotsman snoring loudly. They saw him, and one said, "I've always wondered what a Scotsman wears under his kilt." She boldly walked over to the sleeping man, raised his kilt, and saw what nature had provided him at his birth.

Her friend said, "Well, he has solved a great mystery for us, now. He must be rewarded!" So, she took a blue ribbon from her hair, and gently tied it around what nature had provided the Scotsman, and the two walked away.

Several minutes later, the Scotsman was awakened by the call of nature, and walked around to the other side of the tree to relieve himself.

He raised his kilt, and saw where the blue ribbon was tied. After several moments of bewilderment, the Scotsman said, "I dinna know where y'been laddie ... but it's nice ta'know y'won first prize!"

Three Irish Catholic ladies are across the street from a brothel. One asks, "Isn't that Reverend Brown coming out of there?"

"What a scandal! For a clergyman to sink like that!" the ladies say.

"Isn't that Rabbi Armlestein?" asks another.

They all exclaim, "Oh, that filthy Jew! Disgusting!"

"Isn't that Father Murphy?" asks the third.

"My, my, there must be a very sick girl in there."

Bowing to international pressure not to act unilaterally, the United States reversed course today and promised to consult with its allies before doing whatever the hell it was going to do anyway.

A professor told dirty jokes in class and the women wanted to protest about it. They decided that the next time that the professor started with these kind of jokes they would all leave the class as a group protest.

But a male student overhead and the professor was told of the plan.

At the beginning of the next lecture he said, "In Sweden, a prostitute makes $2000 per night."

All the women stood up and started to leave the class.

He shouted after them, "Where are you going? The plane to Sweden doesn't take off until the day after tomorrow."

The Grand Prix was in full swing, the cars hurtling round the track at death-defying speeds.

The German driver pulled in, and his pit crew had his car finished and out on the track again in eight seconds.

The Italian driver came in, his pit crew changed his tyres, refuelled the car and repaired his carby, all in 11 seconds!

The Aussie car came in. They told him to bring it in on Thursday, leave the keys, and they'd get back to him with a quote.

There are two men working at an adult book and sex aids store. The older man, the owner, announces that he has to go to the bank, and asks his new young sales assistant to watch the shop.

Shortly after the first man leaves, a white woman comes into the store looking for a dildo. The young man is happy to help her and sells her one about six inches long.

After she leaves, a black woman comes in looking for a dildo, and again the assistant is happy to help her and sells her one 10 inches long.

After the second woman leaves, a Polish woman comes in the store looking for a dildo – but something really huge.

The man looks around and shows her several types, but they are not big enough for her. Finally she spots a giant silver one in the corner, and says, "There, that's the one for me."

Later, the owner returns and asks how business went while he was away. The young assistant says, "Great! I sold a white dildo, a black dildo, and that new model silver one."

"What new model silver one?" says the owner.

"The big silver one that was sitting in the corner," says the young man.

"You idiot," says the owner, "that was my thermos containing my soup for lunch!"

During his visit to China, George W. Bush was intrigued by a new telephone which was capable of connecting China with Hell.

He spoke briefly with the Devil, and the call cost him 27 cents.

When he came back home, he found out that this same service was now available in the USA also.

Again he spoke to the Devil but this time he received a bill for $12,000.

George W. was distressed. "How come?" he complained, "that the same call only cost me 27 cents in the China?"

"Well," replied the operator. "Over there it is a local call."

A Russian and an American are talking over a drink.

"When I'm in a good mood I drive a car that is painted a light colour," says the American.

"When I'm busy or have a lot of troubles, I drive a darker colored car.

"And when I go for vacation overseas, I pick a brightly colored car."

"Things are much easier in Russia," says the Russian. "If you are in a good mood, they will give you a ride in yellow car with a blue stripe.

"If you feel bad, the car will be white and the stripe red.

"I was abroad only once, and there I drove a tank."

"Rabbi, what should I do? My son has converted to Christianity."

"I don't know," answered the Rabbi. "Come back tomorrow, and I'll ask advice from God."

The man comes back the next day.

"I can't help you," says the Rabbi. "God told me he has the same problem."

"Rabbi, I don't know what to do. Should I marry my girlfriend or not?"

"It doesn't matter what you do. The result will be the same. You'll regret it anyway."

At the International Meeting for Genetic Scientists, an American scientist reported, "We crossed chickens with cows. The new breed simultaneously produces milk, meat and eggs."

The French scientist reported, "We succeeded in crossbreeding flies and bees. The hybrid flies over the trash fields and produces honey."

The Russian scientist reported, "We crossed a melon with cockroaches. When you cut this melon, seeds run away by themselves."

Abraham sits in front of the Rockefeller Bank and sells oranges. His friend comes and asks to borrow a couple of bucks.

"You know," says Abraham, "Rockefeller and I reached an agreement. He does not sell oranges, and I do not borrow money."

The owner of a Scottish company tells his employees, "You worked very well during this year.

"The company's profits increased dramatically.

"As a reward, I'll give everyone a cheque for 20 pounds.

"And if you work with the same zeal next year, I'll sign them ...

A young English girl trying to impress her American date says, "My genealogy starts from a person who met the Queen. She touched his shoulder and made him a knight."

"Well," says the American, "my genealogy starts from a person who faced an Indian chief. The chief touched his head with a tomahawk and made him an angel."

An American physician asked his Russian colleague, "Is it true that there are cases in your country where a patient was treated for one disease, only to have the autopsy reveal another cause of death?"

"Absolutely not! All our patients die from the diseases we treat them for."

WHAT A BEAUTY

I'VE NEVER SEEN ONE AS BIG AS THAT BEFORE

My dick is so big, it graduated a year ahead of me in high school.

My dick is so big, it has a roadie.

My dick is so big, I have to call it Mr. Dick in front of company.

My dick is so big, it won't return Spielberg's calls.

My dick is so big, it was overthrown in a coup. It's now known as the People's Democratic Republic of My Dick.

My dick is so big, it has casters.

My dick is so big, it lives next door.

My dick is so big, it votes.

No matter where I go, my dick always gets there first.

My dick takes longer lunches than I do.

My dick is so big, it has feet.

My dick is so big, it has investors …

… and a Chairman of the Board.

My dick is so big, we use it at parties as a limbo pole.

My dick is so big, it has an opening act.

My dick is so big, every time I get hard-on I cause a solar eclipse.

If you cut my dick in two, you can tell how old I am.

My dick is so big, Trump owns it.

My dick is so big, I can never sit in the front row. I did sit in the front row once, and conducted the orchestra through the entire score of *Cats*.

My dick is so big, it has its own dick. And even my dick's dick is bigger than your dick.

My dick is so big, it only does one show a night.

My dick is so big, you can ski down it.

My dick is so big, it has elbows.

My dick is so big, I have to check it as luggage when I fly.

My dick is so big, it has a personal trainer.

My dick is so big, it has a retractable dome.

My dick is so big, it has its own gravity.

My dick is so big, it has a basement.

My dick is so big it has cable.

My dick is so big, it violates seventeen zoning laws.

My dick is so big, I can braid it.

My dick is so big, it passes through eleven time zones.

My dick is so big, I can sit on it.

My dick is so big, it can chew gum.

My dick is so big, it only tips with hundreds.

My dick is so big, investors want to build an amusement park on it.

My dick is so big, you're standing on it.

My dick is so big, it only comes into work when it feels like it.

My dick is so big, it plays golf with the Prime Minister.

My dick is so big, it charges money for its autograph.

My dick is so big, the tip of it celebrated the arrival of the new Millennium 40 minutes before my balls did.

My dick is so big, it has an agent.

So, let's have lunch with my dick. My dick's people will call your people …

THIS BLOKE WALKS INTO A BAR SEE...

A bloke who was obviously the victim of a nasty accident comes staggering into the pub with both arms in plaster casts.

"I'll have a beer, thanks mate," he says to the barman. "And could you hold it up to my lips for me?"

"No worries," says the barman.

"Couldn't light a ciggie for me, too, could you?" asks the bloke.

"Not a problem," says the barman.

"Thanks, mate," says the bloke. "Me wallet's in me back pocket, if you'd like to get it out for me."

"There you go," says the barman.

"Cheers," says the bloke. "By the way, where's the toilet?"

And without a moment's hesitation, the barman says, "Go two blocks up the street, turn right and it's the second on the left."

Two fat blokes are sitting in a pub. One says to the other "Your round."

And the other bloke replies, "So are you, ya fat bastard!"

Then there was the bloke who walks into a bar and is surprised to find he's the only customer. He asks for a beer, but the barman says, "I'll just be a few minutes, sir, I've got to change the barrel, help yourself to the savory snacks."

So the man's sitting quietly nibbling the nibbles, when he hears a voice, "I tell you what mate, you're looking really good tonight, that suit is really you."

He looks around, but he's still alone.

Then he hears, "And that new haircut, it couldn't be better."

Again he looks around. Nothing.

"And have you lost weight! I don't think I've ever seen you looking so well."

Still no-one about.

After a while the barman returns and the man says, "You won't believe what's happened. I was just sitting here on my own and I heard this voice say I look great, my suit is really me, and that I've never looked so well. And yet there's no-one here"

"Oh," said the barman, "that'll be the nuts, they're complimentary."

An Englishman, Irishman and Welshman walk into a bar. The barman says, "Is this some kind of a joke?"

A drunk is in a bar, lying on the floor and looking the worse for wear. Other hotel patrons decide to be good Samaritans and to take him home.

They pick him up off the floor, and drag him out the door. On the way to the car, he falls down three times.

When they get to his house, they help him out of the car and he falls down four more times. Mission accomplished, they prop him against the door jam and ring the doorbell.

"Here's your husband!" they exclaim proudly.

"Where's his wheelchair?" asks the puzzled wife ...

A pirate with a peg leg, a hook and an eye-patch walks into a bar. The bartender says, "Where did you get that peg leg?"

The Pirate replies, "We were swimming one day, on the high seas, when a big shark came up and bit off me leg."

The bartender asks, "Well, where did you get the hook, then?"

The pirate responded, "We were in a battle with Capt'n Bloodeye, and my hand was cut off at the bone."

The bartender asks, "Then where did ya get the eye patch?"

The pirate says, "One day, I looked up at a gull flying over head and it pooped right in me eye."

The puzzled bartender says, "Why would you need an eye patch after that?"

The pirate replies, "First day with the hook ..."

A bloke proposes a one dollar bar bet to a well endowed young lady that despite her dress being buttoned to the neck, he could touch her breasts without touching her clothes.

Since this didn't seem remotely possible, she is intrigued and accepts the bet. He steps up, cups his hands around her breasts and squeezes firmly.

With a baffled look, she says, "Hey, you touched my clothes."

And he replies, "OK, here's your dollar …"

An infamous stud with a long list of conquests walked into his neighborhood bar and ordered a drink. The bartender thought he looked worried and asked him if anything was wrong.

"I'm scared out of my mind," the stud replied. "Some pissed-off husband wrote to me and said he'd kill me if I didn't stop f…ing his wife."

"So stop," the barkeep said.

"I can't," the womanizer replied, taking a long swill. "The prick didn't sign his name!"

A man walks into a bar carrying a small box. He says to the bartender, "How much do you think I could make from a dancing fly?"

"A dancing fly?!" says the bartender. "Let me see it."

The man opens the box and puts a tiny fly onto the bar,

goes over and turns on the jukebox, and straight away the fly begins to dance.

"Hey that's pretty good," says the bartender, "How long did it take to teach him that?"

"Ten years," replies the man "Do you know an agent who could help me make him a star?"

"Sure," says the bartender, "See that man over there on the phone? He's in the entertainment game."

The man puts the fly back in the box, walks over and carefully puts the fly back on the table next to the phone, and patiently waits for the man to hang up.

"Yes, of course I will," says the bloke on the phone. "No, I won't forget. OK, thank you, goodbye, see you."

Bang he goes with the phone on the table.

"Blasted bugs," he says. "Now what is it you want?"

A string walks into a bar and says to the bartender, "Hi, a vodka, please."

The bartender says, "Sorry, we don't serve strings around here."

The string leaves and goes around the corner, ties himself in a knot and ruffles his top and bottom. He goes up to the bartender and again asks for vodka and the bartender says, "Aren't you the string that just came in here?"

The string replies, "No, I'm afraid not!"

A chihuahua, a doberman and a german shepherd are in a bar having a drink when a great-looking female collie comes up to them and says, "Whoever can say liver and cheese in a sentence can have me."

So the doberman says, "I love liver and cheese."

The Collie replies:, "That's not good enough."

The shepherd says, "I hate liver and cheese."

She says, "That's not creative enough."

Finally, the chihuahua says, "Liver alone ... cheese mine."

BUMPER STICKERS GOING AROUND

- This is it, I don't have another car.
- Warning! I brake for hallucinations.
- Honk if you love peace and quiet.
- My son isn't an honor student. He plays poker.
- So many pedestrians so little time.
- Subvert the dominant paradigm.
- This bumper sticker exploits illiterates.
- Today's mood: Irritable.
- Warning: Dates in Calendar are closer than they appear.
- Welcome to California. Now go home.
- When everything's coming your way, you're in the wrong lane and going the wrong way.
- Your kid may be an honor student but you're still an IDIOT!
- Been there – shit happened.
- Boldly going nowhere.
- Cover me, I'm changing lanes.
- Forget world peace. Visualize using your turn signal.
- For Chrissake, hang up and drive.
- He who hesitates is not only lost but miles from the next exit.
- Honk if you want to see my finger.

- I get enough exercise just pushing my luck.
- Sometimes I wake up grumpy; other times I let him sleep.
- Question reality.
- Chemistry professors never die, they just smell that way!
- Boycott shampoo! Demand REAL poo!
- Microbiology lab: Staph only.
- Honk if anything falls off.
- How can I miss you if you won't go away?
- Santa's elves are just a bunch of subordinate Clauses.
- Eschew obfuscation.
- Ground beef: a cow with no legs!
- A waist is a terrible thing to mind.
- Women who seek to be equal to men lack ambition.
- Post cool.
- A man without a women is like a neck without a pain.
- Make it idiot-proof and someone will make a better idiot.
- Atheism is a non-prophet organization.
- Cole's law: thinly sliced cabbage.
- Does the name Pavlov ring a bell?
- Editing is a rewording activity.
- Everyone is entitled to my opinion.
- Gene Police: YOU! Out of the pool!
- Honk if you're ontologically alienated.
- Help stamp out and eradicate superfluous redundancy.
- I used to be indecisive; now I'm not sure.
- My reality check just bounced.

- Rap is to music what paint by numbers is to art.
- What if there were no hypothetical questions?
- Energizer bunny arrested, charged with battery.
- No sense being pessimistic. It wouldn't work anyway.
- The floggings will continue until morale improves.
- The badness of a movie is directly proportional to the number of helicopters in it.
- You will never find anybody who can give you a clear and compelling reason why we observe Daylight Saving Time.
- Anyone who feels the need to tell you that they have an excellent sense of humour is telling you that they have no sense of humour.
- Real women don't have hot flashes, they have power surges.
- I took an IQ test and the results were negative.
- Where there's a will, I want to be in it.
- A penny saved is worthless.
- Dyslexics have more ufn.
- Clones are people two.
- Dear Auntie Em. Hate you; hate Kansas, taking the dog. Dorothy.
- We're staying together for the sake of the cats.
- It's been lovely, but I have to scream now.
- It's lonely at the top, but you eat better.
- My karma ran over your dogma.
- This is not an abandoned vehicle.
- I don't lie, cheat or steal unnecessarily.
- It's as bad as you think and they are out to get you.
- I'm not paranoid. But that doesn't mean they're not looking at me ...

- Life's too short to dance with ugly men.
- Life's too short to dance with ugly women.
- My wife says if I go fishing one more time, she's going to leave me. Gosh, I'm going to miss her.
- Why is 'abbreviation' such a long word?
- My wife ran off with my best mate. Gee, I miss him …
- I is a college student.
- Six munce ago they sed I would never make prufreader, and now I are one …
- Beer isn't just for breakfast any more.
- Sorry, I don't date outside my species.
- Happiness is seeing your mother-in-law's face on the back of a milk carton.
- Is there life before coffee?
- Never play leap frog with a unicorn.
- The weather is here. Wish you were beautiful.
- I Cayman went.
- My other wife is beautiful.
- I need someone really bad. Are you really bad?
- Nuke the unborn baby whales.
- I came, I saw, I did a little shopping.
- There's one in every crowd and they always find me.
- If money could talk, it would say goodbye.
- When you're in love, you're at the mercy of a stranger.
- Just when you think you've won the rat race, along come faster rats.
- If it's too loud, you're too old.
- Wink. I'll do the rest.
- The worst day fishing is better than the best day working.
- Save the whales, shoot the seals.

- I want to be like Barbie, that bitch gets everything she wants.
- Change is inevitable, except from a vending machine
- Time is what keeps everything from happening at once.
- The more people I meet, the more I like my dog.
- Conserve toilet paper, use both sides.
- Rehab is for quitters.
- I get enough exercise just pushing my luck!
- All men are Idiots, and I married their king!
- Work is for people who don't know how to fish.
- I may be fat, but you're ugly – I can lose weight!
- Reality is a crutch for people who can't handle drugs.
- I'm as confused as a baby in a topless bar!
- Learn from your parents mistakes – use birth control!
- We've got what it takes to take what you have got.
- Time is the best teacher; unfortunately it kills all its students!
- Which came first? The woman or the department store?
- How can I miss you if you won't go away?
- I'm not as think as you drunk I am.
- We are born naked, wet and hungry. Then things get worse.
- Lottery: A tax on people who are bad at math
- Very funny, Scotty. Now beam down my clothes.
- Consciousness: that annoying time between naps.
- Be nice to your kids. They'll choose your nursing home.
- Beauty is in the eye of the beer holder.

- Diplomacy is the art of saying 'Nice doggie!' until you can find a rock.
- I'm out of bed and dressed: What more do you want?
- Who cares who's on board?
- Die yuppie scum.
- No radio. Already stolen.
- Question appearances.
- Crime wouldn't pay if the government ran it.
- Want a taste of religion? Bite a minister.
- Flying saucers are real, the Air Force doesn't exist.
- I don't care who you are, what you are driving, where you would rather be or what you have on board.
- My girlfriend can't wrestle, but you ought to see her box!
- He who laughs last thinks slowest.
- We are Microsoft. Resistance is futile. You will be assimilated.
- Jesus is coming, everyone look busy.
- The more you complain, the longer God lets you live.
- 'Don't worry,' they say, 'he's a nice doggie and will lick you to death.' Personally, I find that an even worse option …
- If at first you do succeed, try not to look astonished.
- Help wanted telepath: you know where to apply
- Jesus loves you … everyone else thinks you're a jerk.
- I'm just driving this way to make you mad.
- Out of my mind. Back in five minutes.
- Keep honking, I'm reloading.
- Hang up and drive.
- Laugh alone and the world thinks you're an idiot.

- Lord, save me from your followers.
- Guns don't kill people, postal workers do.
- I said "no" to drugs, but they just wouldn't listen.
- The gene pool could use a little chlorine.
- If we aren't supposed to eat animals, why are they made of meat?
- Jesus paid for our sins ... now lets get our money's worth.
- Friends help you move. Real friends help you move bodies.
- Puritanism: The haunting fear that someone, somewhere, may be happy.
- Ever stop to think, and forget to start again?
- I like you, but I wouldn't want to see you working with subatomic particles.
- I don't suffer from insanity, I enjoy every minute of it.
- Some people are alive only because it's illegal to kill them.
- A bartender is just a pharmacist with a limited inventory.
- Don't take life too seriously, you won't get out alive.
- You're just jealous because the voices only talk to me.
- I'm not a complete idiot, some parts are missing.
- Horn broken, watch for fist.
- How can I be overdrawn, I still have cheques!
- Prevent inbreeding: ban country music.
- It IS as bad as you think, and they ARE out to get you.
- Always remember you're unique, just like everyone else.

- Three kinds of people: those who can count & those who can't.
- All generalizations are false.
- We have enough youth, how about a fountain of smart?
- I love cats … they taste just like chicken.
- I get enough exercise just pushing my luck.
- I didn't fight my way to the top of the food chain to be a vegetarian.
- Sorry, I don't date outside my species.
- OK, who stopped payment on my reality check?
- Few women admit their age. Fewer men act it.
- Give me ambiguity or give me something else!
- Smile, it's the second best thing you can do with your lips.
- Don't drink and drive … You might hit a bump and spill your drink.
- If you are psychic – think "HONK"
- If you can read this, I can slam on my brakes and sue you!
- Don't get me mad! I'm running out of places to hide the bodies …
- You are depriving some poor village of its idiot!
- My hockey Mom can beat up your soccer Mom
- Grow your own dope, plant a man.
- All men are animals, some just make better pets
- Jesus saves, passes to Moses; he shoots, he SCORES!
- Never say anything to a woman that even remotely suggests you think she's pregnant unless you can see an actual baby emerging from her at that moment.
- If you don't like the news, go out and make some of your own.

- Don't steal. The government hates competition.
- Car service: If it ain't broke, we'll break it.
- Could you drive any better if I shoved that cell phone up your ASS?
- Friends don't let friends drive naked.
- He who hesitates is not only lost but miles from the next exit.
- Honk if you love peace and quiet.
- How can I get in your way when you don't even have one?
- I brake for no apparent reason.
- I don't brake.
- I drive way too fast to worry about cholesterol.
- If you lived in your car, you'd be home by now
- My other car has bumperstickers, too
- Welcome to Victoria now go home.
- *On an old, rusted-out car with plastic bags taped over where the rear window should be, parked in a shopping centre*: This is not an abandoned vehicle.
- *On the back of a bikie's vest*: If you can read this, my wife fell off.
- *On a painted-up custom shaggin' wagon:* Don't laugh, your daughter may be inside!
- *On an upside down Jeep:* If you can read this, please flip me back over ...

HOW TO DESCRIBE
THESE . . . ?

James had smelly feet. They stank. In fact, they were so smelly and he was so embarrassed about them that he felt that he would never be able to marry.

Mary had a chronic case of halitosis. Her breath ponged. She was so self conscious about it that she always held a handkerchief in front of her mouth.

One day they met. They began a courtship that progressed without either one of them knowing about the other's problem. James never took his shoes off; Mary never took the handkerchief from her mouth.

They married. On their wedding night James was preparing for bed in the bathroom. He had taken with him all manner of things to quell the smelly feet, and after a session of scrubbing and deodorizing, it was Mary's turn to use the bathroom.

She was equally nervous and had brought with her an array of mouth fresheners and mints to sweeten her breath.

She was in the bathroom when James remembered to his horror that he had left his smelly socks in there. There seemed to be nothing left to do but confess to his smelly feet.

Mary was thinking the same thing. "I must tell him about my condition now," she thought to herself.

She opened the bathroom door, and there stood James.

"I have something I must tell you!" she blurted.

"I know," said James, getting a whiff of her breath that nearly made him pass out, "you have eaten my socks."

One fine morning in Eden, God was looking for Adam and Eve, but couldn't find them. Later in the day God saw Adam and asked where he and Eve were earlier. Adam said, "This morning Eve and I made love for the first time."

God said, "Adam, you have sinned. I knew this would happen. Where is Eve now?"

Adam replied, "She's down at the river, washing herself out."

"Damn," says God, "now all the fish will smell funny."

F... ME DEAD!

English is a funny old language. Pain, pleasure, hate and love. The same word can cover them all.

"F..." just about covers everything.

It can be used as verb both transitive (Tom f...ed Betty).

And intransitive (Betty was f...ed by Tom).

It can be an active verb (Tom really gives a f...).

Or a passive verb (Betty really doesn't give a f...).

It can be used as a noun (Betty is a fine f...).

It can be used as an adjective (Betty is f...ing beautiful).

It can be used to describe the whole spectrum of

emotions:

Aggression:	F… you.
Confusion:	What the f…?
Despair:	F…ed again.
Difficulty:	I can't understand this f…ing business.
Dismay:	Oh, f… it!
Displeasure:	What the f… is going on?
Fraud:	I got f…ed by my insurance agent.
Incompetence:	He's all f…ed up.
Laziness:	He just f…s about.
Passive:	F… me.
Philosophical:	Who gives a f…?
Problem:	I guess I'm f…ed now.
Rebellion:	F… off!
Religious:	Holy F….
Surprise:	F…ing Incredible!

It can be used to tell time – It's five f…ing thirty.

It can be used in business – How did he get that f…ing job?

It can be a prediction – Oh, will I get f…ed!

It can have maternal connotations – as in Motherf…er.

It can be nautical – F… the Admiral.

It can be political – F… Bush.

It can open the door to wonderful relationships – Let's f….

It can be used to enhance the meaning of a word –
        beautif…ingful, terf…ingific or absof…inglutely.

How could anyone be offended when you say f…?

Tell someone, "f… you," today.

But not your mother …

Waiter: Tea or coffee, gentlemen?
First customer: I'll have tea.
Second customer: Me, too. And be sure the glass is clean!
Waiter exits and returns.
Waiter: Two teas. Which one asked for the clean glass?

There were three lunatics who were walking down the road when they came across a huge pile of shit.
The first loony put his eye in it and said, "Looks like shit."
The next one put his nose in it and said, "Smells like shit."
The last one put his tongue in it and said, "Tastes like shit."
They all looked at each other and said, "Lucky we didn't stand in it!"

What did the Mathematician do when he was constipated? He worked it out with a pencil!

A man goes to the doctor. Every time he walks, he farts. He arrives at the doctors and walks in, "Parp! Fumph! Toot! Poop!" go his bowels.
He sits down and the doctor tells him to walk across the room to show him the problem. He walks across the room and again his arse explodes with each stride, "Parp! Fumph! Toot! Poop!" He walks back to his seat, "Toot! Fumph! Parp! Poop!"

He sits down and the doctor says, "I know what I'm going to do!" He goes to his cupboard and brings out a giant pole with a great big hook on the end of it.

The fellow looks in horror and says, "Jeez, Doc, what the bloody hell are you gonna do with that?"

The doctor replies, "I'm going to open the window, of course. This place stinks!"

A guy sits down in a cafe and asks for the hot chilli. The waitress says, "The guy next to you got the last bowl." He looks over and sees that the guy's finished his meal, but the chilli bowl is still full.

He says, "Are you going to eat that?"

The other guy says, "No. Help yourself."

He takes it and starts to eat. When he gets about half way down, his fork hits something. He looks down sees a dead mouse in it, and he pukes all of the chilli back into the bowl.

The other guy says, "That's about as far as I got, too."

AN ACTUAL STORY

Eric Tomaszewski had to tell the sorry tale to amused and bemused doctors in the severe burns unit of Salt Lake City Hospital.

"In retrospect, lighting the match was my big mistake. But I was only trying to retrieve the gerbil," he said.

Tomaszewski and gay partner Andrew (Kiki) Farnom had been admitted for emergency treatment after a felching session had gone wrong.

"I pushed a cardboard tube up his rectum and slipped Raggot, our gerbil, in," Tomaszewski explained. "As usual, Kiki shouted out 'Armageddon.'

That's my cue that he'd had enough. I tried to retrieve Raggot but he wouldn't come out again, so I peered into the tube and struck a match, thinking that the light might attract him."

A hospital spokesman later described to a hushed press conference what happened next.

"The match ignited a pocket of intestinal gas and a flame shot out of the tubing, igniting Mr. Tomaszewski's hair and severely burning his face," he said. "It also set fire to the gerbil's fur and whiskers which in turn ignited a larger pocket of gas further up the intestine, propelling the rodent out like a cannonball."

Tomaszewski suffered second degree burns and a broken nose from the impact of the gerbil. Farnom suffered first and second degree burns to his anus and lower intestinal tract.

It is rumoured that the gerbil has gone off to write about his experiences and is already in discussion with three Hollywood producers.

PICKING YOUR NOSE

1.   *Deep Salvage Pick.*
     Reminiscent of the deep sea exploration to find the
     Titanic, you probe deep into your nasal passages.

2. *Utensil Pick*.
   When fingers, and even your thumb, just aren't enough to get the job done to your satisfaction.

3. *Extra Pick*.
   When you have been digging for nuggets hours upon hours and suddenly you hit the jackpot! Excitement only equalled by winning the lottery.

4. *Depression Pick*.
   When you are sad, and the only way to fill the void is to pick so hard and fast that the agony overcomes your feeling of remorse and depression.

5. *Pick A Lot*.
   What we would call abnormal amounts of picking. Anything in the three digit realm we consider a bit too much for a 24 hour time frame.

6. *Kiddie Pick*.
   When you're by yourself and you uninhibitedly twist your forefinger into your nostril with childlike joy and freedom. And the best part is, there's no time limit!

7. *Camouflaged Kiddie Pick*.
   When, in the presence of other people, you wrap your forefinger in a tissue, then thrust it in deep and hold back the smile.

8. *Fake Nose Scratch*.
   When you make believe you've got an itch but you're really trolling the nostril edge for stray boogers.

9. *Making A Meal Out Of It*.
   You do it so furiously, and for so long, you're probably entitled to dessert.

10. *Surprise Pickings*.
    When a sneeze or laugh causes snot to come hurling out of your nose, and you have to gracefully clean it off your shirt.
11. *Autopick*.
    The kind you do in a car, when no one's looking. Also can mean automatic pick, the one you do when you're not even thinking about it, at work, while talking to a co-worker, during a meeting.
12. *Pick Your Brains*.
    Done in private, this is the one where your finger goes in so far, it passes the septum.
13. *Pick And Save*.
    When you have to pick it quickly, just when someone looks away, and then you pocket the snot so they don't catch on to what you did.
14. *Pick And Flick*.
    Snot now becomes a weapon against your sister and others in range around you.
15. *Pick And Stick*.
    You wanted it to be a "Pick And Flick," but it stubbornly clings to your fingertip.
16. *Pipe Cleaner Pick*.
    The kind where you remove a piece of snot so big, it improves your breathing by 90%.

This guy comes home from work one day to find his dog with the neighbor's pet rabbit in his mouth.

The rabbit is very dead and the guy panics.

He thinks the neighbors are going to hate him forever, so he takes the dirty, chewed-up rabbit into the house, gives it a bath, blow-dries its fur, and puts the rabbit back into the cage at the neighbor's house, hoping that they will think it died of natural causes.

A few days later, the neighbor is outside and asks the guy, "Did you hear that Fluffy died?"

The guy stumbles around and says, "What happened?"

The neighbor replies, "We just found him dead in his cage one day, but the weird thing is that the day after we buried him we went outside and someone had dug him up, gave him a bath and put him back into the cage. There must be some real sick people out there!"

A publican is shutting for the night when there is a knock at the door. He answers, and a tramp asks him for a tooth-pick. He gives him the tooth-pick and tramp goes off.

A few minutes later there is another knock on the door. When he answers there is another tramp there who also asks him for a tooth-pick. He gets the tooth-pick and off he goes.

There is a third knock at the door, and a third tramp. The publican says, "Don't tell me, you want a tooth-pick too?"

"No, I'd like a straw, please."

The publican gives him a straw but is curious as to why he wants it, so he asks the tramp why he does he want a straw and not a toothpick.

The tramp replies, "One of your patrons threw up outside, but all the good stuff is gone already."

A man goes into a bar and asks for shots of drinks. He has a shot of tequila then vomits.

He has another shot then vomits. He does this several times.

A leper comes over and says, "I'm sorry if my appearance is making you sick."

"No, it's not your fault," the man says, "it's the guy next to you dipping his chips in your neck."

SEX LAWS AROUND THE WORLD

Next time you are having a quiet nookie, consider the approach to sex of some other societies around the world:

- In Cali, Columbia, a woman may only have sex with her husband, and the first time this happens, her mother must be in the room to witness the act.
- The penalty for masturbation in Indonesia is decapitation.
- In Hong Kong, a betrayed wife is legally allowed to kill her adulterous husband, but may only do so with her bare hands. The husband's lover, on the other hand, may be killed in any manner desired.
- Most middle eastern countries recognize the following Islamic law: "After having sexual relations with a lamb, it is a mortal sin to eat its flesh."
- In Lebanon, men are legally allowed to have sex with animals, but the animals must be female. Having sexual relations with a male animal is punishable by death.

- In Bahrain, a male doctor may legally examine a woman's genitals, but is forbidden from looking directly at them during the examination. He may only see their reflection in a mirror.
- Muslims are banned from looking at the genitals of a corpse. This also applies to undertakers. The sex organs of the deceased must be covered with a brick or piece of wood at all times.
- There are men in Guam whose full-time job is to travel the countryside and deflower young virgins, who pay them for the privilege of having sex for the first time. Reason: under Guam law, it is expressly forbidden for virgins to marry.
- Topless saleswomen are legal in Liverpool, England – but only in tropical fish stores.
- In Santa Cruz, Bolivia, it is illegal for a man to have sex with a woman and her daughter at the same time.
- In Maryland, U.S.A., it is illegal to sell condoms from vending machines with one exception: prophylactics may be dispensed from a vending machine only "in places where alcoholic beverages are sold for consumption on the premises."

GOING WILD IN THE LIBRARY

The library is usually the place where bookish types, academics, people with inch-thick glasses and little old ladies gather in something approaching total quiet.

They need you in there, to brighten things up. Here are 20 ways to make a day at the library a bit of fun.

1. Read your book upside down.
2. Read your book from right to left, flipping the pages that way to make it obvious.
3. Grab a 1000-page book, thump it down, and begin reading – flipping a page every two seconds.
4. Every so often, yelp in pain, and look at your feet.
5. Break the silence by making a noise as if you have dropped a monstrous fart, then say, "Wow! That was a good 'un!"
6. Read out very loudly and very slowly.
7. While pointing to a very simple word, like 'the', ask the person next to you if he/she can pronounce it for you.
8. Look over your book and say, "You! I know you! You're one of THEM!"
9. Every time the person next to you turns the page, make a beeping noise.

10. Announce the page number each time you turn a page.

11. Glance over your shoulder every few seconds.

12. Do multiple sneezes, at full volume.

13. While looking at your book, turn so you're facing the person. Then, peer over the top of your book, and say, "Peekaboo!!"

14. Hold your book right next to your eyes.

15. Pretend you have a nervous, involuntary tic, which concludes with you shouting, "Oooh-ahhh."

16. Find a thesaurus and say in complete astonishment, "Wow! Did you know that 'negative' and 'no' mean the same thing?"

17. Every few minutes, get up out of your chair, walk around the table, and sit back down.

18. Crawl under the table, and pretend you are asleep, snoring very loudly.

19. Bring a bottle of mouth freshener, miss when you try to spray it into your mouth, get it in your eye, scream in agony, and roll on the floor clutching your eye.

20. Collapse on the floor. Do twenty push-ups, shouting, "Yes, Sergeant, I've been a bad, bad soldier and twenty push-ups will make a man of me." Then get up like nothing happened.

LOVE ... AND MARRIAGE

A woman announces to her friend that she is getting married for the fourth time.

"How wonderful! But I hope you don't mind me asking what happened to your first husband?"

"He ate poisonous mushrooms and died."

"Oh, how tragic! What about your second husband?"

"He ate poisonous mushrooms too and died."

"Oh, how terrible! I'm almost afraid to ask you about your third husband."

"He died of a broken neck."

"A broken neck?"

"He wouldn't eat the mushrooms ..."

A young couple, were in their honeymoon suite on their wedding night. As they undressed for bed the husband, who was a big burly man, tossed his pants to his bride and said, "Here, put these on."

She put them on and the waist was twice the size of her body. "I can't wear your pants," she said.

"That's right!!" said the husband, "And don't you forget it. I'm the one who wears the pants in this family!"

With that she threw him her panties and said, "Try these on."

He looked at her incredulously.

"Go on!" she urged, "Go on."

He reluctantly tried them on and found he could only get them on as far as his kneecap.

He said, "Hell, I can't get into your panties!"

She said, "That's right, and that's the way it's going to be until your attitude changes!"

Then there was the elderly gentleman who had serious hearing problems for years. He went to the doctor who was able to have him fitted for a set of hearing aids that allowed the man to hear 100%.

The old bloke went back in a month to the doctor and the doctor said, "Your hearing is perfect. Your family must be really pleased that you can hear again."

To which the gentleman said, "Oh, I haven't told my family yet. I just sit around and listen to the conversations. I've changed my will three times!"

The doctor had to tell the husband that his wife would have to be admitted to a psychiatric hospital.

"I'm afraid her mind's completely gone," he said.

"I'm not surprised," said the husband. "She's been giving me a piece of it every day for the past 15 years."

I only get five miles to the gallon in my car. My teenage children get the other twenty!

Two parents take their son on a vacation and go to a nude beach. The father goes for a walk on the beach and the son goes and plays in the water.

The son comes running up to his mom and says, "Mummy, I saw ladies with boobies a lot bigger than yours!"

The mother says, "The bigger they are, the dumber they are."

So he goes back to play. Several minutes later he comes running back and says, "Mummy, I saw men with dingers a lot bigger than Daddy's!"

The mother says, "The bigger they are, the dumber they are."

So he goes back to play. Several minutes later he comes running back and says, "Mummy, I just saw Daddy talking to the dumbest lady I have ever seen! And he's looking dumber by the minute ..."

A young husband e-mailed home from his job: "Made foreman. Feather in my cap."

A few days later he wrote: "Made Manager. Another feather."

After weeks of silence he sent: "Fired. Send money for bus fare."

His wife e-mailed back: "Use feathers and fly home"

And did you hear about the couple that, after 20 years of marriage finally achieved sexual compatibility. They both had headaches!

A man observed a woman in the supermarket with a three year old girl in her basket. As they passed the biscuit section, the little girl asked for chocolate biscuits and her mother told her, "No."

The little girl immediately began to whine and fuss, and the mother said quietly, "Now Mary, we just have half of the aisles left to go through – don't be upset. It won't be long now."

Soon, they came to the candy aisle and the little girl began to shout for candy. When told she couldn't have any, she began to cry. The mother said, "There, there, Mary, don't cry – only two more aisles to go and then we'll be checking out."

When they got to the checkout stand, the little girl immediately began to clamor for gum and burst into a terrible tantrum when told there would be no gum purchased. The mother said serenely, "Mary, we'll be through this check out stand in five minutes and then you can go home and have a nice nap."

The man followed them out to the parking lot and stopped the woman to compliment her. "I couldn't help noticing how patient you were with little Mary here," he began, pointing at the little girl.

The mother replied, "She's Jessie. I'm Mary ..."

Marriage is the price men pay for sex. Sex is the price women pay for marriage.

After the party, as the couple was driving home, the woman asks her husband, "Honey, has anyone ever told you how handsome, sexy and irresistible to women you are?"

The flattered husband said, "No, dear they haven't."

The wife yells, "Then what the heck gave you THAT idea!"

A Welshman, a Scot and an Irishman are sitting in a pub a couple of days after Christmas.

The Welshman asks, "What did you give your wife for Christmas?"

The Scot replies, "A diamond ring and a pair of gloves."

"Why the gloves?" asks the Welshman.

"Well, if she doesn't like the ring, she can wear the gloves to cover it," he replied.

"I got mine a necklace and a polo-neck sweater," the Welshman said. "If she doesn't like the necklace, she can wear the polo-neck sweater to cover it".

"Perfectly logical," agrees the Scot.

They then ask the Irishman, "What did you buy your wife for Christmas?"

The Irishman replied, "I got her a handbag and a vibrator"

"That's an odd combination, why those two items?" says the Welshman.

"Well, if she doesn't like the handbag, she can get screwed!"

There was a boy who wasn't developing very well in his 'down-stairs department', so his mum took him to the doctor to get him examined and see if there was anything that could be done.

"Well there isn't much wrong," said the doctor, "but if you feed him lots of toast, it should soon rectify itself."

The next day, the boy comes home from school and there is a huge pile of toast on the table – about twenty pieces high.

"Awwhh, mum, is that all for me?" said the boy.

"No, son, the top two slices are for you – the rest is for your dad!"

A market researcher called at a house and his knock was answered by a young woman with three small children running around her. He asked her if she minded replying to his questions.

She agreed, so he asked her if she knew his company, Ponds. When she answered no, he mentioned that among their many products was Vaseline. She certainly knew of that product. When asked if she used it, she answered "yes."

Asked how she used it, she said, "To assist sexual intercourse."

The interviewer was amazed.

He said, "I always ask that question because everyone uses our product and they always say they use it for the child's bicycle chain, or the gate hinge; but I know that most use it for sexual intercourse, yet they are too sheepish to say so. Since you've been so frank, could you tell me exactly how you use it?"

"Yes," she said, "We put it on the doorknob."

"The doorknob?" the man replied incredulously.

"Yes, to keep the kids out ..."

A dad was explaining the facts of life to his son. He covered the basic biology, and then moved on to the finer points of love-making.

Dad: "All women are different son. One thing to keep in mind is that different women say different things during the act, even if you are doing the same thing."

Son: "What do you mean, Dad?"

Dad: "Their words will vary according to their occupation. For example, a prostitute will tend to say, 'Are you done yet?'"

Son: "I see."

Dad: "On the other hand, a nymphomaniac will ask, 'Are you done already?'"

Son: "Go on."

Dad: "A school teacher will say, 'We are going to do this over and over again until you get it right!'"

Son: "Wow!"

Dad: "A nurse will say, 'This won't hurt one bit.' A bank teller will say, 'Substantial penalty for early withdrawal.' And a stewardess will say, 'Place this over your mouth and nose and breathe normally.'"

Son: "Gee, Dad, and what does mum say?"

Dad: "She says, 'Beige ... beige ... I think we should paint the ceiling beige.'"

Three men are arguing about when exactly does life begin? The first one says, "At the time of conception."

"At the time of birth," argues the next.

"Oh, no," says the third. "Life begins when the wife takes the children and they all leave for vacation."

When the young couple married, the wife put a wooden box under the marital bed and warned her husband not to ever open it until she was dead. Time passed and although the husband was sometimes curious, he never broke trust and looked in the box.

After twenty years the wife became unwell and had to spend a lot of time in hospital undergoing surgery. The husband found the evenings long and uneventful in his wife's absence, and one night he couldn't help himself and opened the wooden box.

Inside he found three eggs and $50,000 in notes. He returned them to the box, but when he wife returned from hospital, he asked her to explain.

"What are the eggs for?" he asked.

She looked at him for a long time, and then finally spoke,

"Every time I have been unfaithful to you and our marriage I put an egg in the box."

After thinking for a bit, the man reasoned that three instances of betrayal in twenty years wasn't too bad in this day and age. "Fair enough. That's okay, darling. But what about the $50,000?" he asked.

The wife replied, "Every time I got a dozen I sold them."

A husband is about to leave on a business trip, "Honey, if my business requires me to stay longer in that town, I'll send you a card."

"Don't bother, dear. I read it already – it's in the pocket of your coat."

Matthew's dad picked him up from school to take him to a dental appointment. Knowing the parts for the school play were supposed to be posted that day, he asked his son if he got a part.

Matthew enthusiastically announced that he'd gotten a part. "I play a man who's been married for twenty-five years."

"That's great, son. Keep up the good work and before you know it they'll be giving you a speaking part."

"**Y**ou and your husband don't seem to have an awful lot in common," said the new tenant's neighbor. "Why on earth did you get married?"

"I suppose it was the old business of 'opposites attract,'" was the reply. "He wasn't pregnant and I was."

Two blokes were out walking home from work one afternoon. "Shit," said the first bloke, "as soon as I get home, I'm gonna rip the wife's knickers off!"

"What's the rush?" his mate asked.

"The bloody elastic in them is killing me …"

This bloke called Chris goes over to his friend's house, rings the bell, and the wife answers.

"Hi, is Tony home?" he asks.

"No, he went to the store."

"Well, you mind if I wait?"

"No, come in."

They sit down and the friend says, "You know Tina, you have the greatest breasts I have ever seen. I'd give you a hundred bucks if I could just see one."

Nora thinks about this for a second and figures what the hell – a hundred bucks. She opens her robe and shows one. He promptly thanks her and throws a hundred bucks on the table.

They sit there a while longer and Chris says, "They are so beautiful I've got to see the both of them. I'll give you another hundred bucks if I could just see the both of them together."

Nora thinks about this and thinks what the hell, opens her robe, and gives Chris a nice long look. Chris thanks her, throws another hundred bucks on the table, and then says he can't wait any longer and leaves.

A while later Tony arrives home and his wife says, "You know, your weird friend Chris came over."

Tony thinks about this for a second and says, "Well, did he drop off the two hundred bucks he owes me?"

Little James tells his mother how much fun he and his father had while she was interstate for five days on a business trip.

"Everyday Aunt Miriam visited us and brought candy for me. Daddy entertained her with wine, and then they did the same thing you and Uncle Dick do when dad is out of town."

"Get this," said the bloke to his mates. "Last night while I was down the pub with you blokes, a burglar broke into my house.

"Did he get anything?" his mates asked.

"Yeah, a broken jaw, six teeth knocked out, and a pair of broken nuts. Poor bastard. The wife thought it was me coming home drunk."

Then there was the bloke who decided that it was time to teach his son how to say prayers. This included choosing someone special and asking for God's blessing for that person.

The first night the little boy said his prayers, he ended with, "And God, please bless my puppy." However, the next morning the little dog ran out the door and was killed by a car.

That night the little kid asked, "God, please bless my cat."

And, sure enough, the next morning the cat slipped out and took on the biggest dog in the neighborhood and lost. They buried him in the back yard.

When the kid asked God to bless his goldfish, the fish was found floating upside down on the top.

That night the little kid ended with, "God, please give an extra special blessing to my father."

Well, the father couldn't sleep. He couldn't eat breakfast in the morning. He was afraid to drive to work. He couldn't get any work done because he was petrified. Finally quitting time came and he walked home, expecting to drop dead any minute.

When he arrived home, the house was a mess. His wife was lying on the couch still dressed in her robe. The dishes from breakfast were still on the table, and nothing had happened all day.

The father was furious. He yelled at his wife, telling her that he had had the worst day of his life and yet she hadn't even gotten dressed.

She looked at him and said, "Don't go on, darling, my day was far worse. The postman had a heart attack and died on the front porch!"

A husband was coming out of anaesthesia after some tests in the hospital. His wife was sitting at his bedside.

His eyes fluttered open, and he murmured, "You're beautiful."

Flattered, his wife continued her vigil while he drifted back to sleep.

Later he woke up and said, "You're cute."

"What happened to beautiful?" the wife asked him.

"The drugs are wearing off," he replied.

MASHED TATORS AND OTHERS

- Some people never seem motivated to participate, but are content to watch others do everything. These layabouts are called "Speck-Tators."
- Some people never do anything to help, but are gifted at finding fault with the way others do things. These types pick on everybody and are called "Comment-Tators."
- Some are always looking to cause problems and really get under your skin. They can't help themselves and are always looking for a fight. They are called "Aggie-Tators."
- There are those who are always saying they will do something for you, but somehow, they never get around to doing it. There's always a reason to put it off until another time. We call them "Hezzie-Tators."
- Some people put on a front and act like someone else. They make out as if they are richer or more handsome or more powerful than they really are. They're called "Emma-Tators."
- Finally, there is that other group of smart-arses that, really, can't keep their hands off themselves. They're called "Mastur-Tators." Or something like that, you know what I mean …

DIVORCE ME, YOU BASTARD!

A man was reading the paper when an ad caught his eye. It loudly announced, "Porsche! New, $500!"

The man thought that it was very unusual to sell a Porsche for $500, and he thought it might be a joke, but he said to himself, "It's worth a shot."

So he went to the lady's house who was selling the Porsche and she led him into the garage. Sure enough, there was an almost brand new Porsche.

"Wow!" the man said. "Can I take it for a test drive?"

"Sure," answered the lady. Unlike what he expected, the man found that the car ran perfectly.

When he got back to the lady's house, and handed over the $500, he asked her, "Why are you selling me this great Porsche for only $500?"

Then the lady replied with a laugh, "My mongrel of a husband just ran off with his big-busted, blonde secretary, and he told me, 'You can keep the house and the furniture, just sell my Porsche and send me the money.'"

The miserly husband was berating his long suffering wife about the bills. "Look at the water usage. It's exorbitant. You spend far too much time in the bath, you're obsessive about keeping those children clean. And the electricity bill is up in the three digits."

He went on, "You have the lights on all night doing the sewing you take in, and not to mention the ironing business you have going at home. It just burns up the electricity and you expect me to pay for it."

"And," he exploded, holding out another bill, "look at this massive gas bill. You and all those suicide attempts!"

A farmer walked into a lawyer's office. The lawyer asked, "May I help you?"

The farmer said, "Yes, I want to get one of those divorces."

"Well do you have any grounds?"

"Yes, I got about two hundred acres."

"No, you don't understand, do you have a case?"

The farmer said, "No, I don't have a Case, but I have a John Deere."

The lawyer said, "No, I mean do you have a grudge?"

"Yeah I got a grudge. That's where I park my John Deere."

"No sir, I mean do you have a suit?"

"Yes sir, I got a suit. But I only wear it to church on Sundays."

Fuming, the lawyer said, "Well sir, does your wife beat you up or anything?"

"No sir, we both get up about 4:30 am."

Finally, the lawyer says, "Okay, let me put it this way. Why do you want a divorce?"

"Well, I can never seem to have a meaningful conversation with her ..."

YOU KNOW YOU ARE A CHILD OF THE EIGHTIES IF

1. You had a Swatch watch.
2. You had a crush on one of the New Kids on the Block.
3. You wanted to be on *Star Search*.
4. You can remember what Michael Jackson looked like before his nose fell off.
5. You can name at least half of the members of the Brat Pack.'
6. You wore a banana clip.
7. You wore slap on wrist band.
8. You thought Jon Bon Jovi's hair was cool.
9. You had slouch socks, and puff paint on your shirt.
10. You know the profound meaning of "Wax on, Wax off."
11. You can recite the whole script for *Grease* and *Grease 2*.
12. You have seen at least 10 episodes of *Fraggle Rock*.
13. You know that another name for a keyboard is a Synthesizer.'
14. You hold a special place in your heart for *Back to the Future*.

15. You had big hair, crimped, combed over to the side.
16. You wore spandex pants.
17. You owned an extensive collection of Cabbage Patch Kids.
18. You wore fluorescent clothing.
19. You could break dance.
20. You wished you could break dance.
21. You remember when ATARI was a state of the art video game system, especially the Ping Pong game.
22. You own any cassettes.
23. You believed that by 2000 we'd all be living on the moon.
24. You own any of the CareBear Glass collection from Pizza Hut.
25. Poltergeist freaked you out.
26. You carried your lunch to school in a *Gremlins* lunchbox.
27. You pondered why Smurfette was the only female Smurf.
28. You remember when *Saturday Night Live* was funny.
29. You wanted to have an alien like Alf living in your house.
30. You wore biker shorts underneath a short skirt and felt stylish.
31. You wore tights under shorts and felt stylish.
32. You spent countless hours trying to perfect the Care-Bear stare.
33. You had Wonder Woman or Superman underwear.
34. Partying "like it's 1999" seemed SO far away.

POLICE & CRIME

A squad car driver was covering a quiet beat out in the sticks, when he was amazed to find a former lieutenant on the police force covering the same beat.

He stopped the car and asked, "Why, Smithson, this wouldn't be your new beat way out here in the sticks, would it?"

"That it is," Smithson replied grimly, "ever since I arrested Judge McGonigal on his way to the masquerade ball."

"You mean you pinched his honor?" asked the officer.

"How was I to know that his convict suit was only a costume," said Smithson.

"Well," mused the officer, "this is life, there's a lesson in this somewhere."

"That there is," replied Smithson. "Never book a judge by his cover …"

A burglar had been casing a particular house for some time. Finally, he saw the owners leave for what appeared to be an extended holiday.

That night he broke in through a basement window. He was trying to find his way in the dark when he heard what seemed to him to be the crackly voice of a very old woman saying, "Shame on you! I see you, and Jesus is watching you!"

Startled, the burglar snarls back, "Shut up, Grandma, or you're gonna get hurt! And none of that religious crap, either."

He shines his flashlight all around, but no Grandma.

Again the voice, "Shame on you! I see you, and Jesus is watching you!"

The burglar warns again, "I'll get you Grandma, and don't think any of that religious stuff is going to scare me."

Finally, the beam of the flashlight finds a large cage, and in it a parrot. Relieved, the burglar turns around and starts toward the stairs, only to spot an enormous growling, slobbering doberman, its teeth bared, waiting at the top.

The crackly voice comes from the cage, "Go straight for his nuts, Jesus!"

Then there was the farmer who had been involved in a terrible road accident with a large truck. He ended up in court fighting for a big compensation claim.

"I understand you're claiming damages for the injuries you're supposed to have suffered?" said the counsel for the insurance company.

"Yes, that's right," replied the farmer, nodding his head.

"You claim you were injured in the accident, yet I have a signed police statement that says that when the attending police officer asked you how you were feeling, you replied, 'I've never felt better in my life.' Is that the case?"

"Yeah, but ..." stammered the farmer.

"A simple yes or no will suffice," counsel interrupted quickly.

"Yes," replied the farmer quietly.

Then it was the turn of the farmer's counsel to ask him questions. "Please tell the court the exact circumstance of events following the accident when you made your statement of health," his lawyer said.

"Certainly," replied the farmer. "After the accident my horse was thrashing around with a broken leg and my poor old dog was howling in pain. This cop comes along, takes one look at my horse and shoots him dead.

"Then he goes over to my dog, looks at him and shoots him dead too.

"Then he comes straight over to me, with his gun still smoking, and asks me how I was feeling.

"Now, mate, what the hell would you have said to him?"

Three convicts were on the way to prison. They were each allowed to take one item with them to help them occupy their time while incarcerated.

On the bus, one turned to another and said, "So, what did you bring?"

The second convict pulled out a box of paints and stated that he intended to use his time to paint anything he could.

He asked the first, "What did you bring?"

The first convict pulled out a deck of cards and grinned and said, "I brought cards. I won't be bored. I can play poker, solitaire and gin, and any number of games."

The third convict sat quietly aside, grinning to himself.

The other two noticed and asked, "Why are you so smug? What did you bring?"

The guy pulled out a box of tampons, smiled, and said, "I brought these."

"What can you do with those?" the others asked, puzzled.

He grinned and pointed to the box and replied, "Well according to the box, I can go horseback riding, swimming, roller-skating ..."

Somebody actually complimented me on my driving today. They left a note on the windscreen that said, 'Parking Fine.'

So that was nice.

---

20 STATEMENTS TO AVOID WHEN YOU'VE BEEN PULLED OVER

1. Officer, could you hold my beer, please, while I look for my licence?
2. Wow, you must've been doin' about 125 mph to keep up with me. Good job!
3. Gee, Porky, I thought you had to be in relatively good physical condition to be a police officer.
4. Sorry, Officer, I didn't realize my radar detector wasn't turned on.
5. You're not gonna check the trunk, are you?
6. I was trying to keep up with traffic. Yes, I know there are no other cars around. That's how far ahead of me they are.
7. Gee, Officer! That's terrific. The last officer only gave me a warning, too!

8. Listen, pal, I pay your salary!
9. I only had three officers Mr. Beer …
10. Want to race to the station, Sparky?
11. On the way to the station let's get a six pack.
12. You'll never get those cuffs on me … you big pussy!
13. Come on write the friggin' ticket, the bar closes in twenty minutes!
14. How long is this going to take? Your wife is expecting me.
15. Hey big boy, is that your nightstick or are you just glad to see me?
16. You know, I was going to be cop, too, but I decided to finish seventh grade instead.
17. So, uh, are you on-the-take, or what?
18. Do you know why you pulled me over? Good, at least one of us does.
19. So are you still a little crabby because your mother didn't let you play with your gun when you were little?
20. Hey, aren't you one of the Village People …?

All the toilet seats mysteriously disappeared from the Police station last night. The Police have nothing to go on!

A young man, sporting a skinhead hair-style, had started to work on a farm. The boss sent him to the back paddocks to do some fencing work, but come evening, he's half an hour late.

The boss gets on the CB radio to check if he's all right.

"I've got a problem, boss. I'm stuck 'ere. I've hit a pig!"

"Ah well, these things happen sometimes," the boss says. "Just drag the carcass off the road so nobody else hits it in the dark."

"But he's not dead, boss. He's gotten tangled up on the bull-bar, and I've tried to untangle him, but he's kicking and squealing, and he's real big boss. I'm afraid he's gonna hurt me!"

"Never mind," says the boss. "There's a .303 under the tarp in the back. Get that out and shoot him. Then drag the carcass off the road and come on home."

"Okay, boss."

Another half an hour goes by, but there's still not a peep from the kid. The boss gets back on the CB. "What's the problem, son?"

"Well, I did what you said boss, but I'm still stuck."

"What's up? Did you drag the pig off the road like I said?"

"Yeah boss, but his motorcycle is still jammed under the truck …"

A highway patrolman waited outside a popular bar, hoping for a bust. At closing time everyone came out and he spotted his potential quarry.

The man was so obviously inebriated that he could barely walk. He stumbled around the parking lot for a few minutes, looking for his car. After trying his keys on five other cars, he finally found his own vehicle.

He sat in the car a good ten minutes, as the other patrons left. He turned his lights on, then off, wipers on, then off. He started to pull forward into the grass, then he stopped.

Finally, when everyone had left, he pulled out onto the road and started to drive away.

The patrolman, waiting for this, turned on his lights and pulled the man over. He administered the breathalyser test, and to his great surprise, the man blew a 0.00.

The patrolman was dumbfounded. "This equipment must be broken!" he exclaimed.

"I doubt it," said the man. "Tonight I am the designated decoy!"

A man in his 40's bought a new BMW and was out on the interstate for a nice evening drive. The top was down, the breeze was blowing through what was left of his hair, and he decided to open her up.

As the needle jumped up to 80 mph, he suddenly saw flashing red and blue lights behind him. "There's no way they can catch a BMW," he thought to himself and opened her up further.

The needle hit 90, 100 ... then the reality of the situation hit him. "What the hell am I doing?" he thought and pulled over.

The cop came up to him, took his license without a word, and examined it and the car. "It's been a long day," said the cop, "this is the end of my shift, and it's Friday the

13th. I don't feel like more paperwork, so if you can give me an excuse for your driving that I haven't heard before, you can go."

The guy thinks for a second and says, "Last week my wife ran off with a cop. I was afraid you were trying to give her back."

"Have a nice weekend," said the officer.

OXYMORONS

The A to Z of oxymorons – sublime examples of superb self-contradiction.

- Advanced BASIC.
- Airline food.
- British fashion.
- Business ethics.
- Childproof.
- Christian Scientists.
- Civil War.
- Computer jock.
- Computer security.
- Diet ice cream.
- Extinct life.
- Found missing.
- Freezer burn.
- Friendly fire.
- Genuine imitation.
- Good grief.
- Government organization.
- Happily married.
- Holy war.
- Honest politician.
- Jumbo shrimp.
- Legally drunk.

- Living dead.
- Loners Club.
- Military intelligence.
- New classic.
- New York culture.
- Peace force.
- Plastic glasses.
- Political science.
- Postal service.
- Rap music.
- Religious tolerance.
- Sanitary landfill.
- Small crowd.
- Soft rock.
- Software documentation.
- Synthetic natural gas.
- Taped live.
- Temporary tax increase.
- Tight slacks.
- Working vacation.

OLD PEOPLE

An old man gets on a crowded bus and no one gives him a seat. As the bus shakes and rattles, the old man's cane slips on the floor and he falls.

As he gets up, a seven-year-old kid, sitting nearby, turns to him and says, "If you put a little rubber thingy on the end of your stick, it wouldn't slip."

The old man snaps back, "Well, if your daddy did the same thing seven years ago, I would have a seat today."

My grandfather was a lucky man. He died in his sleep. Unfortunately, the passengers in his car at the time were not so lucky, and died screaming and yelling ...

"How are you grandpa?" asks his grandson who is visiting him in hospital.

"Feeling fine," says the old man.

"What's the food like?"

"Terrific, wonderful menus."

"And the nursing?"

"Just couldn't be better. These young nurses really take care of you."

"What about sleeping? Do you sleep OK?"

"No problem at all. I get nine hours solid every night.

At 10 o'clock they bring me a cup of hot chocolate and a Viagra tablet, and that's it. I go out like a light."

The grandson is puzzled and a little alarmed by this, so rushes off to question the Sister in charge.

"What are you people doing?" he says. "I'm told you're giving an 85-year-old Viagra on a daily basis. Surely that can't be true?"

"Oh, yes," replies the Sister. "Every night at 10 o'clock we give him a cup of hot chocolate and a Viagra tablet. It works wonderfully well.

"The hot chocolate makes him sleep, and the Viagra stops him from rolling out of bed."

Three old men are sitting on the porch of a retirement home. The first says, "Guys, I have real problems. I'm seventy years old. Every morning at seven o'clock I get up and I try to urinate. All day long I try to urinate. They give me all kinds of medicine but nothing helps."

The second old man says, "You think you have problems. I'm eighty years old. Every morning at eight o'clock I get up and try to move my bowels. I try all day long. They give me all kinds of stuff but nothing helps."

Finally the third old man speaks up. "Mate, I'm ninety years old. Every morning at seven sharp I urinate. Every morning at eight o'clock I move my bowels. And every morning, bang on nine, I wake up."

"When I'm eighty," the man says to his wife, "I plan on finding myself a pretty twenty-year-old, and I'll have myself a real good time."

"When I'm eighty," replies the wife, "I plan on finding myself a handsome young twenty-year-old stud. I think that I'll find that twenty goes into eighty a lot easier than eighty goes into twenty!"

Senior citizens at a retirement village are exchanging notes about their ailments.

"My arm is so weak I can hardly hold this coffee cup."

"Yes, I know. My cataracts are so bad I can't see to pour the coffee."

"I can't turn my head because of the arthritis in my neck."

"My blood pressure pills make my dizzy."

"I guess that's the price we pay for getting old."

"Well, it's not all bad. We should be thankful that we can still drive!"

An older timer was in at the doctor's for his annual check-up. His doctor was amazed.

"Holy cow! Mr. Edwards, I must say that you are in the greatest shape of any sixty-year-old I have ever examined!"

"Did I say I was sixty?"

"Well, no, did I read your chart wrong?"

"Damn right you did! I'm eighty five!"

"Eighty five! Unbelievable! You would be in great shape if you were thirty! How old was your father when he died?"

"Did I say he was dead?"

"You mean he's not dead?"

"Damn right! He's one hundred and six and going strong!"

"My Lord! What a healthy family you must come from! How long did your grandfather live?"

"Did I say he was dead?"

"No! You can't mean ..."

"Damn straight! He's one hundred and twenty six, and getting married next week!"

"One hundred and twenty six! Truly amazing, Mr. Edwards! But gee, I wouldn't think a man would want to get married at that age!"

"Did I say he *wanted* to get married?"

There was this guy who really took care of his body. He lifted weights and jogged six kilometres every day.

However, when he looked in the mirror he noticed that he was suntanned all over, with the exception of his penis.

He decided to do something about it.

He went to the beach, undressed and buried himself in the sand, leaving only his penis sticking out to face the sun.

Two little old ladies were strolling along the beach. Upon seeing the thing sticking out of the sand, one lady began to move it around with her cane, remarking to the other little old lady, "There really is no justice in this world."

The other little old lady said, "What do you mean?"

"Look at that! When I was twenty, I was curious about it.

"When I was thirty, I enjoyed it.

"When I was forty, I asked for it.

"When I was fifty I paid for it.

"When I was sixty I prayed for it.

"When I was seventy I forgot all about it.

"Now that I'm eighty the damn things are growing wild!"

The officer pulled over an elderly driver and asked, "Didn't you realise your wife fell out of the car a couple of miles back?"

"Thanks," the old gent said, "I thought I had gone deaf."

There was a nice old lady who was considering a week's sunny vacation at a particular campground. However, she wanted to make sure of the accommodation first.

Uppermost in her mind were toilet facilities, but she couldn't bring herself to write "toilet" in a letter.

After considerable deliberation, she settled on "bathroom commode," but when she wrote that down, it still sounded too forward. So she rewrote the letter to the campground, and referred to the "bathroom commode" as the "B.C." "Does the campground have its own B.C.?" she wrote.

The campground owner was baffled by the euphemism, so he showed the letter around to several people, but they couldn't decipher it either.

Finally, the campground owner concluded that she must be referring to the local Baptist Church, so he sat down and responded:

"Dear Madam,

"I regret very much the delay in answering your letter, but I now take pleasure in informing you that a BC is located nine kilometres north of the campground, and is capable of seating 250 people at one time. I admit that it is quite a distance away if you are in the habit of going regularly, but no doubt you will be pleased to know that a great number of people take their lunches along and make a full day of it. They arrive early and stay late.

"The last time my wife and I went was six years ago, and it was so crowded that we had to stand up the entire time we were there. It may interest you to know that right now there is a supper planned to raise money to buy more seats. The supper is going to be held in the basement of the BC.

"I would like to say that it pains me very much not to be able to go more regularly, but it is surely from no lack of desire on my part. As we grow older, it seems to be more of an effort, particularly in cold weather!

"If you do decide to come down to our campground, perhaps I could go with you to the BC the first time, sit with you, and introduce you to all the other folks.

"Remember, we are widely known as a friendly community, so come on down and we will all enjoy the BC together."

Visiting the modern art museum an old lady turned to an attendant standing nearby.

"This, I suppose, is one of those hideous representations you call Modern Art?"

"No madam," replied the attendant. "That one is called a mirror."

An elderly man was dying and in his last few moments he asked the priest to take him down to the kitchen where his wife was baking.

The priest carried the old man down and pushed through the kitchen door to see the table laden with home made cakes, cooling on wire trays.

The old man feebly reached for one. His wife smacked his hand, saying, "Hands off! They're for the funeral!"

A man goes to the doctor with a very bad case of sunburn. The doctor prescribes Viagra.

"I didn't realize that Viagra was a treatment for sunburn," said the man.

It isn't," replied the doctor, "but it will stop the sheets from hurting your legs ..."

One evening a family brings their frail, elderly mother to the local nursing home in Dublin and leaves her as planned, hoping she will be well cared for.

The next morning, the nurses bathe her, feed her a tasty breakfast including All Bran and some toast, and set her in a chair at a window overlooking a lovely flower garden.

She seems okay, but after a while she slowly starts to lean over sideways in her chair. Two attentive nurses immediately rush up to catch her and straighten her up.

Again she seems okay, but after a while she starts to tilt to the other side. The nurses rush back and once more bring her back upright.

This goes on all morning.

Later on the family arrives to see how their dear sweet mother is adjusting to her new home. "So Ma, how is it here? Are they treating you all right?" they ask.

"It's pretty nice," she replies. "Except them feckers won't let me fart."

Two old ladies were out for a walk when a streaker ran past them. One of the old ladies had a stroke. The other missed.

A man moves into a nudist colony, without telling his mother exactly what it is. He receives a letter from his mother asking him to send her a current picture.

Too embarrassed to let her know that he lives in a nudist colony, he cuts a picture in half and sends her the top part.

Later he receives another letter asking him to send a picture to his grandmother. The man cuts another picture in half, but accidentally sends the bottom half.

He is really worried when he realizes that he sent the wrong part, but then remembers how bad his grandmother's eyesight is and hopes she won't notice.

A few weeks later he receives a letter from his grandmother. It says, "Thank you for the picture. But I reckon you should change your hair-style ... it makes your nose look too long."

An old man visited his doctor to complain of deafness in his left ear. "I could hear perfectly well last night," the man said.

The doctor shined his light into the man's ear.

"What have we here," he said and, inserting a fine pair of tweezers' withdrew a woman's tampon.

"Good grief!" said the patient. "May I use your phone doctor?"

"Certainly, but who are you going to call?"

"My wife – to tell her where my hearing aid is!"

Two old men suffering from short term memory loss were sitting on the steps of the old-age home when an ice cream van drove past.

"Gee," said the first old codger. "I'd love an ice cream right now."

"Would you like me to get you one?" asked the second old bloke.

"Are you joking?" the first old fart snapped back. "You'd forget my order straight away."

"No I wouldn't," replied the second."

"All right, then," said his mate. "I want a double cone with mint ice cream and choc chips, and a cherry on top."

The second old bloke repeated the order flawlessly.

Five minutes later he walked back carrying two meat pies. The first old bloke looked at the pies in disgust then yelled, "I knew I should've gone myself. You forgot the bloody sauce!"

An elderly couple, still very loving after all these years, is shocked when the woman's doctor says she has a heart condition that could kill her at any time. She is to avoid stress, including never, ever having sex again, as the strain would be too much.

The couple reluctantly try to live by these rules. Both get really horny over time, however, and the husband decides he'd better sleep downstairs on the couch to guard against temptation.

This works for a few weeks, until late one night when they meet each other on the stairs. She's coming downstairs, he's heading up.

"Honey, I have a confession to make," the woman says, her voice quavering. "I was about to commit suicide."

"I'm glad to hear it, sweetie," the man says, "Because I was just coming upstairs to kill you!"

A social-worker visit one of his elderly clients, Mrs Smith. He rings the door-bell and Mrs Smith appears.

"Good day, Mrs Smith. I just thought I would drop by and see how you're doing"

"Oh hello, come on in and we'll have some tea."

While sitting at the coffee table, the social worker notices a bowl of almonds on the table. "Mind if I have one?" the social worker says.

"Not at all, have as many as you like."

After a few hours the social worker looks at his watch and alarmed at how long he has been visiting.

He says to Mrs Smith, "Oh my goodness, look at the time. I must be going. Oh, but dear me, I have eaten all your almonds. I'll have to replace them next time I visit."

To which Mrs Smith replied, "Oh don't bother. Ever since I lost all my teeth, it's all I can do just to lick the chocolate off them."

Two octogenarian men are talking in the park. The first one looks at his watch and says, "I must go now, it's time to meet my wife for sex."

The other man says, "We're in our eighties now, how do you still manage to get it hard?"

"By eating a lot of rye bread," comes the reply. "That makes it hard as a rock."

The other man simply has to try it and goes to the bakery. He asks the girl for ten loaves of rye bread.

The girl asks if it's for a party and he replies, "No, it's all for me."

The girl says, "All for you? It's going to get hard."

The man replies, "God, everybody knows about it, but me!"

An old man and his wife have gone to bed. After a few minutes the old man lets out a loud fart and says, "One-nil."

His wife rolls over and asks, "What in the world was that?"

The old man says, "A goal. I'm ahead one-nil."

A few minutes later the wife lets one go and says, "Goal! One all."

The old boy farts again. "Goal! I'm ahead 2-1 now."

Now starting to get the hang of it, the wife quickly farts again and says, "Goal! 2-all."

The old man tries to fart again, but cannot. Trying desperately not be out done by his wife, he gives it everything he has to get out just one more fart. He strains a little too hard and shits in the bed.

The wife asks, "Now what in the world was that?"

The old man replies, "Half-time, switch sides!"

IF IT CAN GO WRONG
IT WILL

1. An original idea can never emerge from a committee.
2. When the product is destined to fail, the delivery system will perform perfectly.
3. The success of any venture will be helped by prayer, even in the wrong denomination.
4. When things are going well, someone will inevitably experiment detrimentally.
5. The "think positive" leader tends to listen to his subordinates' premonitions only during the post mortems.
6. The deficiency will never show itself during the dry run.
7. Information travels more surely to those with a lesser need to know.
8. Clearly stated instructions will consistently produce multiple interpretations.
9. The lagging activity in a project will invariably be found in the area where the highest overtime rates lie waiting.
10. Give a sub-committee specific instructions on how to design a horse, and they will surely produce a camel – or at least the feasibility study giving the go-ahead …

SWITCH THAT LIGHT BULB ON

Q. How many Irishmen does it take to screw in a light bulb?

A. Fifteen. One to hold the bulb and the rest to drink whisky until the room spins.

Q. How many feminists does it take to change a light bulb?

A. One to change it, and fifteen to form a support group.

Q. How many Californians does it take to change a light bulb?

A. Six. One to turn the bulb, one for support, and four to relate to the experience.

Q. How many data base people does it take to change a light bulb?

A. Three. One to write the light bulb removal program, One to write the light bulb insertion program, and one to act as a light bulb administrator to make sure that nobody else tries to change the bulb at the same time.

Q. How many folk singers does it take to screw in a light bulb?

A. Two. One to change the bulb, and one to write a song about how good the old light bulb was.

Q. How many surrealists does it take to change a light bulb?

A. Two. One to hold the giraffe, and the other to fill the bathtub with brightly colored machine tools.

Q. How many gorillas does it take to screw in a light bulb?

A. Only one, but it sure takes a shit load of light bulbs!

Q. How many psychologists does it take to change a light bulb?

A. None, the bulb will change itself when it is ready.

Q. What is the difference between a pregnant woman and a light bulb?

A. You can unscrew a light bulb.

Q. How many managers does it take to change a light bulb?

A. Three. One to get the bulb and two to get the phone number to dial one of their subordinates to actually change it.

Q. How many IBM types does it take to change a light bulb?

A. 100. Ten to do it, and 90 to write document number GA8762439-001, Multi-Tasking Incandescent Source System Facility.

Q.   How many gays does it take to screw in a light bulb?

A.   Two. One to screw it in, and the other to say
       "Fabulous!"

Q.   How many professors does it take to change a light
       bulb?

A.   Only one, but they get three tech. reports out of it.

Q.   How many people from Calabria does it take to
       change a light bulb?

A.   Three. One to change the bulb, one to witness, and
       the third to shoot the witness.

Q.   How many programmers does it take to change a
       light bulb?

A.   None. That's a hardware problem.

Q.   How many public servants does it take to change a
       light bulb?

A.   That's proprietary information. Answer available from
       AT&T on payment of license fee.

Q.   How many graduate students does it take to screw in
       a light bulb?

A.   Only one, but it may take upwards of five years for
       him to get it done.

Q.   How many "Real Men" does it take to change a light
       bulb?

A.   None. "Real Men" aren't afraid of the dark.

Q.   How many "Real Women" does it take to change a light bulb?

A.   None. A "Real Woman" would have plenty of real men around to do it.

Q.   How many Jewish mothers does it take to change a light bulb?

A.   None. ("That's all right ... I'll just sit here in the dark ...")

Q.   How many Polacks does it take to change a light bulb?

A.   Just one, but you need 6000 Russian troops in case he goes on strike!

Q.   How many Marxists does it take to screw in a light bulb?

A.   None. The light bulb contains the seeds of its own revolution.

Q.   How many Army Generals does it take to change a light bulb?

A.   1,000,001. One to change the bulb, and 1,000,000 to rebuild civilization to the point where they need light bulbs again.

Q.   How many med students does it take to change a light bulb?

A.   Five. One to change the bulb and four to pull the ladder out from under him.

Q. How many Christians does it take to change a light bulb?

A. Three, but they're really one.

Q. How many jugglers does it take to change a light bulb?

A. One, but it takes at least three light bulbs.

Q. How many feminists does it take to change a light bulb?

A. That's not funny!

Q   How many supply-side economists does it take to screw in a light bulb?

A. None. If the government would just leave it alone, it would screw itself in.

Q. How many strong men does it take to screw in a light bulb?

A. 115. One to hold the bulb and 114 to rotate the house.

Q. How many gods does it take to screw in a light bulb?

A. Two. One to hold the bulb and the other to rotate the planet.

Q. How many cops does it take to screw in a light bulb?

A. None. It turned itself in.

Q. How many surgeons does it take to change a light bulb?

A. None. They would wait for a suitable donor and do a filament transplant.

Or three. They'd also like to remove the socket as you aren't using it now.

Q.   How many veterinarians does it take to change a light bulb?

A.   Three. One to change the bulb and two more to complain that an MD makes ten times as much for the same procedure!!

Q.   How many physiotherapists does it take to change a light bulb?

A.   None. They just give the dead bulb some exercises to do and hope it will be working a bit better the next time they see it.

Q.   How many nuclear engineers does it take to change a light bulb?

A.   Fifty-one. One to install the new bulb, and fifty to figure what to do with the old one for the next 10,000 years.

Q.   How many lawyers does it take to change a light bulb?

A.   How many can you afford?

Q.   How many football players does it take to change a light bulb?

A.   The entire team! A team is only as good as its weakest link.

Q.	How many lesbians does it take to screw in a light bulb?

A.	Three. One to screw it in, and two to talk about how much better it is than with a man.

Q.	How many thought police does it take to screw in a light bulb?

A.	None. There never *was* any light bulb.

Q.	How many accountants does it take to screw in a light bulb?

A.	What kind of answer did you have in mind?

Q.	How many civil servants does it take to change a light bulb?

A.	45. One to change the bulb, and 44 to do the paperwork.

Q.	How many mystery writers does it take to screw in a light bulb?

A.	Two. One to screw it almost all the way in and the other to give it a surprising twist at the end.

Q.	How many existentialists does it take to screw in a light bulb?

A.	Two. One to screw it in and one to observe how the light bulb itself symbolizes a single incandescent beacon of subjective reality in a netherworld of endless absurdity reaching out toward a cosmos of nothingness.

Q.   How many junkies does it take to change a light bulb?

A.   Who says it's dark?

Q.   How many consultants does it take to change a light bulb?

A.   I'll have an estimate for you a week from Monday.

Q.   How many technical writers does it take to screw in a light bulb?

A.   Just one, provided there's a programmer around to explain how to do it.

Q.   How many doctors does it take to change a light bulb?

A.   That depends on whether it has health insurance.
     None. They just tell it to take two aspirin and come round to the surgery later.
     None. They only sign the death certificate and phone the mortuary.
     None. They would diagnose depression and prescribe benzodiazapines.
     Only one, but he has to have a nurse to tell him which end to screw in.
     Three. One to find a bulb specialist, one to find a bulb installation specialist, and one to bill it all to Medicare.

THE ELEVATOR – THE A TO Z OF MAKING YOUR NEXT TRIP EXCITING

Do you find trips in the lift dull and boring? Here's a few ideas to make your next journey an interesting experience – for you and the other passengers.

- As soon as other people get in, start listening to the elevator walls with a stethoscope.
- After staring at the floor numbers, put a voice on that is straight out of *The Omen* and declare to everyone else in the lift, "Thirteen is my favourite number …"
- See if you can get a mexican wave started.
- Airily bring a chair along, and then sit quietly, with one hand down your crotch.
- Ask each passenger getting on if you can please push the button for them.
- Ask in a loud voice, "Does this stop at Madam Lash's floor?"
- At your floor, strain to pull the doors open, then act embarrassed when they open by themselves.
- Bet the other passengers you can fit a tampon up your nose.

- Bring on board a blanket and clutch it protectively, sucking your thumb.
- Casually lean over to another passenger and whisper: "They're still watching me!"
- Draw a little square on the floor with chalk and inform the other passengers that this is your personal space.
- Frown and mutter, "Have to go … I've gotta go to the …" then groan, and say, "Oops!"
- Greet everyone getting on with a warm handshake and ask them to call you field marshall.
- Grimace painfully while smacking your forehead with the palm of you hand and muttering, "Shut up, damn it, all of you, just shut UP!"
- Hand out pamphlets with religious tracts to each passenger.
- Holler, "Whoa there!" whenever the elevator descends.
- Lean nonchalantly against the button panel.
- Let rip with a magnificent burp, and then say. "Mmmm … *very* tasty!"
- Loudly blow your nose, and offer to show the contents of your hanky to everyone.
- Make explosion noises when anyone presses a button.
- Make race car noises when anyone gets on or off.
- Meow occasionally.
- Moan from the back, "Oh, no, that damn motion sickness again!"
- Offer name tags to everyone getting on the elevator. Wear yours upside-down.

- On a long ride, sway side to side at the natural frequency of the elevator.
- Open your briefcase, peer inside and ask, "Got enough air in there?"
- Play the harmonica.
- Pull your gum out of your mouth in long strings.
- Say, "Ding!" at each floor.
- Say, "I wonder what all these do" and push the red buttons.
- Sell Girl Scout cookies.
- Shadow box.
- Shave. Preferably by lathering up and then using a battery-powered razor.
- Announce in a devil's voice to all other passengers, "I need to find a more suitable host body."
- Show other passengers a wound and ask if it looks infected.
- Sing "Mary had a little lamb" while continually pushing buttons.
- Stand silent and motionless in the corner, facing the wall, without getting off.
- Stare at a passenger and announce, "You're one of THEM!" and move to the far corner of the elevator.
- Stare at your thumb and say, "I think it's getting larger."
- Stare, grinning, at another passenger for a while, and then announce, "I've got new socks on!"
- Start a sing-along version of "I Am The Walrus."
- Wear "X-Ray Specs" and leer suggestively at other passengers.
- Wear a glove puppet on your hand and talk to other passengers via it.

- When the elevator is totally silent, look around and ask the person next to you, "Is that your beeper I can hear?"
- Whistle the first seven notes of "It's a Small World" ad infinitum.

THE WORLD OF SPORT

While touring a small South American country, a woman was taken to a bullfight.

"This is our number one sport," the guard explained.

The woman was horrified at the thought and said, "Isn't it revolting?"

"No," the guide replied, "that's our number two sport."

Posh and Becks had somehow managed to lock their keys in their car. Beckham was trying to unlock the door with a coat hanger.

Posh said, "Oh come on David, it's starting to rain and the roof on our convertible is down ..."

Two men are hiking in the mountains. One suddenly stops, removes his hiking boots, and starts putting on sneakers. The other asks why he is doing that. The first man answers, "I thought I heard a bear."

The second argues, "You can't outrun a bear, not even with sneakers."

The first responds, "No, but I only need to outrun you!"

What do you do if a professional gridiron player throws a pin at you? Run, because he's got a grenade in his mouth.

One day, John was walking down the main street of London when he came across an American Indian with full head gear on, sitting cross legged on the pavement with a sign written on the back of a beer carton, which said:

Marvo the Marvellous Memory Man.
Give me a dollar, ask me a question.
If I am unable to answer it I shall give you $10.

"Hello!" said John.

"Where I come from it is polite to say, 'How?'" said the Indian.

"Sorry," said John. So he walked away, turned around, came back and tried again.

"How?" he greeted the Indian. He gave him a dollar and then asked, "Who won the Scottish FA Cup in 1945?"

The Indian thought for a bit and gave his answer. "Rangers beat Kilmarnock 1-0."

John was amazed. Ten years passed. John was walking down the same street and this time he saw a massive building with a sign written in neon lights: "Marvo the Memory Man."

John walked in and saw a familiar face, sitting at a table. Remembering his manners, John went up to the man and said, "How?"

The man looked at him and said, "Great cross, bullet header, top left hand corner ..."

Posh and Becks arrive from their holiday at Heathrow. A mini-cab driver asks them where they have been.

"I've been away in America, doing some sight seeing and shopping, and we ate in this wonderful restaurant," said David.

"Oh what's it called?" asked the driver.

"Oh what was it called, don't tell me, er, name a London railway station"

"Euston?"

"Nah, nah, nah!"

"Paddington?"

"Nope"

"Victoria?"

"Yeah, that's it! Victoria, what's the name of that restaurant?"

Three members of a golf club were arguing loudly while the fourth member of their group lay dead in a bunker. A club official was called to calm the row. "What's the trouble here?" he asked.

"My partner has had a stroke and these two bastards want to add it to my score."

A LAYMAN'S GUIDE TO THE VOCABULARY OF SKIING

Alp Mountains in Europe and other countries that are often used for skiing. Depending on your accent, it can also be a shouted request for assistance …

Skier One who pays an arm and a leg for the opportunity to break same …

Stance Your knees should be flexed, but shaking slightly; your arms straight and covered with a good layer of goose flesh; your hands forward, palms clammy, knuckles white and fingers icy; your eyes a little crossed and darting in all directions. Your lips should be quivering, and you should be mumbling, "Am I f…ing stupid or what?"

Thor The Scandinavian god of acheth and painth.

"Ski!" A shout to alert people ahead that a loose ski is coming down the hill. Another warning skiers should be familiar with is "Avalanche!" which tells everyone that a hill is coming down the hill.

Bindings Automatic mechanisms that protect skiers from serious injury during a fall by releasing skis from boots, sending the skis skittering across the slope where they trip up two other skiers.

Bones There are 206 in the human body. No need for dismay, however. The two bones of the middle ear have never been broken while skiing.

Gravity One of four fundamental forces in nature that effect skiers. The other three are the strong force, which makes bindings jam, the weak force, which makes ankles give way on turns, and electromagnetism, which produces dead batteries in expensive ski-resort parking lots. See *Inertia*.

Inertia Tendency of a skier's body to resist changes in direction or speed due to the action of Newton's First Law of Motion. It goes along with these other physical laws:

- Two objects of different mass falling side by side will have the same rate of descent, but the lighter one will have larger hospital and home care bills.
- Matter can neither be created nor destroyed, but if it drops out of a parka pocket, don't expect to encounter it ever again.
- When an irresistible force meets an immovable object, it's a long way for the ambulance driver to get up the slope and unwrap you from around the tree.

Gloves Designed to be tight around the wrist to restrict circulation, but not so close fitting as to allow any manual dexterity. They should also admit moisture from the outside without permitting any dampness within to escape, thus ensuring you have no control or grip whatsoever.

Exercises A few simple warm-ups to make sure you're prepared for the slopes:

- Tie a house brick to each foot and climb 12 flights of stairs sidewards.

- Sit on the outside of a ninth-story window ledge, with your skis on and your poles in your lap, for four hours during a snow storm.
- Bind your legs together at the ankles, lie flat on the floor; then, holding a banana in each hand, try and get to your feet. It's more fun if you are playing Ludo at the same time.

Pre-jump   Manoeuvre in which an expert skier makes a controlled jump just ahead of a bump. Beginners can execute a controlled pre-fall just before losing their balance and, if they wish, may precede it with either a pre-scream and a few pre-groans or a simple profanity.

Shin   The bruised area on the front of the leg that runs from the point where the ache from the wrenched knee ends to where the soreness from the strained ankle begins.

Gluhwein   An ultra-sweet concoction, often drunk warm in vast quantities with the object of dulling the shin pain, or ending up in the sack with a voluptuous snow-bunny, or both.

Traverse   To ski across a slope at an angle; one of two quick and simple methods of reducing speed.

Tree   The other method …

Becks got back to his hotel and decided he would buy a drink from the vending machine in the foyer. When he put his money in, a can of Coke came out. So he put some more money in, and a can of Fanta came out.

He kept putting more money in, and more cans kept coming out.

A long line began forming behind him. Finally, a big Yankee bloke, the next guy in line can't take it any more and says, "Jesus, what's going on, will you hurry up? We want our turn here!"

And Becks says, "No way, man. I'm still winning!"

A travelling salesman is in a small country town, and having done a good morning's work, decides to play a round of golf.

He drives out to the local club, hires a bag of sticks, and asks if there is someone who will not only caddy for him, but has a good local knowledge of the course, so he won't get into too much trouble.

"Certainly," says the pro shop assistant. "Frank's your man. Frank is our oldest member, he is a twelve-time club champion, he helped design the course back in the thirties, and he knows every blade of grass. In fact he knows every beetle under every blade of grass."

The man says that is fine, and the assistant tells him to go to the first tee, and that Frank will meet him there.

The salesman arrives at the first tee, and does a few limber-up exercises. Eventually he hears a sound, and turns around to see an old bloke, 97 years old if he is day, tottering towards him. It takes him two minutes to cross the tee.

"You must be Frank?" says the salesman extending his hand.

"I sure am, I know everything about this course," says the old bloke.

The salesman finishes warming up, pulls out his driver, tees up a ball, and swings with all his might.

The ball takes off beautifully, but then starts to develop a curve. It veers dramatically off course, and disappears into the trees and bushes.

The salesman turns anxiously to Frank, who is staring fixedly.

"Frank, Frank, did you see it?"

"Yes."

"Where did it go?"

"I forget ..."

FAMILY LIFE

Yes, it is a wonderful moment when you become a parent for the first time. That little bundle of joy is all yours and is going to mean so much to you.

That little bundle is also going to turn your life upside down! Here's a few tests that will you put you right under the pump:

CAR TEST Forget the Roller. It's the station wagon for you. Buy a chocolate ice cream cone and put it in the glove compartment. Leave it there. Get a pencil. Stick it into the cassette player. Take a family size tub of deep fried chips. Mash them into the back seat. Run a garden rake along both sets of doors. Now, after 130,000 miles and a second engine, try and trade it in.

DRESSING TEST Obtain one large, unhappy, live giant squid. Stuff it into a small net bag, at all times making sure that all the arms stay inside.

STINK TEST Smear honey, peanut butter and soy sauce on the sofa and curtains. Place a fish stick and a hermit crab behind the couch and leave them there for the entire summer.

FEEDING TEST   Obtain a large plastic milk jug. Fill halfway with water. Suspend from the ceiling with a cord. Start the jug swinging. Try to insert spoonfuls of soggy cereal into the mouth of the jug, while pretending to be a helicopter. Now dump part of the contents of the jug over your head and the rest on the floor.

INGENUITY TEST   Take a toilet paper tube. Turn it into an Easter candle. Use only sticky tape and a piece of foil. Take an egg carton. Using a pair of scissors and pot of paint, turn it into a happy rhino. Take a milk carton, an empty box of Cocoa Puffs, a ping-pong ball, and make an exact replica of the Eiffel Tower.

LAND-MINE TEST   Get a giant box of Lego. Get your partner to spread them all over the house. Put on a blindfold. Endeavour to walk to the kitchen. Do not scream because this would wake a child at night.

NIGHT TEST   Prepare by obtaining a small cloth bag and fill it with 8-12 pounds of sand. Soak it thoroughly in water. At 3:00pm, begin to waltz and hum with the bag until 9:00pm. Lay down your bag and set your alarm for 10:00pm. Get up, pick up your bag, and sing every song you have ever heard. Make up about a dozen more and sing these until 4:00am. Set alarm for 5:00am. Get up and make breakfast. Keep this up for 5 years. Look happy.

PHYSICAL TEST (Men) Go to the nearest chemist. Set your wallet on the counter. Ask the shop assistant to help herself. Now proceed to the nearest supermarket. Go to the office and arrange for your paycheck to be directly deposited to the store. Purchase a race guide. Go home and read it quietly for the last time.

PHYSICAL TEST (Women) Take a large beanbag and attach it to the front of your clothes. Leave it there for nine months. Now remove 10 of the beans. Try not to notice your closet full of clothes. You won't be wearing them for a while.

SHOPPING TEST Borrow one or two small animals, such as goats, ferrets or Tasmanian devils, and take them with you as you shop. Always keep them in sight and pay for anything they eat or damage.

WARN-OFF TEST   Find a couple who already have a small child. Lecture them on how they can improve their method of bringing their child up, including patience, discipline, table manners and toilet training. Enjoy this experience. It will be the last time you will have all the answers.

A LETTER FROM A LOVING SON

Dear Dad,
$chool i$ really great. I am making lot$ of friend$ and $tudying very hard.
With all my $tuff, I $imply can't think of anything I need, $o if you would like, you can ju$t $end me a card, a$ I would love to hear from you.
Love,
Your $on.

Dear Son,
I kNOw that astroNOmy, ecoNOmics, and oceaNOgraphy are eNOugh to keep even an hoNOr student busy. Do NOt forget that the pursuit of kNOwledge is a NOble task, and you can never study eNOugh.
Love,
Dad

A DICTIONARY FOR PARENTS

AMNESIA: Condition that enables a woman who has gone through labor to *ever* have sex again.

BOTTLE FEEDING: An opportunity for Dad to get up at 2am too.

DEFENSE: What you'd better have around the yard if you're going to let the children play outside.

DROOLING: How teething babies wash their chins.

DUMB WAITER: One who asks if the kids would care to order dessert.

FAMILY PLANNING: The art of spacing your children the proper distance apart to keep you from falling into the financial abyss.

FEEDBACK: The inevitable result when a baby doesn't appreciate the strained carrots.

FULL NAME: What you call your child when you're mad at him.

GRANDPARENTS: The people who think your children are absolutely wonderful even though they're convinced you're not raising them right.

HEARSAY: What toddlers do when anyone mutters a dirty word.

IMPREGNABLE: A woman whose memory of labor is still vivid.

INDEPENDENT: How we want our children to be as long as they do everything we say.

LOOK OUT!: What it's too late for your child to do by the time you scream it.

PRENATAL: When your life was still somewhat your own.

PREPARED CHILDBIRTH: A contradiction in terms.

PUDDLE: A small body of water that draws other small bodies wearing dry shoes.

SHOW OFF: A child who is more talented than yours.

STERILIZE: What you do to your first baby's dummy by boiling it and to your second baby's dummy by blowing on it. By the third you don't care if the dog licks it for you.

STOREROOM: The distance required between the supermarket aisles so that children in shopping carts can't quite reach anything.

TEMPER TANTRUMS: What you should keep to a minimum so as to not upset the children.

THUNDERSTORM: A chance to see how many family members can fit into one bed.

TOP BUNK: Where you should never put a child wearing Superman jammies.

TWO-MINUTE WARNING: When the baby's face turns red and she begins to make those familiar grunting noises.

VERBAL: Able to whine in words.

WEAKER SEX: The kind you have after the kids have worn you out.

WHODUNIT: None of the kids that live in your house.

WHOOPS: An exclamation that translates roughly into "get a sponge".

TOILET HUMOUR

Two men are occupying booths in a public restroom, when one calls to the other, "There is no toilet paper over here – do you have any over there?"

The second man replies, "No, sorry, I don't seem to have any, either."

The first man then asks, "Well, do you have a magazine or newspaper?"

The second man says, "No, sorry!"

The first man pauses, then inquires, "Do you have change for a twenty?"

Late one night, an alien spacecraft landed near a deserted gas station. One of the aliens came down the ramp, looked around, and walked over to one of the gas pumps.

He demanded, "Earthling! Take me to your leader!"

The gas pump did not reply. The alien became agitated and again demanded, "Take me to your leader!"

The gas pump remained silent.

Frustrated, the alien went back to the spacecraft where he was confronted by the captain,

"Report what you have found out about earthlings," demanded the captain.

"I contacted an earthling, but he would not cooperate."

"I will have to deal with this earthling myself," said the captain.

"Yes sir. Be careful sir, I have a feeling there could be trouble."

The captain left the ship and approached the gas pump.

"Earthling, you will cooperate. Take me to your leader."

The gas pump remained unresponsive.

"Very well!" The captain drew his blaster. "If you do not respond by the count of three, I shall be forced to fire on you. One. Two. Three."

ZZZZZT. WHAM! The gas pump exploded, knocking the alien over. The captain jumped up and got back to the ship as fast as he could.

"Quickly! Make ready to depart!"

"Yes sir. What happened sir?"

"I fired on the earthling and it responded very forcefully."

"Sorry sir, I was afraid that might happen."

"How did you know that there would be trouble?"

"Well sir, I assumed that anyone who can take his dick, wrap it around his feet and stick it in his left ear is probably going to be one bad bastard."

Have you heard about the butcher who backed in to the bacon-slicing room and got a little behind in his customers' orders?

"I see," said the blind man as he pissed into the wind. "It's all coming back to me now."

A football player walked into a motel on a rainy night. He asked the manager for a room for one night.

The manager said, "I only have one room left and I don't think you would want it."

The football player asked, "Why not?"

"It's haunted."

"Well, I'll kill the ghost or whatever is in it."

The manager agreed to hire the room and gave him the key. That night when the football player was just getting settled, he heard a voice. He listened and heard it again.

It said, "If the log rolls over, we all will drown."

With that, the footballer ran out of the room screaming.

The next night a woman came in and wanted a room. The manager did not argue with her as the place was full except for the one room. So she took the key and went to her room.

As she got settled in she heard, "If the log rolls over we all will drown."

She took a look around and realized it was coming from the bathroom. She looked in the toilet and saw three ants singing on a turd, "If the log rolls over we all will drown."

What did the cannibal do after he dumped his girlfriend? Wiped his butt!

A dwarf walks into a bar and slips over a piece of shit on the floor. He walks off, thinking nothing of it.

A few minutes later a huge man walks in and falls over the same piece of shit.

The little dwarf shouts out, "I just did that."

And the big man kills him.

Two guys are in a locker room and the one guy starts laughing. The other man says, "What is so funny?"

The man says, "There is a cork in your butt. How did it get there?"

"Well, I was walking down the street and I tripped over a lamp and a Genie came out. He said to me, 'You will be granted one wish.'"

"And?" says the other man.

"I was so surprised that all I could reply was, 'No Shit!'"

A young courting couple are out for a romantic walk along a leafy country lane. They walk hand in hand and, as they stroll, the young man's lustful desire rises to a peak.

He is just about to get frisky when the young woman says, "I hope you don't mind, but I really do need to have a piss."

Slightly taken aback by this vulgarity, he suggests she go behind a hedge. She nods in agreement and disappears behind the hedge.

As he waits, he can hear the sound of tight white panties

sliding down voluptuous legs and he imagines what loveliness is being exposed. Unable to contain his animal thoughts a moment longer, he reaches through a gap in the foliage, and touches her smooth, bare leg.

He gently brings his hand further up to her thigh until suddenly, and with great astonishment, he finds himself gripping a long, thick appendage hanging between her legs.

He gasps in horror, "My God Mary have you changed your sex?"

"No," she replies, "I've changed my mind, I'm having a shit instead."

Three vampires walk into a bar. One orders a blood on the rocks. Another orders a double blood. The third simply asks for a mug of hot water.

"Why didn't you order blood like everyone else?" asks the bartender.

The vampire pulls out a tampon and says, "I'm making tea!"

20 CHARACTER INDICATORS AT THE URINAL

Next time you are having a slash in public urinal, guys, check out the following tell-tale characteristics to understand the make-up of those sharing this intimate moment with you:

TIMID: Boarding school memories come back to him, and simply cannot piss if someone is watching, so flushes urinal, rushes out and comes back later.

TOUGH: Bangs dick on side of urinal to dry it.

ABSENT-MINDED: Opens his jacket, pulls out his tie, pisses in his pants.

CHILDISH: Pisses directly in bottom of urinal, likes to see it bubble.

FRIVOLOUS: Plays stream up, down, and across urinal, especially if there is a fly he can hit.

EGO-TRIPPER: Plays stream in the shape of his initials.

PISS-POT: Holds his left thumb very carefully in his right hand, wobbles unsteadily on feet, pisses in his pants, and does not notice.

CONCEITED: Holds two inch dick like it is a baseball bat.

CONTENTED: Flops out ten-inch dick, stands back, puts hands on hips, and radiates warm smile to all around him.

FAT BASTARD: Stands right on edge, fumbles to get fly open, and eventually takes an unsighted shot at the stainless steel. Usually pisses on shoes. Hopefully his, and not yours.

CROSSEYED: Looks discreetly sideways to see how the other guy is hanging.

SCIENTIST: Sprays directly into hygiene "lollies" and looks earnestly for chemical reaction.

SNEAKY: Farts silently while pissing, acts innocent, knows that some innocent poor bugger in a nearby stall will cop the blame.

GROANER: Luxuriates in the expulsion of the fluid, and wants everyone to know. "Ooooooh, yes, that feels sooooo good."

DRIPPY: Shakes, inspects, shakes, inspects, and shakes again, to ensure every last drop is out, and that there will be no tell-tale stain on his beige pants.

SOCIABLE: Joins his mates in an enjoyable communal piss whether he has to go or not.

WORRIED: Not sure of where he has been or what he has been up to lately, so makes a quick inspection for any tell-tale signs of overuse or oncoming rash.

CONVERSATIONALIST: Starts chat with bloke next to him with: "So, this is where the big knobs hang out ...?"

INDIFFERENT: With all spots being in use, he shrugs and pisses in the sink.

EFFICIENT: Waits until he needs to have a crap, and then does both ...

Did you hear about the pissed dung beetle that fell off his stool ...?

25 REASONS WHY BEER IS BETTER THAN A WOMAN

1. Beer never gets a headache.
2. Your beer will always wait patiently for you in the car while you play football.
3. You don't have to wine and dine beer.
4. Beer doesn't get jealous when you grab another beer.
5. You can enjoy a beer all month long.
6. Beer stains wash out.

7.   When your beer goes flat, you toss it out.

8.   Hangovers go away.

9.   A beer label comes off without a fight.

10. Beer is never late.

11. When you go to a bar, you know you can always pick up a beer.

12. After you've had a beer, the bottle is still worth 5 cents.

13. A beer won't get upset if you come home and have another beer.

14. If you pour a beer right, you'll always get good head.

15. A beer always goes down easy.

16. You can share a beer with your friends.

17. You always know you're the first one to pop a beer.

18. Beer is always wet.

19. Beer doesn't demand equality.

20. You can have more than one beer a night and not feel guilty.

21. You can have a beer in public.

22. A beer doesn't care when you come.

23. A frigid beer is a good beer.

24. You don't have to wash a beer before it tastes good.

25. If you change beers you don't have to pay alimony.

WHEN LIFE IS CRUEL

Johnny comes in from school very upset and crying. When comforted by his mother, he says that he has had a dreadful day as the other kids were teasing him and calling him names.

"What were they calling you, darling?" asked his mother sympathetically.

"They called me square head," sobbed little Johnny.

"Don't you worry," retorted his mother. "They must like you as they are being very nice. What they really mean is that your head is a big, ugly and deformed one."

These two green beans are crossing the freeway when one of them was hit by a semi. His friend scrapes him up and rushes him to the hospital.

After hours of surgery the doctor comes in and says, "I have good news and bad news."

The healthy green bean says, "OK, give me the good news first."

The doctor says, "The good news is that he's going to live."

"So," says the green bean, "what's the bad news?"

"The bad news is he'll be a vegetable for the rest of his life …"

Welcome to the psychiatric hotline, please choose from the following menu at anytime:

- If you are obsessive-compulsive, please press 1 repeatedly
- If you are co-dependant, please ask someone to press 2
- If you have multiple personalities, please press 3, 4, 5, and possibly 6
- If you are paranoid delusional, we know who you are, stay on the line so we can trace this call
- If you are schizophrenic, listen carefully and a little voice will tell you which number to press
- If you suffer from indecision, press the number of your choice
- If you are delusional and hallucinating, be aware that thing in your hand is alive and may bite your head off.

How can you tell a blind man in a nudist colony? It's not hard.

PICKING UP

12 SURE-FIRE PICK-UP LINES (WITH NO GUARANTEES …)

1. I wish you were a door, so I could bang you all day long.
2. Nice legs. What time do they open?
3. Do you work for the post office? I thought I saw you checking out my package.
4. You have 206 bones in your body, want one more?
5. I'm a bird watcher and I'm looking for a big breasted bed thrasher, have you seen one?
6. I'm fighting the urge to make you the happiest woman on earth tonight.
7. I'd really like to see how you look when I'm naked.
8. You must be the limp doctor, because I've got a stiffy.
9. You, me, whipped cream and handcuffs. Any questions?
10. Those clothes would look great in a crumpled heap on my bedroom floor.
11. Hi, the voices in my head told me to come over and talk to you.
12. (Lick finger and wipe on her shirt) Let's get you out of those wet clothes.

TRAVEL TALES

Tourist: "Have you lived here all of your life?"
Local: "Not yet."

Then there is the feller who saves his money, travels to
Spain, and goes to Pamplona during the wonderful
Running of the Bulls Festival.

After his first day there, he goes out late in the evening
for dinner, like the locals do, and chooses a nice-looking
restaurant in a busy street. Unfamiliar with the language, he
orders the house special and is brought a plate with
potatoes, vegetables, and two large, round meaty objects.

"What are these?" he asks, pointing to the big round
things.

"Cojones, senor," the waiter replies.

"What are cojones?" the man asks.

"Cojones," the waiter explains, "are testicles. These are
the testicles of the bull that lost at the arena this
afternoon."

At first the man is taken aback, but decides that seeing as
he is in Spain, he should try the local delicacies. To his
surprise, it is delicious.

The next night, he comes back again, and decides that

seeing as he enjoyed the meal the previous night, he will try it again. He even uses the right word.

"Cojones," he orders.

"Certainly, senor," says the waiter, who rushes off and returns with a plate with the potatoes, vegetables, and the two large, round meaty objects.

The man eats the dish and loves it. So much so, he decides to come back again the next night and order it again.

"Cojones," he orders.

"Certainly, senor," says the waiter, who rushes off and returns with a plate with the potatoes and vegetables. But this time, instead of the meat being the usual two large, round objects, there are two tiny little pieces, each not much bigger than a walnut.

The man looks astounded. "What's this?" he asks the waiter.

"Cojones, senor," the waiter replies.

"No, no," the man objects. "I had cojones yesterday and the day before, and they were much bigger than these. Much bigger!"

"Senor," says, the waiter explains, "the bull does not lose every time …"

DEAR TRAVEL DIARY,

Mon. 23rd   Came aboard, met everyone. There are many interesting and good-looking men aboard this ship. This will be fun.

Tues. 24th   Everybody seems to be making passes at me. I enjoy being the centre of attention, but I have no intention of becoming involved in a ship board romance.

Wed. 25th   Tonight I have been invited to sit at the captain's table.

Thurs. 26th   I enjoyed having dinner with the captain but he made some lewd passes at me and made some improper suggestions. I refused. I do not intend to have a shipboard romance.

Fri. 27th   The captain persists. He says that unless I agree to come to his cabin, he will sink the ship.

Sat. 28th   Last night I saved 1,245 lives …

The duty free shop at Dublin Airport has some pretty amazing stock. For example, there are the water proof tea bags; the one piece jigsaws and the inflatable dart boards.

The grand final of the football season was on in town and the young man was torn between going to a high class prostitute or buying tickets to the big match.

He eventually decided on the football, but he had left his decision so late that they only had $180 tickets left for sale.

"What!" he exclaimed, "I could have gone to the best brothel in town for that money!"

"Ah, that may be so," said the attendant, "but you

wouldn't have got one hundred minutes of action-packed play and a brass band at half time, would you?"

A tourist asks the guide, "When does the Loch-Ness monster show up?"

"Usually after the fifth shot of whisky."

A travelling salesman was about to check in at a hotel when he noticed a very charming lady giving him the eye.

In a causal manner he walked over and spoke to her as though he had known her all his life. Both walked back to the desk and registered as Mr and Mrs.

After a three-day stay he walked up to the desk and informed the clerk that he was checking out. The clerk presented him with his bill for $1600.

"There is a mistake here," he protested. "I have been here only three days."

"Yes," replied the clerk, "but your wife has been here a month."

B ucko and Gascoigne were travelling together when their car broke down in the middle of nowhere.

They could see a light burning dimly in the distance and so they approached a farm house. It was owned by a beautiful, but lonely widow named Sue.

About nine months later Bucko rang his mate, Gascoigne and asked, "Do you remember that night we broke down and had to seek help at the farmhouse? You didn't by any chance slip into our kind host's bed room, did you? And, you didn't tell her that your name was Bucko, did you?"

"Sorry mate," mumbled Gascoigne, knowing that he'd been caught out.

"Oh, don't be sorry, old buddy. She died and left me the farm."

A crowded United Airlines flight was cancelled. A single agent was assigned to re-book a long line of unhappy inconvenienced travellers. She was doing her best when suddenly an angry customer pushed his way to her desk.

He slapped his ticket down on the counter and shouted, "I don't want to stand in line. I have to be on this flight and it has to be first class and right now!"

The young agent replied, "I'm sorry, sir, I'll try to help you but I've got to help these folks first. I'm sure we'll be able to work things out for you."

The angry passenger was unimpressed and unrelenting. He asked loudly, so that all the passengers could hear, "I don't want to stand in line! Do you have any idea who I am?"

Without hesitation, the agent smiled and grabbed her public address microphone. "May I have you attention, please," her voice bellowed through the terminal. "We have a passenger here who does not know who he is! If anyone can help him identify himself, please come to the gate."

With the crowd laughing hysterically, he glared at her and screamed, "F... you!"

Without flinching, she smiled and said, "I'm sorry, sir, but you'll have to stand in line for that too!"

MAJOR RULES FOR DIETING

1. If you eat something, and no one else sees you eat it, it has no calories.

2. When drinking a diet soda while eating a candy bar, the calories in the candy bar are cancelled by the diet soda.

3. When you eat with someone else, calories don't count as long as you don't eat more than they do.

4. Foods used for medicinal purposes *never* count. Example: hot chocolate, brandy, toast, and Sara Lee Cheesecake.

5. If you fatten up everyone else around you, then you look thinner.

6. If you are in the process of preparing something, food licked off knives and spoons have no calories.

LOVE THOSE LAWYERS . . .

At a convention of biological scientists one researcher remarks to another, "Did you know that in our lab we have switched from mice to lawyers for our experiments?" "Really?" the other replied, "Why did you switch?"

"Well, for three reasons. First, we found that lawyers are far more plentiful. Second, the lab assistants don't get so attached to them. And thirdly there are some things even a rat won't do. However, sometimes it is very hard to transfer our test results to human beings."

A New York man was forced to take a day off from work to appear for a minor traffic offence. He grew increasingly restless as he waited hour after endless hour for his case to be heard.

When his name was called late in the afternoon, he stood before the judge only to hear that court would be adjourned for the next day and he would have to return.

"What for?" he snapped at the judge.

His Honor, equally irked by a tedious day and the sharp query, roared, "Fined two hundred dollars for contempt of court. That's what for!"

Then, noticing the man checking his wallet, the judge said, "It's all right. You don't have to pay now."

The young man replied, "I'm just seeing if I have enough for two more words!"

The Pope and a lawyer find themselves together before the Pearly Gates. After a little polite small talk, St. Peter shows up to usher them to their new Heavenly station.

After passing out wings, harps, halos and such, St. Peter shows them to their new lodgings. Peter brings them down on the front lawn of a huge palatial estate with all sorts of lavish trappings. This, Peter announces, is where the lawyer will be spending eternity.

"Holy Mary", the Pope thinks, "If he's getting a place like this, I can hardly wait to see my heavenly reward!"

Peter leads the way but the landscape below begins to appear more and more mundane until they finally land on a street lined with brownstone houses.

Pete indicates that the third stairs on the left will take the Pope to his new domicile and turns to leave, wishing the Pontiff his best. The Pope is quite taken aback and cries out, "Hey Peter! What's the deal here? You put that lawyer in a beautiful estate home and I, spiritual leader of the whole world end up in this dive?"

Peter looks at the Pontiff with amusement and replies, "Look here old fellow, this street is practically encrusted with spiritual leaders from many times and from many religions. We're putting you here with them so you can all get together and discuss dogma and philosophy. That other guy gets an elegant estate, because he's the first lawyer ever to make it up here!"

Avery successful lawyer parked his brand-new BMW in front of his office, ready to show it off to his colleagues. As he got out, a truck passed too close and completely tore the door off of the driver's side.

The counsellor immediately grabbed his cell phone, dialled 911, and within minutes a policeman pulled up. Before the officer had a chance to ask any questions, the lawyer started screaming hysterically. His BMW, which he had just picked up the day before, was now completely ruined and would never be the same, no matter what the panel beater did to it.

When the lawyer finally wound down from his ranting and raving, the officer shook his head in disgust and disbelief. "I can't believe how materialistic you lawyers are," he said. "You are so focused on your possessions that you don't notice anything else."

"How can you say such a thing?" asked the lawyer.

The cop replied, "Don't you know that your left arm is missing from the elbow down? It must have been torn off when the truck hit you."

"Ahhh!" screamed the lawyer. "Where's my Rolex!"

A small town prosecuting attorney called his first witness to the stand in a trial – a grandmotherly and elderly woman. He approached her and asked, "Mrs. Jones, do you know me?"

She responded, "Why, yes, I do know you Mr. Williams. I've known you since you were a young boy. And frankly, you've been a big disappointment to me. You lie, you cheat on your wife, and you manipulate people and talk about them behind their backs. You think you're a big shot when you haven't the brains to realize you never will amount to anything more than a two-bit paper pusher. Yes, I know you."

The lawyer was stunned. Not knowing what else to do he pointed across the room and asked, "Mrs. Williams, do you know the defence attorney?"

She again replied, "Why, yes I do. I've known Mr. Bradley since he was a youngster, too. I used to baby-sit him for his parents. And he, too, has been a real disappointment to me. He's lazy, bigoted, he has a drinking problem. The man can't build a normal relationship with anyone and his law practice is one of the shoddiest in the entire state. Yes, I know him."

At this point, the judge rapped the courtroom to silence and called both counsellors to the bench. In a very quiet voice, he said with menace, "If either of you asks her if she knows me, you'll be in jail for contempt within five minutes!"

A man went to a brain store to get some brain for dinner. He sees a sign remarking on the quality of professional brain offered at this particular brain store. So he asks the butcher:

"How much for engineer brain?"

"Three dollars for one hundred grams."

"How much for doctor brain?"

"Four dollars for one hundred grams."

"How much for lawyer brain?"

"One hundred dollars for fifty grams."

"Why is lawyer brain so much more?"

"Do you know how many lawyers you need to kill to get one ounce of brain?"

O'Reilly, a dishonest lawyer, bribed a man on his client's jury to hold out for a charge of manslaughter, as opposed to the charge of murder which was brought by the state.

The jury was out for several days before they returned with the manslaughter verdict.

When O'Reilly paid the corrupt juror, he asked him if he had a very difficult time convincing the other jurors to see things his way.

"I sure did," the juror replied, "the other eleven wanted to acquit."

AND FINALLY …

Q.   What happens to a lawyer when he takes Viagra?

A.   He gets taller …